Christopher
            Christmas 2001

JAMES ALLEN is familiar to television audiences as ITV Sport's man in the pit lane. He co-wrote Nigel Mansell's bestselling autobiography *The People's Champion*, writes on Formula 1 for the *Financial Times* and is a columnist for *F1 Racing* magazine. Born into a racing family, he has worked in the sport as a writer and broadcaster for ten years. He lives in west London with his wife, Pip.

With love from
        Mum and Dad.

MICHAEL SCHUMACHER

Driven to Extremes

JAMES ALLEN

BANTAM BOOKS

London • New York • Toronto • Sydney • Auckland

MICHAEL SCHUMACHER: DRIVEN TO EXTREMES
A BANTAM BOOK : 0553 81214 9

Originally published in Great Britain by Partridge,
a division of Transworld Publishers

PRINTING HISTORY
Partridge edition published 1999
Bantam Books edition published 2000

5 7 9 10 8 6 4

Set in 11/13pt Goudy by Falcon Oast Graphic Art

Bantam Books are published by Transworld Publishers,
61–63 Uxbridge Road, London W5 5SA,
a division of The Random House Group Ltd,
in Australia by Random House (Pty) Ltd,
20 Alfred Street, Milsons Point, Sydney, NSW 2061, Australia,
in New Zealand by Random House New Zealand,
18 Poland Road, Glenfield, Auckland 10, New Zealand,
and in South Africa by Random House (Pty) Ltd,
Endulini, 5A Jubilee Road, Parktown 2193, South Africa.

Reproduced, printed and bound in Great Britain by
Clays Ltd, St Ives plc.

CONTENTS

PREFACE

This is the story of two critical years in the life of one of the most brilliant and controversial racers in history.

After his attempt to win the 1997 World Championship by ramming Jacques Villeneuve off the road, Michael Schumacher was, quite rightly, vilified by the world's press. His quest the following year to rebuild his battered image seemed to me to have all the elements of a classic human drama. As a sub-plot to his mission to end Ferrari's twenty-year World Championship drought, it made for an irresistible story. He failed twice again to win the title and the jury is still out on whether he will ever be able to remove the stain the Jerez incident left on his record. That he is one of the greatest drivers in the sport's history is certain. That he is the most controversial is also beyond doubt.

Michael Schumacher polarizes opinion. To his fans he is an icon, a forceful, charging virtuoso, who can do things with a racing car other racers can merely dream of. To his enemies he is a ruthless, arrogant hypocrite, who never admits his mistakes and who finds it virtually impossible to be gracious, either in victory or defeat. He is often dismissed as robotic, but those who know him well are familiar with an honest, caring human being.

His career at Ferrari has been magnificent but flawed. The greatest name in racing has structured its entire team around him, fulfilled his financial demands and built cars in which he can challenge. His victory in the 1999 Monaco Grand Prix made him the most successful driver in Ferrari's seventy-year history and gave him a stranglehold on the World Championship, but then a leg-breaking accident at Silverstone ended Ferrari's dream once again.

His subsequent comeback had all the elements which have defined him as a man and a racer. Speed and brilliance on the track; controversy, bad feeling and dark rumours off it.

This book attempts to look beyond the caricature and to discover the man behind the public image. The question I am most often asked by members of the public is, 'What is Michael Schumacher like as a person?' The answer is human. I hope that this book will provide some useful insights into his character and background.

I am grateful to many people for their help on this book. My colleagues at ITV: Martin Brundle, Murray Walker, Gerard Lane and Ted Kravitz. From the Formula 1 media centre: journalists Michael Schmidt, Pino Allievi, Eric Silbermann, Gerald Donaldson, Mike Doodson, Roger Benoit, Stan Piecha, Andrew Benson, Jochen Mass, Raffaele Dalla Vite, Andrea Cremonesi.

I would especially like to thank Michael Schumacher and Heiner Buchinger for agreeing to help me and the 'inner sanctum' at Ferrari; Eddie Irvine, Jean Todt and Ross Brawn for being so open.

Thanks also to:

Stefania Bocchi, Nigel Wollheim and Tim Watson at Ferrari, Pat Symonds at Benetton, Trevor Foster at Jordan, Ron Dennis, Mika Hakkinen and David Coulthard at McLaren for being accessible.

Francesca Liversidge and Sadie Mayne at Bantam Books.

Jon Holmes, Sally Coxon at Marquee Group.

Sarah Wood for help with translation.

I am indebted to my father Bill for help with the manuscript, and also to Mary, my Mum and to Sue and Dan for their support.

This book was written partly in Italy and partly in Britain. Thanks to Annice Resnick at Fontanella and to Brian and Anne Calvert at Crow Park.

And most of all thanks to my wife, Pip, for her help and patience. Normal service is now resumed, sweetheart.

James Allen
London

ONE THE EDGE OF GREATNESS
Jerez, Spain, October 1997

It had been an incredible day. In the grandstands opposite the pits many of the crowd had sat for hours after the final qualifying session of the season, skin tingling from the Spanish sun, heads woollied by a steady consumption of beer. As they watched the mechanics on the other side of the track carefully taking the cars to pieces, they all had their own theory about how it came about that Michael Schumacher, Jacques Villeneuve and Heinz-Harald Frentzen had recorded exactly the same qualifying time.

'It's simple,' said one, 'the drivers have found the absolute limit of the car.'

It was a satisfying sporting theory, and might explain why the two Williams cars had equal times, but how could the Ferrari, an inferior car for pretty much the whole season, have the same limits? It did not satisfy the more cynical among them, who had their own intricate conspiracy theories to explain away this unique accident of circumstance.

Most ran along the lines that Formula 1 is fixed: not a sport any more, just business. Just look at what the organizers had done to Jacques Villeneuve in Japan two weeks before, giving him a one-race ban so we could have this high-profile showdown in Jerez with only one point between him and Michael Schumacher. And now they had set the same time? Come off it, who was writing the scripts here?

* * *

The flags in the grandstands fluttered in the evening sunshine, mostly the same red, yellow and black banners which thousands of fans had carried throughout the summer to the great race tracks of Europe: Silverstone, Nürburgring, Monza and Hockenheim. They bore simple messages of support like, '*Schumi, Weltmeister*' (Schumi, World Champion) and '*Schumi gib gas*' (Give it some gas).

Although most of the crowd in the stands were German, there were plenty of enthusiastic and knowledgeable Italian fans, known as *tifosi*, and a lot of cheerful English fans, bearing equal allegiance to Schumacher, Villeneuve and to the out-going champion, Damon Hill. The Spanish, with no home driver in the field and no real interest in the sport, had largely stayed away. The Germans and Italians had come for similar reasons: to see Schumacher win Ferrari's first World Championship since 1979. Since then Ferrari had been beaten mostly by themselves, but also by the Williams and McLaren teams, who had dominated Grand Prix racing for almost two decades. Only the Benetton team had broken the stranglehold, in 1994 and 1995, when Schumacher was their driver. But now the German hero was at Ferrari, and with five wins during the season he had brought himself and the Prancing Horse to the brink of the dream world title.

Schumacher relishes a challenge, and to bring back the title to Ferrari when they had been denied it so long was his greatest challenge to date. The Italians called this pursuit of a dream, '*la sfida*' and it had captured the imagination of the whole country.

For the *tifosi*, '*la sfida*' is the most important element of sporting drama. Being a *tifosi* means appreciating the effort a driver makes to win and drawing satisfaction from the emotions you feel when watching that effort; with the Italians emotions are always near the surface. You then reward this effort with your enthusiasm and support. Like a matador facing up to a bull by staring deep into his furious eyes, so Schumacher would be expected to face up to his challenge tomorrow and thrill a whole nation with his efforts.

In the eyes of the *tifosi*, Schumacher was a great champion, perhaps one of the greatest ever to drive a Ferrari. They expect victories from their drivers and when he arrived the year before as a proven champion, he had put his hard-earned number one on the nose of the car and immediately offered them victories. After five seasons of poor results, he represented hope and perhaps also proof that Ferrari, or as it was known in Italy, the Scuderia, was getting its act together. Schumacher had won many great victories; he was a true fighter, who considered a Formula 1 race like a boxing match. He would never give up, even when victory seemed impossible, and in his battles with Damon Hill, Jacques Villeneuve and, all too briefly, Ayrton Senna, he had shown he had all the qualities of a great fighter.

But now, two seasons into his career as a *Ferrarista*, although he had acquired the respect and admiration of the *tifosi*, he still did not yet have their love. They respected the talent, the effort and the commitment, but that was it. Other Ferrari drivers in the past had been loved from the moment they signed for the team: Mario Andretti, Clay Regazzoni, Jean Alesi and especially Gilles Villeneuve, Jacques' late father.

These were the heroes of the *tifosi*, part of the folklore of Italy. All had shown great effort behind the wheel of a Ferrari, yet perversely none had won a World Championship for the team, nor had they been particularly successful in a Ferrari. Regazzoni won five races in the 1970s, Villeneuve six, while more recently Alesi, who left the team when Schumacher arrived, had just one win to show for his five years with Ferrari. So although the *tifosi* would be in heaven if Schumacher won the title for them tomorrow, it would not necessarily make them love him. Only time would tell whether they would love him or not.

On the other side of the track, in the pit lane, the normal Saturday-night routine was edged with expectation. As the mechanics of the two teams went through their pre-race preparations the atmosphere in the two garages told its own story.

The Williams mechanics worked purposefully, pausing to chat to each other or to mechanics from other teams who dropped in from time to time to exchange a joke or spread a rumour. Everyone seemed calm, as you would expect from a team which had got used to the idea of winning. In the past five years, Williams had won three World Championships and nearly forty races, and they had been in this position so many times before, it had become the norm.

The competitive spirit in Formula 1 is not confined to drivers and team owners, the mechanics are in it to win as well. They do not work all night to rebuild a car just for the money. Nor do they stand in the pit lane with a wheel gun in their hand as a car bears down on them at 70 m.p.h. just for the fun of it. They are there to win. Success breeds loyalty and Villeneuve's crew were rallied behind him, every bit as hungry as their driver to put one over on Schumacher and Ferrari. They were here to get the job done.

It had been a tough season for them. Villeneuve had dropped the ball a few times, but so had they. The speed of their work in pit stops was still no match for the Ferrari team, who were better drilled and had played some tactical master strokes during the year. But Williams had built the best car, and Villeneuve had gone out and driven the wheels off it at times, which was all they asked for. Very much his own man, he was not a driver to spend the evening before a race chatting to his crew, preferring to maintain a slight distance from 'the boys', which some of them regretted.

Many of the mechanics had harsh words to say about Schumacher's driving ethics, especially those who had been with the team at the end of the 1994 season – the last time Williams had gone head-to-head with Schumacher for the championship. On that occasion, under pressure from their number one, Damon Hill, Schumacher had made a mistake and gone off the road into a wall. He then steered his damaged Benetton into a collision with Hill, putting him out of the race and the championship. Schumacher and Benetton later claimed that the damage from his collision with the wall had made the car undriveable; the steering had gone and Damon was simply in the wrong place at the wrong time. The Williams mechanics weren't so sure.

The stewards had decided that there was nothing untoward in what had happened and so Schumacher kept his title. Although this had left a bad taste in some people's mouths, by and large it was accepted without fuss. People had just wanted the 1994 season to be over. It had been the season when death had showed its face in Formula 1 after an absence of many years and everyone in the sport wanted to put it behind them and move on. Three years on, there were many people in the Williams garage who were looking forward to payback time.

In the Ferrari garage next door, the significance of 'la sfida' seemed to be felt with every bolt tightened and every part examined. Ferrari had been in the wilderness for so long they couldn't remember what success smelled like, let alone how it tasted. Apart from Alesi's win in Canada in 1995 and Gerhard Berger's success at Hockenheim the previous year, they had been largely uncompetitive for six seasons – a lifetime in Formula 1. Schumacher's arrival in 1996 had brought fresh expectation, but a fragmented and disorganized technical department had given him a disappointing car which was both slow and unreliable.

They hadn't been sure what to expect in 1997, but they had given themselves a fighting chance by designing a car which looked just like a Williams and occasionally went like one. They had also brought in the two architects of Schumacher's success at Benetton, Ross Brawn and Rory Byrne. The pair had developed a good working relationship with Schumacher. Brawn, the tall, owlish technical director, oversaw all aspects of the design and manufacture of the Ferrari and set the pace for development of the car; Byrne actually designed the car and experimented with ways of improving it.

Over the past six seasons, Brawn had also developed an almost telepathic understanding with Schumacher during races. His tactical brain dreamed up daring race strategies, and with Schumacher's ability to push the car to the limit for long periods of time, the two had amassed many stunning victories. Now the 'A team' was back together at Ferrari, and although everyone thought it would be 1998 before their organized, methodical approach showed results, they had come very close to the title in their first season together.

At the start of the year the Ferrari was well off the pace of the Williams, but with intensive development as the season progressed it became more competitive. As an added boost, their chief rival, Williams, had shot themselves in the foot a few times during the season. In Monaco, Villeneuve was sent out onto a wet track on slick tyres because the team believed it would stop raining. In Canada, he made a beginner's mistake and crashed out of the lead in the opening laps. Another poor tyre choice in the rain meant Villeneuve struggled in Belgium.

On each occasion, Schumacher and Brawn pounced on the opportunity and scored a memorable win. But there had been disappointments too for Ferrari, like the Nürburgring where, under intense pressure, Schumacher seemed confused at the start and put himself in a risky position heading for the first corner. He was hit from behind by his brother, Ralf, and retired on the spot. And in Austria Schumacher was given a stop-and-go penalty for passing Heinz-Harald Frentzen under yellow flags – a rare unforced error.

Ferrari's technical department had pushed hard in the second half of the season, but perhaps the team confused itself by doing too much testing and they were embarrassingly off the pace at the *tifosi*'s home track in Monza. Publicly, everybody at Ferrari was saying how delighted they were to have got this close to the title after such an inauspicious start to the season. Privately, they all burned with the desire to win it.

Darkness fell around the circuit, but the pit lane buzzed with the bright lights and activity from the garages. Gianni Petterlini, the head mechanic on Schumacher's car, removed his training shoes and climbed into the cockpit. He raised his right index finger, the starter motor whirred and the freshly changed engine burst into life. He sat, blipping the throttle, staring intently at the read-out on the dashboard. Each time he blipped it, the engine barked loudly and the 750 horse-power of the V10 engine rocked the car gently on its support stands. He tried hard to look detached, unaffected by where he was and by what he was doing, but the little boy in him must have imagined he was Schumacher racing to the finish line at Jerez, to the roars of the *tifosi*.

Schumacher earned around $20 million a year for sitting in that seat, many times more than the combined salaries of the whole Ferrari team. But he had won races for them that no other driver could have won, races the car did not deserve to win. Tomorrow, they felt, he would surely do it again.

One final tearing scream from the engine and the systems check was over. Everything looked fine. Petterlini hopped out of the cockpit, slipped his shoes back onto his feet and moved on to the next job.

The man whose seat he had just occupied was already back in his hotel with his wife, Corinna, and their baby, Gina-Maria. Schumacher had left the track after another high-pressure day, which had ended with a marathon technical briefing with the engineers, lasting from 3.15 p.m. to 9.15 p.m., with only a couple of short breaks. Before that there had been the post-qualifying press conference which, after the sensational events of qualifying, was a highly charged affair.

Crammed into a stuffy side room of the press office, the two championship rivals, along with Heinz-Harald Frentzen, the third driver to set an identical time, parried questions from the media. The air was hot and still, the forced intimacy of the surroundings and the intensity of the championship battle served to make the atmosphere seem closer.

The two contenders were giving nothing away. Villeneuve had perhaps betrayed his true state of mind earlier that morning in the pit lane, when he went over to lambast Schumacher's team-mate, Eddie Irvine, for cutting him up on the track, a small piece of gamesmanship which rattled Jacques before qualifying. Villeneuve was convinced Irvine had been waiting around trying to block him on a quick lap. 'Irvine is mentally deficient enough to repeat it in the race,' said Jacques coolly. 'Everyone knows he's a clown, but there's no point in playing like that. He's not fighting me for the championship.' The pressure was building.

Of the two, Schumacher had seemed outwardly the more nervous all weekend. Throughout his career he had always attempted to minimize the pressure on himself by projecting it onto others. His critics called this his 'psychotricks'. He had done it often in the past, particularly to Damon Hill during their intense rivalry. And before the start of the 1997 season he had heaped the pressure on Frentzen, who had replaced Hill at Williams. Sensing an opportunity, Schumacher had said that it was Frentzen and not Villeneuve whom he feared the most, suspecting that Frentzen might be fragile mentally and highly susceptible to pressure. It was a brutally cunning compliment, ensuring that Frentzen would not be allowed to play himself in gently at his new team, but would have the spotlight on him from the outset. Schumacher had set him on the road to falling apart mentally before the season had even started.

Although he wouldn't want to admit it, in Villeneuve Schumacher had probably found his match in terms of mental toughness. After his father Gilles' death when Jacques was just twelve he had grown up to be his own man and he cherished his individuality. He had made some mistakes under pressure in his brief thirty-three-race Grand Prix career, but he had also shown that he would stand up to anything Michael threw at him. His bold passing move around the outside of Schumacher in Portugal the previous season had been a reminder that he wasn't afraid of close combat. So on this particular Saturday afternoon, Schumacher confined his psychotricks with Villeneuve to a simple two-liner out of Villeneuve's earshot: 'Villeneuve complains too much. It shows he's very nervous and is really feeling the pressure of this title battle.'

Only once did Schumacher find himself on the back foot during the press conference. Mindful of the fact that, with a one-point lead, any collision like the 1994 incident would hand him the title, a German radio journalist asked him whether we were likely to see any funny business at the first corner. Schumacher pursed his lips. 'I absolutely refute that kind of talk,' he said. 'In sport, you must be, above all, fair. I want to win in a legal way, like a gentleman with good sportsmanship. For sure, in motor racing you shouldn't give presents and you should fight hard from start to finish. But we are both fighting for a World Championship and I want to think that we will be correct and legal.'

When it was over the journalists filed out of the fetid room, back to their desks to write or broadcast their stories to the waiting world. There was much to reflect upon. Many had been in Adelaide three years before and had formed their own opinions of Schumacher's tactics that day. Many had also been in Suzuka in 1990 when Ayrton Senna deliberately drove Alain Prost off the road at 130 m.p.h. into the first corner to win the title. Would it happen again tomorrow? The sport's governing body, the FIA, had made it clear they would not tolerate that kind of behaviour.

Nevertheless, a few of the more cynical members of the press felt that, if it meant Ferrari winning the world title and as long as it didn't look too deliberate, he might just get away with it. But this was just idle speculation. Only the two people at the centre of the story knew what they would be prepared to do to win. And they weren't telling.

A few copies of *Newsweek*, the American weekly magazine, were lying around on desks in the press office. Formula 1 has only a small following among sports fans in America and virtually no following among the mainstream readers of *Newsweek*. And yet the front cover of the latest issue carried a large photo of Schumacher with the headline, FORMULA FERRARI – WHY MICHAEL SCHUMACHER IS ON THE EDGE OF GREATNESS. The story was spread over six pages and told how Schumacher had brought glory back to Ferrari. It was hard to understand why the American editors considered this story worthy of pushing President Clinton's visit to Latin America and the forthcoming China/US summit off the cover.

Perhaps more than anything else, *Newsweek*'s interest

reflected the worldwide fascination with the mystique of Ferrari, and by extension the significance of this title battle. Perhaps Schumacher was indeed on the 'verge' of greatness, but 'on the edge'? It seemed to imply something else altogether. Whatever happened tomorrow, clearly this would be no ordinary motor race.

Like his rival, Villeneuve had been in a championship showdown before. He had won the IndyCar title at the final hurdle in 1995, and the following year, his first in Formula 1, he took the World Championship down to the wire, eventually losing out to Damon Hill. If the pressure was getting to him, he didn't let it show. Perhaps the events of Suzuka a couple of weeks before, where he'd been banned for a race for ignoring a caution flag, had strengthened his sense of purpose. The frustration of seeing an eight-point lead transformed into a one-point deficit must have been unbearable. Yet Jacques seemed to have turned the situation around in his mind. The pressure was off him now and had been replaced by a clear understanding of where his challenge lay.

'The situation is very clear,' he said before leaving the circuit for the evening. 'Only by staying in front of Michael can I win the world title. So when it comes to strategy I only have one option: to keep him behind me. This eases the tension. I have to counter-attack and that's all.

'Of course, if it goes badly, I'll lose everything . . .'

TWO JEREZ PART ONE

Villeneuve is closing, closing, and then suddenly he's there, making a desperate lunge to Schumacher's right as they approach the corner.

The Ferrari reacts and moves away from the collision, but then has a change of heart and swerves to the right and . . . impact. The right front wheel of the Ferrari bounces off the bodywork of the Williams and the car slides powerlessly off the track. The Williams moves away from the brawl, like a terrier who's just taken on a much bigger dog. It checks itself for signs of damage, snorts and continues on its way. The Ferrari flops onto the sand, its pomp and potency gone. It's all over.

And yet the story is just beginning. Two-tenths of a second have decided a World Championship, two turns of a steering wheel have condemned a great champion.

Schumacher climbs out of the Ferrari and trudges through the sand to safety. The race continues. Villeneuve must finish at least fifth to be the new World Champion.

Schumacher stands on a low wall, his helmet in his hand. No athlete looks more forlorn than a racing driver removed from the action. He stands and watches. Three years earlier he had stood like this, waiting to see whether Damon Hill's Williams would come round again after their collision in Adelaide. It had not reappeared and then one of the marshals had told him that Hill was out of his car. He hadn't known how to react then, and his face had betrayed a confused mixture of all the emotions he thought a new champion should display. Now his face showed no emotion at all as Villeneuve's car passed by again and again and again, leading the race with less than twenty laps to go.

The race had started so well. Schumacher got the better start from the cleaner side of the track and beat Villeneuve to the first corner. Better still, Villeneuve had run slighty wide and Frentzen had nipped in between them. On his new tyres Schumacher was able to pull away. The tyres were the story of the race. Practice had shown that for three or four laps they performed brilliantly, then the performance tailed off. Schumacher had read this well and had saved three new sets for the race, enough for a new set at each of his two pit stops.

Villeneuve had not planned it so well and was forced to start on a used set of tyres. Schumacher would have the advantage in the early stages, he knew that. But he would just have to push like mad when he got his new tyres after the pit stops. He would play the long game.

He passed Frentzen for second place, but could make no impression on Schumacher. The pace was brutal, both drivers pushing as hard as their cars and tyres would allow. Every lap was driven with the intensity of a qualifying lap. It was such an equal contest that at one point they once again recorded exactly the same lap time. Mathematically that sort of coincidence should happen once every thirty years, not twice in two days!

Twenty-three laps into the race, after Schumacher and Villeneuve's first round of pit stops, Frentzen found himself in the lead with the two McLarens behind him, and here a little subterfuge began to come into play: one of the sub-plots which make Formula 1 such an intriguing sport and which confirm the old saying that what happens off the track is often far more interesting that what happens on it.

Before the race, the McLaren boss, Ron Dennis, had met with his old adversary Frank Williams and had assured him that his two drivers would not cause Villeneuve any problems. The two men had been rivals for years, but rivals with a healthy respect for each other. Both men had started at the bottom of the pile – Dennis as a mechanic, Williams as a used-car dealer – and through sheer force of will both had made themselves Grand Prix winners and multi-millionaires. Between them they had carved up most of the spoils in Formula 1 for the last twenty years. During that time, new rivals had threatened to break up the established order, but they had seen most of them off.

There is little love lost between competitive people at the top of any sport, least of all Formula 1, and over the years Dennis and Williams had fought, protested, poached drivers and staff and caused each other many sleepless nights. But they were also bound together by their shared values as racers. They had got into the racing game for the same reason – to win; and they shared the same ideals about what is and is not acceptable in the pursuit of victory.

Ferrari hadn't troubled them in the recent past, but now, with Michael Schumacher as their driver, they posed a major long-term threat. This was no problem in itself, but Dennis and Williams were suspicious of the Ferrari management, particularly its relationship with the people who control the sport, who made no secret of the fact that they badly wanted to see Ferrari win the title. But *how* badly they wanted it and whether they were prepared to help them achieve it was a subject of concern for the other teams.

Throughout the season there had been insinuations from some of the teams and the press about illegal devices on the Ferrari, and before Jerez rumours were circulating that there was something suspicious about Schumacher's miraculous starts. Did he have some form of electronic launch control on the car? There had been similar doubts about his Benetton car in 1994 and, then as now, people who were convinced that something fishy was going on would not listen to the counter-argument that Schumacher had practised his start technique religiously until he'd perfected it. It was not his fault if other drivers hadn't bothered to do the same. Still the rumours persisted.

Illegal electronics in Formula 1 are like drugs in athletics. Everyone has access to them, some may use them, but it's a very hard thing to prove. However, it's remarkably easy to start a rumour that another team is using them, and it's impossible for the team in question to prove that they are clean. A typical rumour might go, 'Team X has a clever piece of software which controls wheelspin and is therefore illegal. But it's so clever the FIA can't find it.' Hard to prove if there's no evidence, hard to defend for the team accused. If the other teams and the press want to believe it, they will, even if Schumacher denied it, as he did.

Launch-control devices, which minimize the amount of wheelspin off the startline, are a clear breach of the rules and in 1997 Schumacher's Ferrari had been through the same technical checks by FIA scrutineers as all the other cars and received a clean bill of health. But this didn't stop the rumours. Nor did Schumacher's start that day in Jerez. The Ferrari went from 0–100 km/h in 2.92 seconds – the fastest recorded start since the turbo-engined days ten years earlier. Perhaps sensing trouble ahead, Williams and Dennis agreed to join forces at Jerez against the common foe.

In the early stages of the race Mika Hakkinen made no attempt to pass Villeneuve, despite the fact that his McLaren was faster than the Williams. But as the race unfolded it began to look like Dennis and Williams had agreed to more than a simple pact of non-interference. First Dennis himself came to the back of the Williams garage to pass a message to Frank's son, Jonathan. Shortly afterwards Dennis's partner, the multi-millionaire industrialist Mansour Ojjeh, dropped in to speak to Frank and Williams's technical director, Patrick Head. The substance of their discussion was that the McLarens would not push Villeneuve in the early stages, and that later they would protect him by keeping Irvine's Ferrari behind them.

Villeneuve's biggest fear was Irvine: the man was just so hard to read. His fanatical loyalty to Ferrari made him a threat if he were to get close, but surely he wouldn't try anything stupid.

In the previous race at Suzuka, Irvine had driven brilliantly, breaking out of the peloton and helping his team-mate to victory like a Tour de France cyclist. Far more was riding on the result of this race. Villeneuve and Williams were right to worry, but as it transpired Irvine would not be the problem.

During his brief spell in the lead, Frentzen slowed the field by almost two seconds per lap to allow his team-mate, Villeneuve, to close the gap on Schumacher. When Frentzen made his first pit stop, the battle for the race and the world title became a direct confrontation. Villeneuve had a look down the inside at Dry Sack corner, a slow right-handed corner. Schumacher covered it easily and held on to the lead.

Schumacher was the first to make the final pit stop and Villeneuve came in a lap later. The race now entered its decisive phase. Villeneuve pushed his car to the limit. Curiously Schumacher did not respond and the gap fell from 2.6 seconds to under a second. Did Schumacher have a problem?

Ross Brawn claims not: 'There was no problem with the car. We had agreed earlier that we needed to take it easy on the tyres. Michael was doing a couple of easy laps to settle the new tyres in, because we'd had a few painful experiences in 1997 with blistering tyres and we couldn't afford to let it happen in this race. We were being very conservative, and judging by the way the tyres had been going, we expected any attack from Villeneuve to come at the end of the stint, not the beginning.'

Villeneuve was going for it. He didn't seem to care about his tyres, he was working them to death, knowing that this set of new tyres offered him his only chance of closing the gap on Schumacher. Later in the race, both he and Schumacher knew the performance would drop off, but Jacques didn't care about later, he only cared about seizing the moment.

His attack, when it came, was unexpected. He was fifteen metres behind as Schumacher braked for Dry Sack corner, enough to make him think that Villeneuve wouldn't try anything. But Villeneuve didn't brake, he pointed the car down the inside with his right wheels on the grass and kept on going. As a famous American sports coach once said, 'You've got to be in it to win it,' and Villeneuve was now right in the middle of it.

Schumacher was caught by surprise. He knew from practice times that the Williams was 10 km/h faster at the end of the straight than his Ferrari and that its superior downforce meant that Villeneuve could afford to brake later into a corner when overtaking. All season it had been the same story: whenever the Ferraris were in front, the Williams could close the gap right up in the final 100 metres before a corner, and the Ferrari drivers would never know as they hit the brakes whether they would be overtaken or not. Villeneuve knew it and so did Schumacher, but as he looked in his mirrors shortly before braking, Schumacher thought Villeneuve was too far behind to try anything.

Schumacher knew that if Villenueve could get past now he would be gone, and passing him with a 10 km/h speed disadvantage on the straights would be impossible, however much Villeneuve might have damaged his tyres. But it was also Villeneuve's only chance. He had caught Schumacher napping, and if he didn't go for it now then Schumacher would speed up and passing him would be virtually impossible. It was time for the 1997 World Championship to be decided one way or the other.

So much was riding on this result for both teams, but Williams's three world titles in five years somehow insulated them from the growing razzmatazz. Their engine supplier, Renault, was withdrawing from the sport after this race and would not be making a big song and dance about it if they won again. Ferrari, on the other hand, were ready to trumpet the success of their $100 million investment around the world. All the sponsors were poised with triumphant adverts celebrating their role in the team's glory. The FIAT organization, the tobacco giant Philip Morris and the Shell oil company had all pumped in huge amounts of money and were just twenty laps away from reaping the rewards. The responsibility was enormous and both drivers had felt it keenly throughout the weekend. It was not so much a sporting contest as a corporate summit.

In the back of Schumacher's mind all weekend was one thought: if Villeneuve finishes in front of me the championship is gone. Now, suddenly, the Canadian was alongside him. Two-tenths of a second passed between his initial realization of this – marked by an instinctive turn of the steering wheel to the left, away from the path of the Williams – and the second sharper turn of the wheel to the right, the one which slammed the two cars together, the one which sought to eliminate the predator, the one which screamed out to the watching millions, I must win at all costs.

What leapt into Schumacher's mind during that sliver of time? Villeneuve was coming from so far back and at such an angle that he would not have made it round the corner without using the side of Schumacher's car. So if Michael hadn't turned away initially there would have been a collision which would have been all Villeneuve's fault. 'He was too impetuous,' people would have said afterwards in the paddock. 'Villeneuve was overcommitted.'

But Schumacher's initial instintive reaction to turn away from a collision was followed by a brief period of reflection and the decision to turn into one. Part of his brain must have said, This is the World Championship slipping away from me, and the devil in him took over from there. Much, much later on, months after the furore had died down, Schumacher conceded that, 'In the past that was the way you did it. I mean, if you wouldn't have done it you would have been criticized the other way around. But we live in different times now.'

It's the nearest he has come to admitting he deliberately tried to take out Villeneuve, which looks like the only logical explanation for the accident, and it shows something incredible about Schumacher's mind. Whereas most human beings travelling at that speed would barely have time to see and instinctively react, Schumacher had the time to see, react, reflect, conduct a brief debate with his conscience and then act decisively.

Even as a newcomer to Formula 1, Schumacher seemed to have the wisdom of Solomon during races. During a tense wet/dry race at Spa in 1992, he had been following his Benetton team-mate, Martin Brundle, and noticed that Brundle's wet tyres were beginning to blister. He chose the perfect moment to dive into the pits and change to slicks tyres, and he went on to win, leaving greats like Nigel Mansell and Ayrton Senna floundering. It was the race that announced him not just as a searing talent, but also as a thinking driver.

'He's able to think long and hard,' says Brundle, 'so that when things happen, he's ready for them. I've always held the view that a great driver uses 70 per cent of his mental capacity to drive the car and the other 30 per cent he keeps in reserve to think about things. Whereas a good driver uses 80 per cent and 20 per cent. This enables Michael to take decisions on the hoof. He is a great thinker.'

So if his sole intention had been to take Villeneuve out of the race, then surely he would have been on top of the situation enough to succeed and to make it look like Villeneuve's fault. The best driver in the world with car control like his would not have failed to drive another car off the road in a slow corner like Dry Sack. Suspension parts on Formula 1 cars are built to withstand huge loads vertically, but they shatter like eggshells if you so much as kick them from the side. Even the most limited driver could have taken Villeneuve out of the race from that position if the intention was there.

And there are many other ways he could have done it. According to one driver, he could have let Villeneuve pass him and then in the next corner left his braking a little late, as Ayrton Senna did in Adelaide in 1992, removing Nigel Mansell from the race. Afterwards a few excuses about a soft brake pedal, no obvious proof on either side and he's home free, World Champion. Clearly Schumacher was surprised by Villeneuve's move, but why? Villeneuve had been closing the gap steadily for a lap and a half. Ferrari's technical director,

Ross Brawn, had told him over the radio, 'He's right behind you,' just seconds before the incident. The threat was apparent.

Was he too tired to think? Villeneuve later spoke of seeing Schumacher make mistakes, which he took as tell-tale signs that his rival had succumbed to the relentless pace.

'The mental side was pushing the physical, because the body just wanted to give up. At the same time I noticed that Michael was starting to make mistakes, lock wheels, and so I went for it even more. I knew that that's when I should overtake him, because he was starting to get tired and I knew that he wouldn't react as quickly as earlier in the race. I am happy because he was also beaten physically that day and he's renowned for his physical fitness. I trained very hard in 1997 and that race showed me it was worth it to train.'

This is certainly mischief-making on Jacques' part. Schumacher's fitness has always been the benchmark for Formula 1 drivers, and although Jerez is one of the most physically demanding circuits in the sport, Schumacher was not feeling the strain after just forty-eight laps. Schumacher believes that, if anything, it was the other way round.

'I talked to Jacques after the race and he said he couldn't have kept the pace up much longer because he was physically finished, which wasn't the case for me at all. There's no way that a guy who starts serious training that season can be as fit as someone who's been doing it for years.'

One theory as to why Schumacher was caught out comes from a man who worked closely with him at Benetton and engineered him to his two World Championships, Pat Symonds.

'At Suzuka in 1994 Michael went to sleep in the middle of the race and I don't believe he should have lost to Damon Hill that day. When I say he "went to sleep" I mean he had a lapse of concentration. It had terrible repercussions, because when he went on to the final race in Adelaide he was nervous and he didn't drive his best that weekend. If he'd won Japan as he should have done, then the pressure in Adelaide would have been less. Michael could have come in second and still been champion.

'The manoeuvre he pulled in Jerez was plain madness. The only thing that surprises me is that I don't believe he needed to do it. I'm sure he must have realized that Villeneuve's tyres would be finished and that, although he might have to drive defensively, in a few laps his car would be able to beat Villeneuve's.

'It is possible that he went to sleep again, just like in Japan in 1994. He didn't realize just how rapidly Villeneuve was catching him and left his defensive moves too late. It doesn't happen often, but I think it happened then. Most drivers have regular lapses of concentration, Michael's are very rare.'

But Ross Brawn, who worked alongside Symonds in those Benetton days, denies that this is what happened.

'For sure Michael didn't expect it, none of us did. If we had thought something like that could have happened we would have warned him and given him our opinion on what to do. I don't think he went to sleep, it was just an unexpected move. Two-thirds of the race was down and it was just entering its crucial phase. I'm sure Michael was just thinking about a lot of other things.'

Schumacher goes along with this.

'Within the rules of our sport you can move once to block. I should have done that. I should have gone much earlier to the inside and that would have been it. I shouldn't have given him any chance, but for me it was clear he was well enough behind me and would never try it. In a moment he was there; I reacted far too late to try to take my line and close the door.

'I have thought a lot about it since then and thought, How stupid I was to let that happen.'

THREE JEREZ PART TWO

In the Piazza Liberta in Ferrari's home town of Maranello, 7,000 people turned away at once. A giant diamond-vision screen, which had been erected for the townsfolk, repeated the incident from several different angles: the head-on shot, the side shot, on-board with Villeneuve and then, worst of all, on-board with Schumacher. From this angle there was no doubt about what had happened, and the more they showed it, the harder the verdict became.

A reporter for the daily sports paper, *La Gazzetta dello Sport*, was among the crowd, and sensing a good story he began canvassing opinion.

'Schumacher should have won it for Enzo Ferrari,' said one fan. 'He has ruined everything with this crazy, desperate move. He said that the best man would win and he was right, because now the champion is Villeneuve.'

As the disappointed crowd spilled out of the square, thirty miles away in the hills above Bologna, Ferrari president Luca di Montezemolo and his two children, Clementina and Matteo, closed the front door of their villa behind them, jumped into their car and sped off towards the local airport. An emotional man, di Montezemolo knew that his own feelings of shock and disappointment would be reflected in the pain of the *tifosi* around the world, as well as within the Ferrari team itself. It wasn't the losing of the championship which mattered so much, it was the way it had been lost. What had happened in Jerez was a major deviation from the script he had planned. There had been a wonderful symmetry to it all. 1997 was Ferrari's fiftieth anniversary and what could have been better than to round off a year of celebration with Ferrari's first world title since 1979?

The importance of Ferrari to Italy had been clearly demonstrated in May, when the president of Italy and enthusiasts from all around the world had joined the team for a spectacular party in Rome. Ferraris from the past fifty years were gathered and Schumacher and Irvine had driven their modern Formula 1 cars from the city centre to the Caracalla circuit on the outskirts of Rome, where Ferrari had won its first race in 1947. Schumacher had learned a lot that day about what Ferrari means to the Italian people. He had begun to appreciate that carrying the hopes of Ferrari has more significance than merely driving for a Formula 1 team. It comes with a set of responsibilities that go far beyond sport. But the events in Jerez showed that he had not yet learned enough about what the Italians expect from their heroes.

Di Montezemolo himself had just turned fifty. Here was a man used to success, a man with high expectations whose career to date had been a series of well-chronicled triumphs. Like many high-profile Italians, he adores seeing his name and most recent pronouncements in the papers and he cares greatly about his public image. A flamboyant man, he conceals his hard edge with aristocratic Italian charm. Despite his skinny frame, he cuts an impressive, but nervous figure. He keeps his hair at 1970s length and sweeps his fingers through it theatrically to signify that he has just made an important point. His face contorts as he speaks, partly through a nervous twitch and partly through emotional expression. When he is not speaking, he lifts his head and looks from side to side, as if searching for his wife at a cocktail party. Some people, including Jacques Villeneuve, regard him as rather a ridiculous, emotional figure, but one glance at his CV persuades you otherwise.

A trained lawyer, his connection with Ferrari began in the

early 1970s, when Gianni Agnelli, the uncle of a close friend and, as head of FIAT, one of the most powerful businessmen in Italy, hired him to keep an eye on the Ferrari Formula 1 team, which had become part of the FIAT empire. Di Montezemolo struck up a good relationship with the ageing Enzo Ferrari and with his number-one driver, Niki Lauda, and success followed, with Lauda winning the 1975 and 1977 World Championships.

After that di Montezemolo had taken on various roles in the FIAT empire, including managing director of Cinzano and publisher of *La Stampa* newspaper. His greatest triumph, however, had been as director general of the organizing committee for the World Cup Italia '90, which had been universally considered a great success.

After the death of Enzo Ferrari in 1988, the team went through a painful interregnum period before Agnelli installed di Montezemolo as president in 1991, making him responsible for turning around the fortunes not just of the racing team but also of the road-car operation as well.

He had set to work persuading FIAT and its partners to give the racing team the budget it needed to do the job. He recruited Jean Todt, then head of Peugeot Sport, to run the race team, and between them they had restructured the whole operation and set in motion the chain of events which led to the arrival of Schumacher in 1996. After many false dawns, by 1997 the Prancing Horse had been nursed back to good health.

Di Montezemolo takes immense pride in his racing operation and loves to drop in by helicopter to a test session or for qualifying day at a Grand Prix to bask in the glory of a reinvigorated Ferrari team. He stands on the pit wall for a while, sweeping his fingers through his hair, and occasionally he slaps one of the technicians on the back. Like many Italian men, body contact is important to the president and any opportunity to make physical contact with Schumacher is grabbed, literally, with both hands. On arrival at a test, for example, he will shake hands all round, but kiss Schumacher extravagantly on the cheek.

His usual routine on these visits is to get a full briefing from Todt and then hold an informal press conference. The Italian press join in the game; they cajole and tease him, and try in vain to get something controversial out of him. Instead he bestows little jewels of flowery prose on them and reminds them again and again that the best driver in the world is working for him. 'Without Schumacher this would be a World Championship of taxi drivers,' is one of his more memorable phrases. 'For us he is an amazing piece of good fortune.'

Di Montezemolo had watched the Jerez race on television at home and knew instantly that there was trouble ahead. What would Enzo Ferrari have done in this situation? He would certainly have called Schumacher after the race and ordered him to come to Maranello the following morning at 7.30 a.m. for a short chat, which would probably have lasted until around midday. For Enzo, drivers were merely overpaid employees, a view shared in the modern era by Frank Willams and Ron Dennis.

But Ferrari was different now and Schumacher was different. He was the only genuine superstar in the sport and Ferrari, by its president's own admission, was lucky to have him. Di Montezemolo had given him a degree of freedom and control unimaginable in any other top team. The whole operation was built around Schumacher, and the single goal of all 500 employees was to get him to the top of the championship. The *tifosi* were on-side and there had been plenty of adulation, not least when Schumacher had won at Monza in 1996 and thousands of fans had poured onto the track with giant Ferrari banners. Ferrari had become great again, but now the downside of all of this hysteria had hit home – Schumacher clearly believed that he could do anything he liked on the track in the name of Ferrari and that the Italians would back him. He couldn't have been more wrong.

Di Montezemolo had seen the same TV pictures as the crowds in Maranello and around the world. He had spoken to Schumacher on the phone and immediately he decided to fly out to Jerez to join the team for dinner, both to sympathize with them and to try to make some sense of what had happened. He also wanted to gauge the press reaction and make sure that it didn't cause too much damage to Ferrari's image. And if it came to it, he would make sure that he got some sort of public show of remorse from Schumacher. But by the time he got there it was far too late for that.

As he boarded his private jet, he spoke to a small group of Italian newspapermen, anxious to get the first reaction from the Prancing Horse's mouth. As always, Luca was happy to oblige. 'Schumacher has explained to me what happened. After the second pit stop the tyres were not performing as well as the others and started to blister. The car could not be driven as hard as before. As for the incident, he told me, "I made a big, stupid, naive mistake. I didn't expect Villeneuve to attack me there and yet I left him space to try it. When he caught me out, the anger at having made a mistake made me react instinctively, but it was too late."

'So congratulations to Williams, and apologies to the *tifosi*, that once again Ferrari has obliged them to wait.'

The journalists scribbled down the quotes, the plane doors were shut and *il presidente* was on his way to Spain.

It would be some three hours before the journalists in Jerez heard Schumacher's own reaction to the incident, and when they did, his perspective was quite different from what di Montezemolo had reported. It was also ten times more damaging. After returning to the paddock, he disappeared without comment into the Ferrari motorhome. Summoned by the race stewards to explain himself, he emerged grim-faced and walked across the paddock pursued by an army of photographers, TV crews and journalists. Without saying a word he climbed the stairs of the control tower to the stewards' office. Then he returned to the motorhome to await their decision, again without comment.

Out on the track, the most dramatic Grand Prix for years was approaching its denouement. Before the chequered flag there was one more surprise as Villeneuve slowed on the final lap, allowing Hakkinen and team-mate, David Coulthard, through for a McLaren one-two, clearly the pay-off part of the arrangement between McLaren and Williams.

There was confused joy on the podium for Hakkinen, the cool Finnish driver who had been at death's door after the final race of the 1995 season and who had just had his first ever Grand Prix victory handed to him. It was like giving a starving man a half-eaten sandwich. Beside him, Villeneuve was ecstatic, having just become World Champion. And this wasn't some walkover World Championship, cruising around in the best car; he had defeated one of the sport's greatest champions in a straight fight. Finally he had emerged from behind the shadow of his late father to take his own place in racing history. He may not have won as many friends as Gilles, but he had won far more races, and now he had claimed motor racing's greatest prize, for which Gilles had been fighting in vain when he died. As the unfamilar refrain of the Finnish national anthem played out, in the pit lane below, Villeneuve's mechanics, wearing fluorescent yellow wigs to mock their driver's peroxide-blond hair, sang along heartily, without knowing any of the words.

Jock Clear, Villeneuve's race engineer and a man with just as much competitive spirit as Jacques, clutched his hand to his heart as if it were his own anthem, wiping tears from his eyes. When Villeneuve returned to the Williams garage to thank his crew, Clear rushed up to him and swept him up in his arms. He pressed his forehead to Villeneuve's, and as they danced up and down he repeated over and over again, 'We did him, we fucking well did him.'

In the McLaren-Mercedes area it was party time. The race had been manipulated to give a perfect outcome. Mika Hakkinen, now fully accepting that a win is a win, no matter how it comes, was beginning to enjoy the feeling. It had taken him far too long to win his first race.

Picked out by McLaren boss, Ron Dennis, as long ago as

1992, he had out-qualified the great Senna on one occasion the following year and since then everyone had talked of him as the coming man. But his arrival at McLaren coincided with a steep decline for the team. Their engine partner, Honda, had pulled out unexpectedly at the end of 1992 – Dennis had heard the rumours that they might quit but had been slow to believe them – leaving McLaren flailing around for several years before landing on Mercedes. Hakkinen stayed loyal through the bad times and now Dennis was rewarding that loyalty. The team was on a steep climb back to the front. They had hired Adrian Newey, the designer credited with much of Williams's success and were reportedly paying him £2 million a year – unheard of for an engineer. For 1998, Dennis was confident that all the elements would be in place for a crack at the title. He couldn't afford to have his principal driver wobbling over his first win, so he had worked it out with his other driver, David Coulthard, to pull over and let Hakkinen by.

Coulthard, playing the team game, obliged, sacrificing a certain win for himself. It's against the nature of a racing driver to let another win, especially if it's not explicit in his contract that he is the number-two driver, and after the race David seemed mildly depressed. As we chatted to him in the McLaren area, the stereo in the Mercedes motorhome next door where Hakkinen sat was pumping out the classic song by The Who, 'We won't get fooled again'. David was probably having the same thought, but little did he know what lay ahead in 1998. On a day of heroes and villains, Coulthard was struggling to work out exactly where he fitted in.

A large crowd of journalists had gathered outside the Ferrari motorhome. The villain of the piece was waiting for the stewards to reach a decision on the incident before making any kind of statement. Many had thought he would go to the *parc fermé* at the end of the race, perhaps to apologize to Villeneuve as he climbed out of his car, or at the very least to congratulate him on his first World Championship. That would have been the sporting thing to do. But instead he'd stayed put. Perhaps, like Ayrton Senna, he didn't like the idea of anyone else winning the title. Nigel Mansell, who beat Senna to win the 1992 championship, recalled how, on the podium after winning the title, he was approached by Senna, who said, 'It's such a wonderful feeling, isn't it, Nigel? Now you know why I'm such a bastard, because I don't ever want to lose that feeling or let anyone else experience it.'

There is little doubt that if Schumacher had followed old-fashioned sporting etiquette rather than his own instincts and made a public show of congratulation to Villeneuve as he climbed from his car, then most of what was to happen next would not have occurred. The world would have seen a defeated but dignified champion sportingly acknowledging his conqueror and would have switched off their TV sets secure in the knowledge that the right man had won, that Formula 1 had provided another thrilling race and that Schumacher and Ferrari would be back next year.

So much pain and damage would have been avoided. In the press office, the snorts of derision when the stewards finally announced that it was a 'racing incident' would not have been so bitter. And the whole chain of events which caused the greatest driver of his generation to fall from grace would probably never have happened.

But this was an athlete of the late twentieth century, with a salary of almost $20 million a year, endorsements to match and an entire merchandising industry based around his name and likeness. He had got used to the idea that he was the very best driver in the world. He didn't need yes-men around him to tell him he was the best; he knew it instinctively. He was a driver on another level from Villeneuve and the others, and yet now he had committed a professional foul in the eyes of millions of people and he'd been caught red-handed. With his misdemeanour had gone the big prize. But could he publicly admit weakness and face the fact that he had been beaten at his own game? That, caught by surprise, Villeneuve had made him crack?

Inside his highly disciplined mind he was coming to terms

with his feelings of personal failure and disappointment, putting it into perspective, but there was a wider perspective that he had failed to appreciate, and no-one around him was pointing it out. His isolation was not inspired by the desire to reflect before speaking. His sense of right and wrong had failed him at the crucial time and those closest to him were not looking after his best interests. The whole thing was unravelling fast.

Ironically one of his first visitors after the race was Frank Williams, who came to offer his commiserations. It was a sporting gesture from a man who, since being paralysed in a road accident, lives solely for his racing team and for Formula 1. Just moments before dropping in on Schumacher, Frank had sat outside the Ferrari garage in his wheelchair looking in at the defeated, devasted mechanics slowly packing away millions of pounds' worth of beautifully designed, Ferrari-badged equipment for another year. If he had been able to raise his hands to applaud them for their brave effort that season, like a footballer saluting the away fans, he would have done so. Instead he just nodded his head gently.

Inside the Ferrari motorhome Michael chatted with his wife, Corinna, Ross Brawn, Jean Todt and with his manager Willi Weber. Bernie Ecclestone, the man who runs the commercial side of Formula 1 and who had played such a big part in getting Schumacher to join Ferrari, had also dropped in. They talked about everything except the incident: their families, skiing holidays and Bernie Ecclestone's birthday.

Brawn later admitted that, as they sat there, he was feeling 'very disappointed and still in shock at the way it had ended'. Perhaps the pressure of the weekend had also been too much for Schumacher and he just wanted to talk about something else for a change. But it wasn't the time for that. It was the time for damage limitation. Instead, all sense of reality was in suspension. With hours to think about what to tell the press, Schumacher could normally be relied upon to come up with something good. He may have told Luca di Montezemolo on the phone an hour or so before that he had made a 'big, stupid, naive mistake', but when finally he emerged from the awning of the motorhome and faced the media for the first time, Michael was singing a very different tune.

'Michael, did you have some problem with the car?'

'No. Obviously when he [Villeneuve] was on new tyres he was a bit stronger than me, but I knew I could keep him behind me. Obviously he made a very optimistic attack. It worked for him, but it didn't work for me. But that's racing and I just want to say congratulations to him because he did a very good season. There was good luck and bad luck on both sides, but we believe we have enough reasons to be happy with the performance we showed this year as a team. In my view we have been the number-one team in Formula 1 and that is something Ferrari can be proud of.'

'Michael, be honest, you made a mistake.'

'A mistake, me?'

'In the manoeuvre.'

'No. I braked on the maximum and he braked even later, and with his braking point I wouldn't have made the corner and he wouldn't have made the corner either, so he used me a little bit as a brake.

'But I probably wouldn't have done anything different.'

An enigmatic and troubling phrase. Did he mean 'I would have done the same thing as Jacques, had I been in his shoes', or did he mean, 'If I had my time again I would do exactly the same thing'? The British interpreted it as the former, but then he was speaking our native language. The Italian and German press interpreted the latter meaning and stored it up to use as a weapon against him. They would quote it in their headlines to illustrate his arrogance, SCHUMI: IT WAS NOT MY FAULT, I'D DO IT AGAIN.

Schumacher, who appeared surprisingly upbeat considering what he had been through, had already condemned himself to a pasting in the press by refusing to accept even a shred of blame for the incident. And now this phrase, this simple mis-understanding, was the final straw.

FOUR THE BACKLASH

'Schumi: Germany in shock' – *Bild*, Germany.

'Schumi, what madness!' – *La Gazzetta dello Sport*, Italy.

'The end of the unbeatable image' – *Express*, Germany.

'Schumi pushes the *tifosi* into the vale of tears' – *Berliner Kurier*, Germany.

'Schumacher loses his head' – *The Times*, England.

'Schumacher's ram raid does not stop Villeneuve' – *Frankfurter Allgemeine*, Germany.

If Michael's performance in front of the press after the race had been an object lesson in how not to react to a situation, the press's response the next day and for the next few months was a classic example of how to tear apart a superstar.

It was Michael's great misfortune that Jerez was the final race of the season, because it meant that no new Formula 1 story could come along to divert attention away from what he had done. Worse still, when a big story did come along it was that Bernie Ecclestone had given the British Labour Party a mysterious £1-million donation a few months before the government vetoed a European Community proposal outlawing tobacco advertising. Formula 1 seemed destined for a winter of discontent, with Schumacher's ram raid still at the forefront of people's minds.

With over two months until his new Ferrari Formula 1 car was due to be launched and four months until the start of the 1998 season, there was nothing to look forward to except weeks of vitriol. One magazine claimed it was the 'fastest fall from grace since Canadian sprinter Ben Johnson at the 1988 Olympics'. Almost unanimously, the press in Germany, England and Italy went for the jugular.

The reaction in Italy was telling. The Italian press were furious, not because the championship had been lost, but because of the way Schumacher had conducted himself. Many commentators believed he had let down the Italian people. According to one, his treatment of the Ferrari legend was 'like having a gem in your hands, caressing it, cherishing it and then chucking it in the rubbish bin'.

Candido Cannavo, writing the leader column in *La Gazzetta dello Sport* said, 'We are not crying because we lost, because the World Championship escaped us, or because the eternal wait keeps getting longer. These would be the normal tears of a sports fan. We resent the stain of this naive and twisted Schumacher who tries to drive Villeneuve off the road as he overtakes with an impeccable, courageous, but not rash move. This naive and crazy act demands an apology and public penitence.'

Il Messagero newspaper went further. 'An imperfect murder attempt!' it cried. 'This was a shot in the heart for sport.'

In England, the Fleet Street boys went for Schumacher with gusto. Plenty of British sports stars have felt the sting of the tabloids over the years, for Britain is a country which adoringly builds up its stars in keen anticipation of one day scything them down again. Paul Gascoigne knows all about it, and David Beckham has learned the hard way, after his World Cup gaffe, that hell hath no fury like the British press scorned. Writing in the upmarket *Times*, Michael Calvin said Schumacher had 'lost more than just the world title. He has sacrificed his reputation in an act of such instinctive cynicism that he has forfeited the right to sympathy', while Ray Matts in the tabloid *Daily Mail* reckoned that Schumacher had 'lost the last vestige of his reputation as a sportsman'.

It was in Germany that the condemnation was most surprising. Writing in *Express* newspaper, Wilfred Pastors asked, 'This mistake, is it the end of a legend? What the stewards called a non-punishable racing incident was seen as quite the opposite by millions of TV viewers. It is the end of the World Championship dream and of the image of the infallible driver.' *Die Welt* newspaper described Schumacher as 'a man who likes to walk on the edge of razor blades'.

Willi Weber, Schumacher's manager, described the press coverage in Germany as 'the rats and the envious, crawling out from their holes', but in truth it wasn't all condemnation. Indeed, beneath the surface, something interesting was going on.

Germany's top-selling tabloid paper, *Bild*, was trying to have it both ways. On the front cover the day after the race, it ran a sympathetic headline, EVERYONE PUNISHES SCHUMI, and inside it avoided attacking Schumacher directly, although in one column former driver Hans Stuck wrote, 'The crash was all Schumi's fault. It was his worst defeat. Michael, why did you do it?'

The following day, *Bild* published all the uncomplimentary headlines, articles and letters from other publications, but maintained a non-committal editorial line itself. *Bild*'s editors had been among the first to notice a new phenomenon in German newspaper publishing: if you are nice to the nation's heroes, you sell more newspapers; if you take them apart, you sell fewer papers. Previously it had been thought, as it still is in Britain, that if you took a national icon to the cleaners the public would lap it up. But things were changing in Germany, and with Boris Becker now less in the limelight, Schumacher was Germany's only real international sporting superstar. The logic was clear: you don't sell papers by destroying your only hero.

No doubt the editors had also calculated that by taking a sympathetic stance amid all the criticism, they would be in a good position to negotiate the 'Schumacher exclusive' that everybody wanted – the confessional, the champion pours his heart out to the nation in the pages of *Bild*. But Schumacher and his advisers weren't going to play that game.

He hadn't anticipated such a media backlash. On the Sunday night after the race, as he sat down with di Montezemolo and the whole Ferrari team for dinner at the El Coto restaurant near Jerez, Schumacher was relaxed and relatively cheerful. He expected some criticism, the odd comparison with Adelaide 1994, but nothing on the scale he got.

It was a subdued gathering. The place had been decked out for a different kind of evening. It was rather like a defeated presidential candidate going back to a room bedecked with banners saying, 'Congratulations, Mr President,' and being forced to see the night out there. One wall was adorned with a huge photo of Schumacher and Irvine spraying champagne after their stunning performance in Suzuka two weeks earlier; a frozen image from a time when Ferrari's hopes still sprang eternal. The theme of the evening was bullfighting and the organizers had laid on a mini corrida involving the two drivers. Despite the events of the day it was decided to go ahead with the original plan.

Both men took turns at swirling the red cape and challenging a young bull, and both also showed a good turn of speed, running for the protective barriers when the bull's horns came a little close for comfort. But a good time was not being had by all. Several mechanics found it hard to understand how the drivers could goof around like this after the events of that afternoon. Before leaving the circuit Schumacher had seemed relaxed and had shared a joke with Irvine, who had unearthed a batch of Michael Schumacher baseball caps, made up speculatively by Willi Weber, with the legend 'World Champion 1997'. The joke was on Michael, who shrugged, 'I've accepted it now. There are more important things in life, after all.'

Irvine had put one on and allowed himself to be photographed wearing the cap. But then it ceased to be a joke, because that night the art editor at *La Gazetta dello Sport* scanned the image into the computer, and replaced Irvine's face with Villeneuve's. They ran it large at the top of the front cover and it became the motif for Jerez '97. It said more than all the headlines and leader columns ever could. The Italians were not going to spare the blushes of their defeated champion.

Perhaps a few of the mechanics felt the same way. Most of them are Italian, although the chief mechanic, Nigel Stepney, is an Englishman. He worked for Ayrton Senna for many years at Lotus and has seen it all in motor racing. Hired to instil some discipline into the team and to provide a calming influence at moments of high emotion, in many ways he symbolizes the change at Ferrari as the foreign management team of Todt and Brawn brought in a disciplined English taskforce to kick the Italians into shape. All communication with the drivers and engineers is now conducted in English, but the mechanics get their orders in Italian, so there is no risk of miscommunication.

The Ferrari team had become like a military operation and the change from five years before was noticeable. Now the team always looked sharp during practice and qualifying. Not rushing any tasks, but responding quickly to the clear chain of command and getting Schumacher and Irvine back on track in the shortest time possible. During the race, they carried out the high-pressure pit stops faultlessly and quickly, often beating the Williams team for speed. Although among the lowest-paid mechanics in the pit lane – the honour of working for the Scuderia is reward in itself – they are among the most dedicated. They had bought into the dream peddled by their new foreign managers and had drawn closer and closer to realizing it.

But now that dream was shattered and they were in no mood for a party. Which was no great surprise, as they are not particularly good at partying even when they've won.

After the famous victory at Monza in 1996, with the wild

scenes of celebration in front of the podium and that abiding image of a huge crowd unfurling a giant Ferrari flag, the paddock was a very different scene. In the Ferrari motorhome area, everybody had a small plastic cup of champagne from the podium celebrations. Once that was gone, someone remembered that there were a few bottles of Prosecco left over from the day before when one of the engineers had toasted the birth of his second child. So they drank that. Then they dug out a couple of bottles of Lambrusco and that was it. So much for *la dolce vita*, so much for the great Italian *festa*! The mechanics went back to the garage to pack away the equipment, while Schumacher, his press officer, Heiner Buchinger, and a few others went to the Rothmans motorhome, where the proprietor, the Austrian restaurateur Karl-Heinz Zimmerman, would surely know how to get the party going. Countless bottles of beer and schnapps later, Michael was on the roof, firing the small canon that Zimmerman lets off when one of his drivers has won a Grand Prix, and which once blew out the eardrum of a mechanic who was standing too close.

The mood at the El Coto was mixed and there were a lot of tired faces watching the floor show as the flamenco musicians, drummers and dancers proudly strutted before them. Finally di Montezemolo climbed onto a balcony to address his fallen army. He thanked them for getting so close to the title. He exhorted them not to be too depressed about the way things had worked out, but to take heart from a fabulous season in which they had done better than they could possibly have imagined. Ferrari were once again a competitive force and with continued dedication they would surely capture the crown in 1998.

As they filed out of the resturant, di Montezemolo was collared by a small group of Italian journalists for a quote. Wasn't it true, they asked, that Ferrari had been on the verge of winning the World Championship and that 'the German' had lost it for them?

'Absolutely not. Ferrari *and* Schumacher lost the title. I

believe Schumacher made a mistake,' he said wearily. 'He's a human being and he can make mistakes. He made one in this case, but you should not jump to the conclusion that he tried deliberately to drive his rival off the track. If he had wanted to do that he would have succeeded. I totally refute the idea that he tried to do anything incorrect. He just had an instinctive reaction when he saw he was being overtaken. But it is past. I have thanked the boys for all their work this year and I hope that I helped to raise their morale a little bit.'

Unnoticed, Schumacher slipped away from the restaurant and headed for the hotel, where he dropped in to pay a late-night visit on the new World Champion.

Jacques Villeneuve was most certainly in the mood to party. After the race he had spent a few hours sampling Karl-Heinz Zimmerman's hospitality at Rothmans, where Schumacher had offered him a schnapps, but not an apology, and later he headed off to the Puerto Santa Maria. Renault was hosting its final farewell bash in a nightclub on the quayside and inside it was standing room only. Half of the Formula 1 paddock was inside, most of them thoroughly drunk and demob happy. One of Ferrari's sponsors went to the bar, bought a bottle of champagne, then stood on his seat facing the dance floor and, apeing the new champion, sprayed the whole lot over the dancing throng. What a moron.

Twenty feet away, Villeneuve sat with a small group of friends and soaked up the atmosphere. He looked at home in the nightclub, a regular partygoer whose face fits on any chic VIP list. Villeneuve bobbed his head in time to the music and smiled quietly to himself. Tiny in stature, with small rimmed glasses, baggy clothes and his trademark peroxide-blond hair, he is a self-styled individual, who follows his own trends and maintains an air of mystery about him. In his first year in Formula 1, when the work load wasn't quite so heavy, he would disappear for a week at a time between races, leaving Williams with no contact number. He might be in Montreal, Helsinki, London, or even at home in Monaco with the phone off the hook. But wherever he was he was enjoying himself, keeping his life under control.

Although it was strictly an invitation-only affair, Renault had felt it necessary to place a couple of security goons round his table, and well-wishers approaching to congratulate the new champion found their path blocked by a burly arm. It was a sign of the times and many of those who knew Villeneuve decided not to go through the embarrassment of an exchange with the bouncers. There would be other less public times to say well done.

Jacques is very much his own man and he hates being set up. If he feels people are crowding in on him or trying to make something from being associated with him, he hits the panic button. Celebrity to him is a cross to be borne rather than an end in itself, and when he feels he's being pinned down to something he has no control over, then he gets nasty.

This is exactly what happened in the days following Jerez, when a photograph of Villeneuve and Schumacher partying together at their hotel in the early hours of Monday morning appeared in the German papers. After leaving the nightclub at around 5 a.m., Villeneuve encountered Schumacher at their hotel, the Monte Castillo, and the pair forced the night-watchman to open the bar. They began mixing cocktails. Schumacher had acquired a yellow wig, of the type worn that afternoon by the Williams mechanics, and he wore it as the two rivals tended the bar.

Michael's wife, Corinna, was there, along with some friends of both Schumacher and Villeneuve. At some point a photograph was taken of this friendly scene. Villeneuve later claimed it was taken by Corinna; Schumacher thought it was one of Villeneuve's gang. Either way, the photo was later to find its way into the German press, along with a few quotes from Michael about them being friends. When he saw it, Villeneuve went berserk.

The impression created in the paper was that Villeneuve and Schumacher got along fine, all's fair in love and war, and that Villeneuve did not bear a grudge against Michael over

Jerez. It was a nice, harmless little PR puff, which did Michael a lot more favours than Jacques. But it made Jacques feel set-up and he lashed out.

'It was a private party,' he told *Bild* newspaper. 'Suddenly photos are published and the only person taking photos was his wife. That's no way to carry on. You just don't do that kind of thing. And then I read that Michael says we are friends. He's always on about us being friends. I'm sick of it. He gets on my nerves. We are not friends and never will be. What he did on the track is not important to me. But what he has done here certainly is.'

In his statements immediately after the race at Jerez, Villeneuve had been quite charitable to Schumacher, refusing to criticize the German too much for the incident. After all, he reasoned, the more you denigrate your rival, the less significant the success of beating him becomes, and Villeneuve knew that his achievement in coming from behind to beat the best driver in the world in a straight fight was indeed significant.

But Villeneuve had also played a very subtle psychological game before the race, gently reminding the media that Schumacher had a history of driving people off the track when the title was at stake. He didn't make a big fuss about it, but he nevertheless put Schumacher on a stage so that everyone could watch for the decisive moment. Consequently, for many as they watched the race, there was a feeling of will he, won't he? And when Schumacher did, the impression that Villeneuve had made him crack was irresistible.

Villeneuve knew right away that he had beaten Schumacher at his own psychological game, but at first he did not set out to rub Schumacher's nose in it. The decision to do that came later. It's interesting to look through press cuttings from the aftermath of Jerez. The general tone of revulsion and anger the day after the race is dictated by the opinion of journalists. But in the following days and weeks a pattern begins to emerge as Villeneuve, who initially doesn't seem to think the incident was so bad, realizes the extent of media feeling about it. He hardens his views on Schumacher and later actively fans the flames. Indeed, it's tempting to suggest that the press crucifixion of Michael Schumacher during the winter of 1997 would not have lasted half as long had Villeneuve not wanted it to.

The first green shoots of this change of heart happened the day after the race. Williams's main sponsor, Rothmans, keen to trumpet the good news of their success all over the world, had lined up twenty-one TV interviews for Villeneuve on Monday morning. Sitting in a temporary studio next to the track, the new World Champion would be patched in by satellite to TV shows all over the world and for the next three or four hours he would answer the same questions over and over again – twenty-one times in all.

When he arrived, having snatched barely a couple of hours of sleep, he was very hungover and subdued. When one interviewer asked him how he felt he replied, 'I'd feel a lot better in bed.' But as the mineral water revived him, he began to buck up. Initially he took the line he had used after the race: that it was more or less a racing accident.

'When he came over on me I couldn't go any further because I was already on the grass. Either Michael had his eyes closed or somehow his hands slipped off the wheel or something. I was not really surprised when he turned in on me, it was a little bit expected.'

But as the same questions came raining in, with interviewer after interviewer employing the same language of revulsion about Schumacher's tactics, Villeneuve began to change his story and agree with them.

'What do you think of what Michael did to you, Jacques?'

'I can understand what pushed him to try and drive me off the road. We were fighting for the title. I could have done the same to him in Japan and been champion there, but it's not in my nature. It's a question of character. He reacted instinctively. In a situation like that, even if your brain tells you different, you follow your instincts. And Michael's instinct was to drive me off the road. My character is different. I would never feel good inside if I had tried that. But he lost at his own game.'

As the twenty-six-year-old champion shifted uncomfortably in his seat, wishing he could be anywhere but where he was, it was impossible not to feel a tinge of sadness for him, especially when the inevitable question about his father came up.

'Jacques, were you thinking of your father when you won the title?'

'I don't go racing with my father alongside me. Whatever I may do in races, he will always be my hero. I grew up with Formula 1, but the decision to become a racing driver was mine alone.'

Gilles Villeneuve could make your heart stop with his ferocious attacking style. He could hurl his racing car into positions and attitudes no-one else would dare attempt, let alone repeat. He was the bravest and wildest driver around, and it was totally clear from his first Grand Prix that here was a man who would either be World Champion or kill himself. Every time he climbed aboard his Ferrari he used to kiss his wife, Joanne, and whisper, 'Don't worry, I won't be long.' But one day, when Jacques was just twelve, he didn't come back.

We get used to the idea of racing drivers as heroes. Men of indomitable will, who risk their lives in the pursuit of something impossibly glamorous and inaccessible to the normal man. They thrill us with their bravery and make us quake with fear at their audacity. Other sportsmen, like soccer players, arouse strong emotions in us too, but they don't risk calamity or flirt with the ultimate sacrifice, and this is what elevates ordinary men, whose skill is to drive fast, into gladiators. The media build on this theme with the language of chivalry from bygone times: 'Villeneuve throws down the gauntlet,' or the language of gunslingers – 'World Championship showdown' – and then act surprised when they actually get stuck into each other!

Nevertheless, like the racing heroes of the past, today's drivers take the risks we don't dare to take. But unlike the

Fangios and Nuvolaris, their rewards are salaries large enough to run a hospital for a year. The game provides sporting peaks and troughs, as any good human drama should, and allows a man like Schumacher to show his brilliance and to raise himself above his competitors. But every now and then we are reminded that these are just vulnerable young men, dressed up like cigarette packets, caught up in a corporate game in which they appear in Venn diagrams alongside projected sales targets, while their 'name and likeness' is traded as a commodity, like gold and silver. Every now and then the turbo-charged conveyor-belt of greed, which turns kids into superstars and manufactures ever higher expectations for them, gets a spanner in the works and produces a moment in which even the greatest heroes can't help but fall and even the most expensive PR companies can't save them. Jerez was one of those times.

Jean Todt summed up best where Schumacher went wrong, why the expectations on him were too great and why Jerez was such a watershed.

'We should all remember that, for all his capabilities, Michael is only human and makes mistakes. He over-reacted due to a lack of time to think about it and he said things that he shouldn't have said. But perhaps it was my fault too. Perhaps we at Ferrari should have helped him at that difficult moment. But I think we forgot that with all his ability he is still just a twenty-nine-year-old youngster.'

FIVE THE QUEST FOR REDEMPTION

In the offices of two of motor sport's most powerful men, both self-styled presidents, the screaming press condemnation of Schumacher posed a serious problem.

FIA president Max Mosley, an urbane English barrister with a keen political brain, realized that the stewards' verdict of 'racing incident' made the FIA look stupid. Indeed many commentators had turned the verdict around and questioned the authority of the governing body. Mosley had been in Jerez and had personally addressed the drivers in the pre-race briefing, warning them that they would face the severest penalties if they employed any dirty tricks to decide the championship.

After the race, the facts had been laid out before the stewards and a decision was reached. The prevailing view seemed to be that the season was over, the championship had been won by the 'victim' of the incident, while the 'culprit' had put himself out of the race as a result of the collision. This was punishment enough, it was felt. No need to take the matter any further.

But now that the press were baying for blood, that decision looked weak. The FIA should be seen to act. A statement went out from the FIA offices announcing that Michael Schumacher was summoned to appear before a special FIA disciplinary hearing on 11 November. Clearly the FIA meant business. After all, they would hardly call him in merely to repeat the verdict of the stewards. Most people jumped to the same conclusion: Schumacher was going to be banned for the first half of next season and Ferrari would have no chance of winning the 1998 title either.

Meanwhile, in the office of Ferrari president Luca di Montezemolo the bad press was causing intense pain. In one paper, Placido Domingo, the great opera singer, said, 'I feel really sorry for Ferrari but really ashamed for Michael Schumacher.' The Italian media was calling for Schumacher to apologize to the Italian people in Italian, a language he had hitherto declined to learn. Now the FIA was on the warpath too. It was all too much for di Montezemolo. A press conference would be organized for the following day at Ferrari's base in Maranello. Michael Schumacher would set the record straight.

It was a huge struggle, far more difficult to understand and to steer through than any race he had ever competed in. His life, his whole career, had hardened him in his belief that he knew best. A racing driver is a solitary person, who must always look after number one first and foremost. Pride, egotism and an innate confidence that you are always right, these are the staple attitudes of a great champion. Shame, penitence and humility are like a foreign language and Schumacher now found himself in a truly foreign land. It was a typically Italian pageant, with the sinner being forced to admit his guilt in public and metaphorically being dragged through the streets of the medieval village while the locals throw rotten fruit at him. If Ferrari wanted a good Catholic confession for the $20 million they were paying him, then they certainly got their money's worth.

'I did not try to take him out, I just wanted to win the World Championship,' said the penitent. 'I committed an error of judgement and I will accept from the FIA whatever the consequences may be. People do not expect me to make mistakes. But from what I have seen the reaction has been exaggerated. Worse things have happened in motor races than what happened last Sunday. The '94 incident with Hill was a different thing and I wasn't driving for Ferrari then . . .

'I saw Villeneuve after the race, we shared a bottle of beer and he asked me why I did it. I told him and he listened without bitterness. I didn't apologize to him; I could do that now, but it wouldn't mean anything. I hope that if I do well in the future, it will cancel out this episode. I will explain to the FIA exactly what I have told you today. I am keen to make myself understood. I'm sorry if it has taken me a while.'

Outside the hall, a crowd of a dozen or so fans waited to catch a glimpse of Schumacher. On any other official Ferrari occasion there might be hundreds of *tifosi* at the gates. It was a clear sign of the Italians' dissatisfaction with their star driver. However, despite the obvious local disaffection, in general the public's reaction had been mixed and Schumacher drew comfort from the many letters of support he received from all over the world during this difficult time. They were to bring him to the conclusion that the press reaction did not mirror the public's view, that his true fans would stick with him through thick and thin, and this belief would become his reference point from which to move forward.

As the press filed out of the hall, Pino Allievi, one of Italy's most respected motor-sport writers, spotted an old acquaintance among the crowd of fans. It was the former motor-cycle champion Umberto Masetti.

'Pino,' he said, 'the exact same thing happened to me as happened with Schumacher. Back in 1952 at Spa I was racing against a guy, and he put out his leg and tried to make me fall off. At the end of the race he came to me, apologized and said he hadn't done it deliberately.'

'What did you do?' asked Pino.

'I punched him,' said the old man.

A mobile phone rings and Heiner Buchinger, Schumacher's press officer, answers. The season is over, but for Heiner there is no peace. The phone has not stopped ringing for two days and every call has the same slant. Many of the smaller-circulation German papers, who do not send a correspondent to the races and in the past have showed only a passing interest in what happens on the track, sense an opportunity for a big scoop. With the big papers all having laid into Schumacher, they are bound to be off-limits, so here is their big chance. 'Heiner,' they all say, 'isn't it terrible what they are saying about Schumi? He's completely down. You must do something to build up his image. We could do a nice story, go to Switzerland, nice pics of him, Corinna and the kid. Get Michael to explain what really happened.'

But Heiner isn't having any of it. 'I told them, "No, we are not doing anything special. The new car will be launched on the eighth of January and before that Michael is not doing anything press-wise."'

The quest for the redemption of Michael Schumacher had begun and the Buchinger strategy for repairing a champion's tarnished image was in action – do nothing. While some celebrities might have felt tempted to run to the safe haven of *Hello!*, for an uncritical twelve-page spread with photos of them tending animals, and a story saying how wonderful they really are, Heiner told Michael to go to his house in Norway, shut the doors and not to talk to anyone.

'Michael had spoken the day before at Maranello and got it right for the first time. So things had calmed down a little bit, or let's say they were a bit more balanced. Especially in Italy, where the press had been really hard on him. But you expect that. It's the job of journalists to be critical, to put a certain control on things. The press is powerful but they cannot change everything.

'For me it was clear that there would be a big storm, but only for a limited time. If you start taking action, putting out special stories, it will look like you're making excuses and that doesn't look good. There was a story in one paper which said, "Schumacher will be forgiven, even if it is only when, during a rainy Grand Prix, he once again, thanks to his amazing feel for driving, leaves all the other competitors standing, and then the headlines will once again call him Schumacher the rain god and the sun will shine down on him once more." And that was right. As soon as he started winning again for Ferrari, everyone would forget Jerez. I knew it would happen. So my plan was, sit tight.'

Tall, slightly stoop shouldered, with a black beard, cobalt-blue eyes and a cigarette always on the go, Heiner Buchinger is an experienced journalist with a superb feel for the mood of the F1 press corps and a healthy disdain for the intelligence of many of its members. For many years he was a senior editor on one of Germany's leading car magazines, and he has been employed by Michael since early 1995 and has overseen all his press relations since then, passing out a tip here, a quote there and gently massaging the media. The system works well. Heiner tells it to you straight, and if a journalist needs to know 'Michael's view' on an issue, or wants a line on how the day has gone, Heiner always knows the answer.

Ferrari's press officer, Claudio Berro, looks after all press matters relating to the team and to Eddie Irvine. Anything related to Schumacher is handled exclusively by Buchinger; he is the sole conduit for access to the driver, and Schumacher trusts him to manage his image and to keep him briefed. Heiner speaks regularly with Berro to make sure that an open and unified front is presented. Even the most troublesome journalists find it impossible to get beween Ferrari and its driver, the result being that you don't see many articles about Schumacher's disenchantment with Ferrari, or vice versa.

With a request list to interview Schumacher which comprises half the Formula 1 press corps at any one time, Heiner's job is to filter out the time-wasters and to arrange who gets what. To get an interview you first contact Heiner and then you must be prepared to travel to a specified test track on a specified day, where, true to his word, he will sit you down in front of Schumacher for a twenty-minute slot. Apart from press conferences, Schumacher doesn't do interviews with print media during race weekends; these have become the exclusive domain of the TV networks and Heiner has worked out a system whereby everybody gets the soundbites and longer interviews they need during a race weekend when Michael is not either driving the car or talking to his engineers.

While other drivers, including the top names like Villeneuve, Hakkinen and Hill, rely on the team press officers to keep the media at arm's length, Schumacher has gone one better and hired his own personal expert, just as Ayrton Senna did a decade ago. Senna hired a lady called Betise Assumpcao, whose main job was to spread word of his successes to all the local papers and radio stations in Brazil who could not afford to send their own correspondent to Grands Prix. She was Senna's personal Reuters news wire. After Senna died, Betise packed in her career, married Williams tecnical director, Patrick Head, and had a baby. Just like Betise with Senna, the very fact that Heiner has this role is proof of how much Schumacher cares about his image and what people think of him. He is also proof of the incredible level of interest the media has in Michael. But then, as the sport's only genuine superstar, that's hardly surprising.

Before Michael came on the scene in the early 1990s, Formula 1 had passed through a halcyon period for drivers. The 1980s had featured great names like Niki Lauda, Keke Rosberg, Ayrton Senna, Alain Prost, Nigel Mansell and Nelson Piquet. But by the time Michael had found his feet and begun to win races there was no-one left to race against; they were all gone, most into retirement, Senna tragically to his death.

Suddenly deprived of genuine stars, the sport hurled the best of the rest up the ladder of stardom; here you go, Michael, race against this guy! The intense pressure of expectation fell first on the shoulders of Damon Hill, a solid but unspectacular test driver with Williams who got his big break in racing when Nigel Mansell quit Formula 1 at the end of 1992. Eighteen months later his team-mate was dead and Hill found himself leading the best team in Formula 1. The pressure was hard to bear at times, but he struggled manfully through. Hill's battle with Schumacher provided Formula 1's only box-office appeal in the mid-1990s, the Brit against the German, grit versus genius. It was a decent enough storyline, but beneath it all there wasn't much of a plot. There were some moments of high drama, but it wasn't the same as watching two aces going at each other. It wasn't Ayrton Senna versus Alain Prost or Muhammad Ali versus Joe Frazier.

There was sometimes an element of 'cross your fingers for Damon'; maybe he'd come through, maybe he wouldn't. Meanwhile the robotic Schumacher, brushing aside whiffs of suspicion that illegal devices had been fitted to his Benetton car, notched up the wins and watched his pay cheque grow. This is Formula 1's only genuine measure of stardom and by that measure Schumacher had become the sport's only genuine star. Damon did magnificently and learned to win from the front. But when he tried to argue that his status and track record justified the big pay cheque too, rightly or wrongly, Frank Williams decided that, at Damon's level, drivers are interchangeable.

By this time, Frank had Jacques Villeneuve on his books, a real charger with plenty of promise. With a Williams under him he could give Schumacher a run for his money. Frank also decided to hedge his bets and hire Heinz-Harald Frentzen, who had reputedly been faster than Schumacher in their German Formula 3 days. Being German, Frentzen's recruitment also sent out the right kind of signals to Williams's future engine partner BMW. At the end of his 1996 championship-winning year, despite his proven track record, Damon was dropped. Like any market place, the big buyers know the score, and when the going gets tough, the tough will send you packing. In Formula 1 only one driver can buck the market.

'One thing's for sure,' Williams once said, 'if Michael Schumacher came up for grabs tomorrow, there wouldn't be one team owner who would say no to him, regardless of how bad his reputation is.'

A bad reputation – the easiest thing to acquire and the hardest to shake off. Before the start of the 1995 season, Schumacher hired Heiner Buchinger because he had acquired a reputation during 1994 that he wanted to shake off – the German press had nicknamed him 'Schumel Schumi' and he really hated it. Roughly translated, the adjective '*schumel*' is halfway between crafty and cheat. An uncomfortable grey area, which has the advantage of being suggestive without being libellous.

In an intensely competitive and at the same time complex sport like Formula 1, there is a narrow line, around which only the serious players flirt. It is the line between what is legal and illegal, and winning and losing have often pivoted around this. But whereas in the past winning was the end in itself, in the modern game, the difference between the two is measured in millions of dollars.

The engineers' job is to design the fastest car they can within the rules, while the driver must go as close as he can to the edge of what is permissible on the track in the pursuit of victory. They are two halves of the same thing, namely winning at all costs.

The engineers read the rules with a view to getting around them. The best engineers are paid millions to find loopholes and exploit them. A Formula 1 car designed an inch inside legality will be slow; to get a really fast car you must be within a cigarette paper of legality. Similarly, for a driver, tactics like blocking or the odd nudge in a tight corner can make all the difference. Most drivers learn these tricks in karting. As they rise through the ranks of the sport and the stakes get steadily higher, most forget their old karting tricks. Some don't. Bending the rules only becomes a problem when you start running away from the opposition in races. No-one minds too much whether your car is bent or whether you are a bully boy when you finish in sixth place. But when you win, especially if your team has come from a long way back to challenge the front runners, then suspicion and jealousy inevitably become intermingled. It is easy to start rumours in Formula 1. Information is like oxygen and there are always plenty of people desperate for a breath of the latest intrigue. If you have information you have power, you belong. But rumours will persist only if enough people are prepared to believe them and everyone knows that rumours stick for a reason.

In 1994 Benetton came under intense scrutiny and allegations of cheating surfaced on several occasions. The team was fined heavily, Schumacher was disqualified twice and banned from two races. His season ended when he collided with Damon Hill, some felt deliberately, to collect the World Championship. Schumel Schumi was born.

The FIA had recently banned so-called driver aids – electronic devices which made the car easier to drive – like launch control, which helped to prevent wheelspin at the start of a race. Schumacher's perfect getaways in the first few races of 1994 got many of his competitors murmuring darkly that the car was still fitted with the system. The FIA decided to look into it. But without the computer source codes, they couldn't get into the system to make proper checks.

Benetton refused at first to provide the codes, claiming it would infringe the copyright of their software suppliers, and were fined $100,000. When finally Benetton did release the codes, the FIA discovered that a launch-control program was indeed present, but that it had been disabled. Benetton claimed it had been deactivated before the start of the season and had not been used in 1994. The FIA's computer expert probed further and discovered that, by following a procedure of flicking the gearshift paddles and pressing the throttle and clutch pedals in the correct order, the system could be activated by the driver, who could then hold the car on the startline with the required level of revs, release the clutch and sit there as the synchronized program linking engine and gearbox hurled the car towards the first corner.

At first Benetton explained that the system was used only in testing, then that the sequence for activating it from the cockpit was deliberately complicated to prevent the driver from activating it by mistake. This rather implausible argument strengthened the impression that something fishy was going on.

Ross Brawn, then Benetton's technical director, said that the team had decided it was simpler to deactivate the system than to remove it for fear of corrupting other software programs. He also stressed that Michael had not been made aware of what disabled systems were in the car. Brawn went on to add that Schumacher's perfect starts were the result of hours of careful practice.

In the end the FIA's computer experts concluded that the 'best evidence' suggested that the system had not been used in 1994 and therefore decided not to exclude Benetton and Schumacher from the championship. But by then, like the Starr investigation into President Clinton, the drip, drip, drip of innuendo and rumour had already worn away at Schumacher's reputation, something that still angers him today.

'I would never use an illegal system because there are too many big players involved in Formula 1. I know that in 1994 we didn't have anything illegal, but there was so much talk about it that it almost became like the truth. I was really upset, after victories that we fought and worked for really hard.'

Another contributing factor to the Schumel Schumi tag was Michael's performance at Silverstone, where he overtook pole-position-holder, Damon Hill, on the parade lap, a rather lame attempt at a psychotrick on his rival and an offence for which the rules state he should have been put to the back of the grid. The race stewards failed to do this. However, once the race was well under way they decided that he should be given a ten-second stop-and-go penalty and they put out the black flag to summon him in. According to the rules it was too late to exact such a penalty, but the officials insisted.

The Benetton team management went to argue the legality of the decision with the race director. In the meantime Schumacher, in contact with his team via radio, stayed out in the lead of the race, passing the black flag – and therefore ignoring it – three times. Schumacher later said he hadn't seen the black flag. To the public the race – and by extension Formula 1 as a whole – looked like a giant pantomime, a Keystone Cops sequence of errors, official blunders and bloody-mindedness.

Predictably the FIA threw the book at them, fining the team $500,000 and banning Schumacher for two races. As he had already won six of the eight races so far that year and was the runaway points leader, there were murmurs in the paddock that he was being banned to even up the championship.

Schumacher's reputation was taking a hammering. Benetton's press operation, under the control of managing director, Flavio Briatore, focused most of its efforts on the team as its main concern was the marketing of the Benetton brand. The company is famous for its 'shock' advertising – thought-provoking images like a new-born baby or a man dying of AIDS. In some ways this controversy over its Formula 1 team fitted in well with the brand image. In other ways it was less than ideal, especially for the real racers in the team, for whom marketing was just a necessary evil that paid the bills.

In the middle of all this, Schumacher felt isolated. His own personal interests were not being looked after as he might have hoped. There followed a damning report into a pit-lane fire at Hockenheim, which found that Benetton had tampered with the refuelling rigs by removing a filter. Then he picked up another disqualification in Belgium as part of the car's floor was worn down too much, and then finally he won the title by colliding with Hill in Adelaide. All in all a devastating year for Schumacher's image.

Nevertheless, he had won the World Championship by participating in just twelve of the sixteen races and his many brilliant drives had laid down a marker for the future. Here was the natural successor to Ayrton Senna, not just in terms of his talent, but in his win-at-all-costs approach to racing. Schumel Schumi, on-the-edge Schumi, clever Schumi, don't-get-caught Schumi.

The nickname and the reputation bothered Michael a great deal and he set out actively to lose them. When Heiner Buchinger started his job as Michael's press officer at the start of 1995, he was thrown in at the deep end straight away. Schumacher's victorious Benetton was disqualified from the season-opening Brazilian Grand Prix, along with

Coulthard's second-placed Williams, for fuel irregularities.

'I was in the media centre and everyone was saying, "Schumel Schumi is back. Michael is cheating again." I said to them, "Who do you think mixes the fuel, Michael or Elf? Do you think Michael went to Elf and asked them to mix him some nitroglycerine? Of course not. Why don't you ask Elf what went wrong?" So they did and it worked out quite well. It started to sort out the problem in Germany and after a while we heard no more about Schumel Schumi. But the problem then was the English press.

'Briatore and his press officer, Patrizia Spinelli, divided the English journalists into two camps: friends of Benetton and enemies of Benetton. The problem was there were only two or three friends of Benetton and at least ten of the most influential writers were off-limits. Briatore had very publicly chucked them out of the motorhome and my first job was to repair that. I invited the British journalists to tests and said, "Come in and talk to Michael." I tried to get things on a normal basis and I think that we had a big improvement.'

But behind the scenes Michael had also realized that he would never be truly free of the Schumel Schumi tag as long as he stayed at Benetton. Towards the end of the previous season, he had told the team that he would not continue driving for them if it meant being disqualified all the time and being branded a cheat. That Benetton had not been proven to be cheating was an important factor in his decision not to walk away from the whole thing at the end of 1994, but both he and his manager, Willi Weber, knew the writing was on the wall. Weber renegotiated his contract and the existing three-year deal was dissolved. In its place came a new one-year deal, expiring at the end of 1995.

Weber had no shortage of offers for Schumacher's services for 1996 and beyond. But as well as a huge salary, the chance to go to Ferrari offered something special: the chance to participate in the running of the team, to be the clear number-one driver with a role in the decision-making process. Looking at the wider picture, going to Ferrari would also give him the chance to build a global image, to be popular all over the world, not just in the places where Formula 1 is appreciated.

Most important of all, making Ferrari great again, winning the championship with them after almost two decades in the doldrums, would obliterate any stains that the 1994 season with Benetton may have left on his reputation. The Ferrari team was on its way up – in Jean Todt, the sporting director, they had a strong man in charge and in John Barnard they had one of the most highly regarded designers in Formula 1, although as things turned out Barnard was to prove a great disappointment to Schumacher.

Weber's intuition proved right; the heroic image of a gifted champion striving to return Ferrari to greatness captured the public's imagination, as did his many sublime victories against superior machinery. Di Montezemolo pushed the marketing button and Ferrari flags dominated every track around the world, whereas before they were only predominant at Monza and Imola. Over two seasons, Schumacher rose head and shoulders above the opposition and the stains of his past seemed to have all but disappeared.

Before the Jerez weekend, Buchinger had cause to feel pretty pleased with things. The press had gone big on the story of Schumacher's brilliance. In a sport which rewards technology over human sporting flair, Schumacher stood alone as a driver who could make a difference, turn the form book on its head, strike a blow for humanity against the dominance of technology. TV reports, news and feature articles told of how he had dragged the ailing Ferrari team up to championship level, and most of the public truly believed that if Ferrari won in Jerez it would be Schumacher who had made the difference, whereas if Villeneuve won it would be because he was driving the best car on the grid.

He was seen as a great competitor, but one with a good balance in his life. As the responsible family man, doting on his baby daughter, he embodied traditional values and a scandal-free personal life any politician would kill for. The

Newsweek front cover before Jerez had summed it up; image-wise Michael Schumacher was in great shape.

But after Jerez, in Heiner's words, it all 'turned to shit'. Everything he had worked towards for so long had been destroyed by a split second of madness on the track and by ten minutes of misjudged human reaction to the press that evening. There was nothing Heiner could do to repair the damage quickly. If he convened a press conference on the Sunday night for Michael to explain himself properly, the press would have said, 'But hang on, ten minutes ago he said the opposite.'

Buchinger was back to square one. 'The problem was in those two hours after the race before he spoke, I did not realize that he did not realize what was going on. In the past he had reacted well, like at Monaco in 1996 when he crashed in the race and the Italian press wanted an explanation. At the time, Michael could easily have said the car let him down, but instead he said that it was all his own fault. He had tried something which worked in practice, but it didn't work in the race. So that's why he crashed and he was very sorry.

'I thought he would do this again, but of course he didn't.'

SIX BEHIND THE HEADLINES
Tuscany, Italy, February 1998

The road from Florence to Mugello passes through some of the most beautiful countryside in Europe. The Tuscan hills, lush green with olive groves, vineyards and cypress trees, roll endlessly on. The narrow ribbon of road follows the contours of the hills through villages like Vicchio and Vespignano, birthplace of the thirteenth-century artist Giotto, who could draw a perfect circle. The Mugello region is on the Tuscany side of the Apennine mountains. On the other side is the province of Emiglia-Romagna, home of Parmesan cheese, and the town of Maranello, Ferrari's celebrated headquarters.

The Mugello area is a popular weekend escape for wealthy Florentines, and in summer the roads are packed with tourist vehicles, many from Germany bearing the number plates of cities like Cologne and Stuttgart. The German love affair with Italy goes back to the eighteenth-century writer Goethe, whose descriptions of the Italian countryside, its open people, simple and traditional way of life continue to draw in new generations of Germans today. They own a lot of real estate in this region; warm terracotta villas, farmhouses and summer retreats. Britons may like to believe that Tony Blair's beloved 'Chiantishire' is a spiritual outpost of Her Majesty's empire, but the reality is that German is now the second language of the region.

Just outside the town of Scarperia is the Mugello circuit. It's an impressive facility, owned and managed by Ferrari and built to Grand Prix standards. But it's easy to see why they don't have a Formula 1 race here; the access roads are dire and the traffic jam on race day would make getting out of Silverstone seem like a drive through a ghost town.

It's early February and Schumacher has been back at work for three weeks, honing his new Ferrari F310 for the upcoming season. Over the winter he has had plenty of time to reflect on Jerez and to search his conscience about what really happened. Six weeks have been spent with his family in their home in Norway; the first proper break he has had for several years. After the FIA disciplinary hearing on 11 November, which found him guilty of a 'deliberate but not premeditated' act, he slipped quietly away from the media din and retired to the tranquillity of Scandinavia.

He would like to draw a curtain over the whole Jerez issue and look forward, but Heiner Buchinger has told him that he'll have to keep answering questions about it until the first race in Australia on 8 March. After that he can legitimately say 'enough'. Stoically, he has been receiving journalists and TV crews throughout the tests; one a day for up to twenty minutes at a time. Some get straight to the point, others delay asking the Jerez question.

Schumacher has been quite open and frank about Jerez and what it has done to his image, although there is none of the self-pity in his voice which you hear from footballers and others who fall from grace. He is clearly not going to allow himself to get bogged down in too much negative thought. Heiner Buchinger has played it skilfully, allowing access to the right newspapers, whilst not making it look like a carefully planned rehabilitation.

The *Sun*, Britain's largest circulation newspaper, has already paid a visit and its wily correspondent Stan Piecha has teased more than most out of the fallen idol. Under the headline MONSTER CRUNCH: FANS HATE ME BUT I DON'T CARE SAYS SCHU, Schumacher admits, 'I am going to be the bad guy in some people's eyes for ever, but I have stopped trying to please everyone. It's impossible. Some people treat me as if I had committed the most unforgivable sin. Others look at it as no worse than throwing a piece of paper out of the car window.

'Everyone in their career has done something they wouldn't want to do again. If I could turn the clock back I wouldn't have done what I did, but life must go on.

'I made a mistake. If someone wants to believe that I deliberately tried to take Jacques off the track they will. If you look at the pictures I can understand why some people think this way.

'The truth is I was so determined – so confident of winning the title. It was mine, and then suddenly everything changed. I was fighting until the last minute, trying to protect what I believed was in my pocket.

'The only thing deliberate about my move was to protect my place – not take him out.'

The rain is falling steadily on the almost-deserted paddock. Three large red trucks with Scuderia Ferrari Marlboro scrawled on the side are backed up against the pit building. One of the technicians, wearing the standard-issue Ferrari team jacket and trousers designed by Tommy Hilfiger, listens on his head-phones, takes a final draw on his cigarette and turns back into the garage.

It's great to be back at a race track again. After the winter lay-off, followed by the monotonous optimism of the new car launches, there's always a prick of excitement when the real thing starts.

Launches are amusing but ultimately pointless. There is always the affirmative statement, 'We at team X are confident that this will be our year,' when you know as well as they do that they'll probably fire at least one of the drivers and will be lucky to score a single point all season. The press packs handed out by hired glamour girls speak of the team's 'synergy' and of the sponsors' 'strategic objectives'. Launches are put on mainly to help the sponsors feel good about their investment, but they can also cause embarrassment.

The Stewart team, now entering its second year, had put on a splendid launch at Ford's UK headquarters in Essex. The team principals looked terribly pleased with themselves for having arranged a satellite link-up with some top Ford brass in Dearborn, USA, to whom they addressed their speeches. It was corporate self-preening at its finest, but it made very little copy in the national newpapers the following day. Stewart was devastated, but the truth was there was simply no story. In Michael Schumacher's life, on the other hand, his every move is a story, and never a day goes by without some kind of coverage in the Italian and German papers.

You hear the sound long before you can see where it's coming from – a racing engine, its high-pitched scream rising and falling like a soprano singer practising her scales. But you don't need to be an aficionado to appreciate the urgent insistence of this music. Schumacher is on the track and on the limit in the new Ferrari, attacking the turns. A modern Formula 1 engine revs more than 17,000 times a minute – three times the limit of a normal family car. There is no sound on earth like it and, to the millions of Italians who love the sport, there used to be no sound quite like a Ferrari engine. Until recently, you could easily pick out the shriek of the Ferrari V12 engines among the other teams' V10s, but now those days are gone. Ferrari switched over to the V10 format three years ago with the attitude, 'If you can't beat them, join them.'

It was quite a break with the past. One of Enzo Ferrari's many idiosyncrasies was his edict, after seeing a V12 Packard at Indianapolis in 1914, that a real racing engine should always have twelve cylinders. For almost fifty years, apart from brief periods when the rules dictated that V6 was the way to go, Ferrari engines were V12.

But Ferrari was now a very modern team and all pretence of doing things differently had long been abandoned. Since the early 1960s British teams had done most of the winning in Formula 1 and the sport's Silicon Valley of technology had grown in the UK. After several flirtations with it, Ferrari had now committed itself to move with the times and sporting director, Jean Todt, had bought in the winning technology, much of it from Britain, and hired the expertise to use it. The team had sent out a clear message in January, holding their 1998 launch against the backdrop of the new wind-tunnel at Maranello. 'Here we are,' they appeared to be saying, 'no longer just the team of the heart, but now also of the head.'

The fruit of that steady build-up of technical power was out on the track on this wet February morning, with Michael Schumacher at the wheel. But there were difficulties. After three weeks of testing, the 1998 car still had some worrying reliability problems. They were only niggling things, but the bedrock of any championship campaign is reliability. The team knew that only by extensive testing would they iron out the problems with this car before the season started. So the decision had been made to stay near the factory, rather than head for sunnier test venues, like Barcelona, where the opposition were. It was a slight gamble in that they would have little idea of where they stood relative to the opposition. If they found at the first race in Melbourne that they were miles off the pace, it would be too late to do anything about it. Another unfortunate side effect of the decision was that it sowed the seed in their opponents' minds that Ferrari had something to hide, that it was working on things which pushed the boundaries of legality. The phoney war – later to develop into a full-blown cold war with McLaren – had begun.

Looking back, the launch of the car in early January at Maranello had not been a good omen for the season. There had been a noticeably smaller press contingent that in previous years and very few of the German media bothered to make the trip. The three or four who did come said that German travel agents were reporting a 40 per cent downturn in Grand Prix bookings compared to the previous winter. To Michael Schmidt, one of the country's leading Grand Prix writers, it was a clear indication that the sport was in decline in Germany.

'There were less journalists in Maranello and the papers

71

who didn't send anyone were not picking up the story from the news agencies. I think the editors had decided that F1 is not a proper sport any more, with the scandal over Schumi trying to drive Villeneuve off the road to win the championship. I thought then that the figures for the TV [a record German audience of sixteen million had watched Jerez] and the whole media attention on F1 had peaked and that it would never be reproduced again.'

Many editors around the world had been unhappy about Schumacher's punishment for Jerez after the FIA disciplinary hearing in November. The FIA's World Council's verdict – that Schumacher driving into Villeneuve was 'deliberate, but not premeditated' – was clever but flimsy reasoning. In their view, the second turn of the wheel was intended to take Villeneuve out, but there hadn't been time for him to *think* about it first. They reasoned that the second turn of the wheel was also instinctive. It was clever diplomacy but it glossed over a key point: surely the 'instinctive reaction' was Schumacher's initial turn of the wheel *away* from Villeneuve, so how could he have had two conflicting instincts?

The punishment was a different matter. He was disqualified from the 1997 points table and, rather than a fine, he was given a spell of community service, helping promote the FIA's message about road safety. To the media, some of whom had campaigned for a ban, this was a mere slap on the wrist.

The *Sun* newspaper in England had said, 'This decision is a licence to kill; Schumacher carry on ramming.' Many commentators had expected a ban of three to six races, but the reality was that without its only genuine superstar on the grid for the opening races of 1998 Formula 1 would be committing financial suicide.

The promoters in Melbourne, where the first race was due to take place, were understood to be concerned about ticket sales if Schumacher wasn't there and TV executives worried about how far audience figures would drop without the Red Baron in the field. Formula 1's box office appeal for 1998 looked pretty thin if you removed Schumacher's Ferrari from the equation. In any case, a sport like Formula 1 thrives on needle and it was far better to have the controversial German on site, with the potential for a new polemic, rather than sulking at home in Switzerland. FIA president, Max Mosley, defended the decision to take away points retrospectively rather than to ban Schumacher.

'It's no use imposing a penalty that isn't a deterrent. There is no driver competing in 1998 who would not be ready to accept a ban in 1999 if it meant he could win the World Championship in 1998.'

Curiously, there had been no talk from the FIA of Schumacher being charged with bringing the sport into disrepute, which, judging by the press coverage, seemed to be his greatest sin. This aspect was quietly swept under the carpet, although one or two of the cheekier papers suggested that, with this lame judgement, the FIA itself had brought the sport into disrepute. But the FIA and its commercial mandarin Bernie Ecclestone were in an awkward position because they were aiming to float the commercial arm of the sport for almost $2 billion in 1998 and they needed Schumacher and Ferrari on the grid, firing on all cylinders.

Ferrari, along with Mercedes, was one of the few brand names that the majority of likely investors would have heard of. The sport's credibility as a business proposition depended partly on Ferrari looking strong. Paralysing the team's championship hopes by removing Schumacher from the equation – even for one race – was a non-starter of an idea. Besides, the flotation plans had been damaged enough already by the European tobacco advertising ban, which was due to come into force in the early twenty-first century, and by the furore over Ecclestone's £1-million donation to the British Labour Party. Potential investors had also been concerned about disunity among the teams: Williams and McLaren were objecting to the terms of the new Concorde Agreement, which binds the teams into the sport for ten years. Against the backdrop of these serious concerns, the Schumacher issue could be seen largely as a creation of the media; a fly in the ointment, to be resolved quickly and pragmatically.

At the height of the furore Bernie Ecclestone was quoted in a British newspaper as saying, 'I can take the heat. Listen, I've got promoters and television to think about. Michael was a silly boy, but they want him at the races. People will forget about this soon enough.'

This was the sound of money talking. A curtain had been drawn over Jerez. The people who run Formula 1 were looking forwards.

In reality the FIA's penalty was extremely severe. Viewed objectively it amounted to the first time in the history of Formula 1 that a driver had been disqualified from a championship for a deliberate foul. It was almost unprecedented in any sport. Whatever records Schumacher may go on to break, however many wins he may accrue, however much glory he may bring to Ferrari and however great a legend he may leave behind him, the history books will show that he was the first man to be thrown out for attempting to foul an opponent. It is a fact.

Far from being a slap on the wrist, it put a permanent stain on his character as a sportsman and Schumacher knew it. 'Jerez is the black spot on my image,' he said at the time. 'I will have to carry it around and live with it, but hopefully there will be some brighter moments in the future.' The one positive thing to come out of the FIA tribunal was that everyone now knew where they stood. 'Perhaps this judgement should have come ten years earlier,' Schumacher reflected sadly. In the light of what had happened a few years earlier, he was entitled to feel somewhat aggrieved. History will also show that in 1989 Alain Prost was World Champion and that the following year it was Ayrton Senna. Further reading will reveal that in 1989 Prost collided with Senna in a slow chicane at Suzuka to win the title, although he never admitted it was deliberate. He received no censure and kept his title.

The following year, at the same venue, Senna launched his car into Prost's in a 130 m.p.h. kamikaze attack, and yet he received no punishment and was also allowed to keep the title. A year later Senna made an astonishingly emotional and foul-mouthed confession – but no apology – and still he kept the title and still no disrepute charge was brought against him.

A few years on, Senna and Roland Ratzenberger were dead, the sport had yet to recover and, outwardly at least, a spirit of political correctness had been embraced. In this new and different climate, Schumacher with his old values had tried to ram Villeneuve off the road and he was being made to pay heavily for it. Perhaps he hadn't realized that the climate had changed, but then, as one of the foremost spokesmen on safety and a leading light in the Grand Prix Drivers' Association, which consults with the FIA on circuit safety, he should have known those days were gone. Perhaps there was something in him that made him forget this at the crucial moment.

Martin Brundle, Schumacher's former team-mate at Benetton and a contemporary of Senna and Prost, put it succinctly: 'Schuey's just like Senna and Prost. He has a natural gift and the incredible self-belief that goes with it. These guys are winners who will push the limits beyond everyone else. They have the most intense, almost dangerous desire, and *need*, to win at all costs and somehow they convince themselves that they are not wrong. They'll talk you through the story and they are actually quite convinced that they are not wrong.

'Look at Senna and Prost in Japan those two years. Both were convinced they had done the right thing. Senna drove Prost off the road, but he could construct a solid reason – even twelve months later – why that wasn't wrong! I think Schumacher did the same in Jerez. I can understand his point of view, he'd be thinking, Hang on, I've seen drivers run guys off the road in the past and people thought they were real racers. Gilles Villeneuve would have been hero-worshipped for something like that! In other words he believed that those kind of moves made you a respected gung-ho racer and he was shaken rigid by the reaction he got. Michael's problem is that he's on a pedestal, and in today's era of political correctness he's learned the hard way that things have changed.'

Brundle's analysis comes to mind as, sitting in his private mobile gym, which follows him to all the winter tests, Schumacher attempts to explain Jerez.

'In the past, that was the way you did it. If you wouldn't have done it you would have been criticized the other way around. Nevertheless, we live in different times and you have to adapt to the situation.'

Different times indeed, but another key difference from the Senna/Prost scenario is that Schumacher *lost* the title as a result of his foul – punishment enough in the view of his allies. Punishable offences are generally where the perpetrator has gained an unfair advantage out of the incident. That did not happen in this case.

Also, with Senna driving into Prost there was an implicit understanding that Prost had done it to him the year before, so there was a sort of rough justice about it, in a strangely human way, which made it almost forgivable. If your neighbour throws a brick through your window, you feel entitled to throw one back through his. Schumacher did not have this symmetry. With Senna the motive was revenge, one of the most uncontrollable, yet understandable human emotions.

Schumacher's move at Jerez, on the other hand, was an act of unprovoked violence, which made even those who didn't believe he'd driven into Hill deliberately in 1994 claim he'd now done it twice. One other crucial thing separated Schumacher from Senna. The Brazilian was prepared to take risks with other people's lives and frequently frightened his rivals with games of chicken at 180 m.p.h., often punting them off the road. Nigel Mansell was once so incensed by a terrifying move Senna had made at Spa that he charged into Senna's garage and lifted the Brazilian off his feet! Controversial as he may be in many of his moves, Schumacher tends to do all his rough stuff at low speeds. Like Prost, he admits to feeling fear in a racing car and is not a fan of unnecessary risk, as would be shown time and again in 1998.

Schumacher looks fresh and primed. His thick neck reminds

one of a racehorse. Fatigue comes across his face only when the subject of Jerez is brought up. It's as if he feels he has to sit in the stocks for a few minutes while visitors throw eggs and fruit at him. Once the conversation moves on to fresh topics, his features lighten and he sits erect and confident, his jaw protruding like an American president posing for his sculpture on Mount Rushmore.

It is always slightly surprising to be in close physical proximity to Schumacher as you are reminded of how small and slight he is. He is neither muscular nor bulky in any way. And yet he looks impossibly fit. His golden skin, drawn tight across his small, sculptured face, oozes well-being. His big green-brown eyes fix you while you talk and you feel that, unlike many drivers, who seem always to be looking for a distraction, Michael is giving you his full attention. His life is well organized and compartmentalized; when he's driving he gives it 100 per cent of his attention with no distractions. When he's being interviewed it is the only thing that matters. He has one of the most uncluttered minds I have ever encountered, which he claims is entirely natural and not the product of any mental training techniques. He has no need of sports psychologists. His memory is outstanding, enabling him to recall the minutest details of incidents or races from years gone by. His mastery of English is sufficient to express himself and to make himself understood and, as he spends quite a bit of his time explaining his side of some fresh controversy, this is no bad thing.

He uses his hands a lot when speaking. You always expect a racing driver's hands to be remarkable in some way and yet Schumacher's are small and quite normal in appearance. They are clearly very strong and he has a firm handshake. When you look at them and imagine the tremendous control they are able to exert over a car at high speed, then they do seem remarkable.

The celebrated American photographer Annie Leibowitz was once commissioned to do a portrait of the soccer hero Pelé. She photographed only his feet – the tools of his trade.

A racing driver needs excellent co-ordination between his feet and hands. The feet decide whether a corner is to be taken flat or whether a slight lift may be advisable, while the hands decide the trajectory the car will take into that corner. They also wave at chequered flags and uncork champagne bottles.

Schumacher is adamant that his reputation has not suffered as much as the media might believe and feels that the public are still behind him despite Jerez.

'It came out after the Jerez race that there was a support towards myself of 78 per cent staying behind me and really supporting me, so I mean the media makes one thing, but the real fan and the people outside are having a different thought. If you look in the first moment, the Italian *tifosi* have been very emotional, but as soon as they calm down they are as normal as are the German fans and they stay behind us and they support us.

'The real fans are the ones who stay with you whether you win or you lose. I believe that most people do not reduce the season to one race. I'm aware that the season ended badly for me, but I have to look to the future. I made a mistake and I can't correct that wrong. All I want to do is win the championship and repay the team.'

It is strange to look at Schumacher and to realize that he's speaking as a loser. Although he has lost badly in races in the past, most notably Japan in 1994, where Damon Hill scored his greatest triumph over him, he hadn't lost something as significant as a world-title showdown before and certainly never in such humiliating circumstances.

When a great champion loses, you are never quite sure what to expect. Perhaps they aren't sure either; losing isn't something they spend time contemplating. You almost imagine them going off the rails in some way. No outsider is privy to the internal dialogue of a champion mourning his loss. Schumacher is often accused of being more like a robot than a human being and it was clear in the immediate aftermath of Jerez that he had attempted to park his error in the appropriate space and move on. The analysis had come later; too much later.

But true greatness often manifests itself in defeat and the manner in which it's accepted. Many people were surprised by Muhammad Ali's reaction after he'd lost his heavyweight world title to Joe Frazier at Madison Square Garden, in the days when boxing titles meant something. Ali had once said that if he ever lost all boxing would end, but, as he told writer George Plimpton in the book *Shadowboxing*, he had learned what it was to lose.

'Oh they all said that if he ever loses, he'll shoot himself, he'll die; but I'm human. I've lost one fight out of thirty-two. I don't think about it as much as I thought I would. The world still turns. I've got to keep living. I'm not ashamed. The title was taken away from me. I'm the one who has to get it back.'

There are echoes of Ali's words as Schumacher weighs up the expectations for 1998: 'I would never say, "I am the best." I'm not arrogant like that. Obviously Mr Villeneuve won the World Championship, so he is the best at the moment. It's up to us to prove he is wrong.

'After what happened last year, our target is to win the World Championship. But whether we can do it or not, who can tell? We will do our best and we hope it will be enough. It's not that we *have* to win it, or that the world will go under if we don't win.'

The words of a pragmatist and not the sort of language Schumacher would have come out with in his early career, before the birth of his daughter. Even before she was born there were signs that fatherhood would change him. In late 1996 he had admitted that the podium scene when he'd won at Monza that year was the most amazing experience of his life, 'except for the day I found out that I was going to be a father'. Now, after his winter of discontent, he was asking us to believe that he had mellowed and that winning wasn't everything to him.

'I really messed up. That I am criticized for Jerez is OK, but you know I am not God and I am not an idiot. I always see things down the middle and that means I take praise as well as blame, within reason. In the first instance it was quite easy for me to put the thing to the back of my mind. What then followed, the public debate, the reaction in the press and from the FIA, that caused me to think a little more deeply, so the painful aftermath was stronger than the initial, spontaneous reaction.

'I've certainly got something to put right, that's clear, but on the other hand, there's never anything that one should totally regret. Look at the season as a whole. I had some good performances. It's not as if I messed up the whole season; it was just one race that went wrong and nobody would have turned a hair if it had been for tenth place. What is special about Jerez is that the World Championship was at stake and every racing driver in my place would have tried everything to win the championship.'

Ali's ability to accept defeat was probably eased by the immense trials he had been through in his life, the political battles he got himself involved in, like refusing to fight in Vietnam or being thrown out of his beloved Muslim sect. He had been through a lot of suffering in his life and losing was just another form of it. It cannot be easy to accept defeat when you believe that you are the greatest. Like Ali, Schumacher is no ordinary human being. He doesn't have the charisma of Ali, nor does he create the excitement that most of Ali's fights generated – a feeling that something far more significant than a mere boxing match was taking place. On the one hand Schumacher often seems appalled by the significance some people attach to his actions as a sportsman, on the other he revels in the superiority that his reputation gives him. But now, he wanted to play down the significance of Jerez and in some ways of the title battle as well. I'm just a racing driver, he seemed to be saying. I do what I do because I love it, not for the hysteria which my winning or losing creates.

One wonders whether the pursuit of a sporting prize is worth all the pressure and vitriol the modern athlete is forced to endure. Money has changed all sport, by raising the stakes and making the players rich. But it has also made it acceptable for the media to say what they like about those sporting heroes and to sit in judgement, not just on their performances but on their characters and private lives, too.

Schumacher got into Formula 1 because he loved driving go-karts, was exceptionally good at it and car racing was a natural progression. He didn't start racing cars in order to become a multi-millionaire and world-famous celebrity; those things came with the territory. The pressure created by fame and wealth on this scale has destroyed many people. Ali thrived on it and Schumacher has learned to deal with it. His feet are firmly on the ground and he knows that however big the headlines about him are, his equilibrium is good because he has got the funda-mentals in his life right. With such a solid footing, he is blown over by neither adulation nor opprobrium.

'One shouldn't get too carried away with all this. Up until now I was always in the sunshine of the media, perhaps even a little too much. Now I'm in the shadows, but I know that the sunshine isn't far away.'

Like Ali, Schumacher is in many ways a prisoner of his own sucess. Sometimes he is dragged down by it, at other times he is able to use it to his own ends as a psychological advantage over his rivals. He understands that his greatness is based not just on a sublime and unusually consistent ability, but also on a character that makes a virtue of rubbing people up the wrong way. He always seems to find a way to generate controversy and he arouses strong, conflicting emotions in people all over the world. He doesn't show his contempt for his rivals in an extrovert way – like the demented poems and taunts of Ali – he simply lets his image and reputation speak for him while he methodically goes about his business. But the two approaches have the same origin – he is 100 per cent mentally driven.

Although he denies it, one of his greatest skills is the way he allows people to believe in their own preconceptions about him: that he is arrogant, ruthless and superior. This gives him a psychological advantage over most of his rivals before he's even sat in his car. According to Martin Brundle, 'He psyches people out just by the way he carries himself around the paddock. He glistens with health, and his totally relaxed demeanour and look of total confidence around the paddock just kills the opposition. He's already done his job before he gets in the car.'

After Jerez, you couldn't help but wonder whether that image had been undermined. Michael had traded for so long on the idea that he was the perfect driver, didn't make mistakes very often, was superior in strategy, ability, fitness and nerve. But in Jerez he had panicked, cracked under pressure, lost his nerve. Worse still, he had appeared human.

His self-belief may have persuaded him that he was not in the wrong and that people would forgive him for it, but the reality was that many people, including himself, couldn't believe it had happened to him. The public now saw that he was beatable. Villeneuve was stoking the fire of doubt, crowing that Schumacher was beatable. Going into the 1998 season, the $10-million question would be, Did Schumacher believe it, too?

A week later. It is midnight in the McLaren factory and the new car is being assembled for the following day's launch. With most of its rivals already well advanced with their test programmes, it is late to be launching a car. But there's a palpable air of confidence around the workshops. Everybody has a real sense of purpose and expectation as they work. Team co-ordinator, Jo Ramirez, who has been with McLaren for many years, says that the atmosphere in the team is 'the best since Senna was with us'.

Their confidence is well founded. Adrian Newey joined the team the previous summer from Williams and made improvements straight away.

The team had grown more competitive in the second half of 1997, culminating in Hakkinen's win at Jerez. With Newey's track record as designer of four of the last six championship-winning cars, great things were expected from this new McLaren-Mercedes.

Ron Dennis, the highly driven boss of the team, won seven World Championships in the eight years running up to 1991, but they were with ace drivers Niki Lauda, Alain Prost and Ayrton Senna. Neither Hakkinen nor Coulthard, though highly rated, can be considered in that league, but in 1998 they will be challenging a man who is.

Norbert Haug, competitions director of Mercedes-Benz, watches alongside Dennis as the 'Silver Arrow' car is assembled. He has known Schumacher since he was a boy and worked with him on the Mercedes junior team. Now they are adversaries, for Haug's McLaren-Mercedes Silver Arrows aim to destroy Schumacher's and Ferrari's title hopes in 1998. When told what Schumacher had said about the world not 'falling under' if Ferrari didn't win in 1998, he snorted.

'I don't believe it and neither should you. Let me tell you something about Michael Schumacher: he is a man who spends his every waking hour thinking about beating the opposition into the ground.'

SEVEN THE REAL MICHAEL SCHUMACHER

According to Ferrari president Luca di Montezemolo, one of the positive things to come out of Jerez was the realization that Michael Schumacher is a human being and not a robot. 'I've always liked him,' said the president, 'but I find that after this accident I like him even more. Michael explained to me what happened and I understood his motives.'

Schumacher was often criticized in the past for being a streamlined product of sponsors and PR men, but now he'd acquired some edges, things for people to hook into. He had become a personality. But the question remains, What is he like as a person?

Some racing drivers show the person they really are to the outside world; what you see is what you get. Others build a wall around their private self and develop a public face. Niki Lauda, Mario Andretti and Gerhard Berger are in the former camp. The impression the public has of the man is broadly accurate, this is who they really are. Schumacher is in the latter camp. He has divided his life firmly into two parts: the racing driver and the family man. The result is that the press and public feel they know the driver, but have very little idea of the man. Unusually he has taken this further than most, to the extent that even work colleagues, who know him well as a racing driver, do not really know the private Schumacher.

'The only people who get through are the ones I want to get

through. There is no point in allowing people to write about my private life because even if the first story is nicely written, it will be picked up by other papers and changed around. Different slants get put on it and all of a sudden it's not so nice. I have had too many experiences of things starting out nice and then being turned against me.'

Nevertheless, Michael was impressed with a story he saw in *Paris-Match* during 1997 about Damon Hill's home life in Dublin with his wife, Georgie, and their three children. He liked the way the story was handled and the photos of Damon playing his guitar and he asked Heiner Buchinger whether he could organize something similar. Before Heiner had the chance to arrange it, Jerez happened.

Eddie Irvine, Schumacher's team-mate at Ferrari for three seasons, is not surprised that many of his colleagues don't feel they know the man: 'I think I know him, but I couldn't honestly say. And he probably thinks he knows how I am, but he couldn't say. In this business there are very few people you want to have knowing what you're really like; it's not in your best interests. If you're playing chess you don't tell your opponent your next move beforehand, do you?'

At an early stage in his Formula 1 career, Michael had to build a protective wall around himself so he would not be destroyed. His main problem was that he came to Formula 1 very young, aged just twenty-two, and his youthful exuberance was in stark contrast to the band of hardened professionals he was up against, both on the track and in the press office. The war between Prost and Senna had subsided from the bitter days of 1989/90, but there was still a great deal of nastiness and contempt in the air and, as always, the politics of Formula 1 were almost impossible for a young man to navigate alone.

'Formula 1 is very political, but I think it seems it more to the media because they report the politics; I don't get involved. When I was in sportscars and Formula 3 I used to read the stories, because there weren't as many then, of course. After a while I stopped reading about what was going on behind the scenes. Nowadays I don't know all the intrigues behind the scenes in Formula 1 and I don't want to know, because it would be too distracting.'

Initially the media warmed to this brilliant young talent and rejoiced in his exuberant celebrations on the podium, which he seemed to reach at virtually every race. But the honeymoon period is short and the press will always try to set heroes against each other if the opportunity arises. With his extreme self-confidence and formative attempts at psychotricks Michael seemed a willing participant in the hype.

It cut both ways; with no-one experienced at handling the media to guide him, Michael fell for some simple traps and came off badly. But he used the media too, for example, when he suggested to a group of British newspaper journalists just before the 1994 European Grand Prix that Damon Hill was not a gentleman and certainly not a worthy championship rival. He added that had Ayrton Senna still been alive he [Schumacher] would have really had something to think about. His suggestion that Hill was 'not a number-one driver and was thrown into the job' was particularly lacking in taste, given the circumstances of Senna's death and Damon's brave attempt to rally the Williams team from its pit of despair.

It made great copy and probably had a small effect on Hill, but it was very undignified and seemed to highlight a disparity between the high-class driver that Michael clearly was and the mean, low-grade cheap shot of a person he appeared to be. It is easy to see why he was so frustrated; he had been hammered by allegations about Benetton's performance and the suspicions of cheating; he'd been suspended for two races and watched a huge points lead evaporate. Damon Hill now had a real chance of beating him to the title. The frustration and anger at what had happened could have destroyed Schumacher, but instead he fell back on his endless reserve of self-confidence and lashed out. Not for the first or last time Michael had had entirely the wrong human reaction, and it added insensitivity and meanness to the charge of arrogance.

The sport needed good rivalry and a Brit-versus-German battle, with all its historic associations, was an added bonus.

But it didn't need a bitter feud like the one that had lasted for five years between Ayrton Senna and Alain Prost, especially not now, as it was still struggling to get over Senna's death. That feud had been entirely emotionally driven, but the two drivers never belittled each other's abilities. Do that, simple logic dictates, and you belittle your own achievement when you win.

Michael is not an emotionally driven racing driver, he is entirely mentally driven. But out of the cockpit it seemed as though the real man had stepped out from behind his stream-lined PR façade to show his true colours. And like his initial public reaction to the Villeneuve incident at Jerez three years later, it was foolish, ill-considered and damaging only to him-self. As one of his colleagues put it, 'Michael's driving is in the very highest class, but the way he carries himself after in-cidents like Jerez is in the lowest class. He must bring that side of himself up to the higher level as well. Senna was much stronger in this way than Schumacher. Perhaps he was wiser or better educated.'

Martin Brundle isn't so sure: 'He's less streetwise than some, but I don't think it's relative to education. His intellect is equal to any of the greats, like Senna or Prost before him; you cannot question his intellect. I just wonder sometimes whether he would understand some of the reactions better if he were a bit more streetwise. But then again if you're looking for Joe Regular, then Joe Regular doesn't race at the front of Grands Prix and earn twenty million pounds a year. He can't be normal and do what he does.'

Jochen Mass was Germany's leading Formula 1 driver before Schumacher came along, and as team-mates in the Mercedes sportscar team the two became firm friends. Today he remains one of Schumacher's closest confidants, in private as well as public life. He sees both sides of Schumacher's character.

'I feel that perhaps his comparative immaturity in terms of not being able to admit a fault might be considered a weak-ness, but of course it isn't. He's dedicated and keen and when he makes a mistake he analyses it a hundred times before he can admit he made a mistake. We can call this a character failing if we want to, but it isn't really, because in private he's a great guy – very soft and generous.'

Ross Brawn too feels that the scrutiny of Michael's character is too harsh. 'Michael is a grossly misunderstood person. He does have a side to him, but so does everybody; nobody's perfect. But if you look at everything; he has this incredible talent, he's very fair to the people he works with, he's very honest and truthful with the team, and when you consider his position – here's a guy who's gone from nothing to having everything – he's handled it pretty well. Nobody else has had to deal with that. No-one else has ever had to come from where he started to where he is now in such a short time and he's had to deal with all the pressures.'

Schumacher's dual life is part of a strict discipline. He keeps the private person hidden from public view and seems able to flick between the two with ease. He has developed the ability to switch on and off, and from this comes not just his focus as an athlete but also his ability to relax.

German newspaperman Michael Schmidt has known him throughout his career, but only once has he caught a glimpse of the private, relaxed Schumacher.

'He's only a private person when he's away from the media. The moment he sees someone from the media the switch goes into the other programme and he puts on the public face.

'There is a small group of us who bet on how many laps Schumi's Ferrari will cover in the race. Bernie Ecclestone is involved and Heiner Buchinger and it's good fun. Last year we had a dinner at Spa and we invited him because we said, "Look we have fun out of you, come and have some fun out of us." So he accepted.

'Bernie was in great form, telling jokes about how Ferrari was cheating all the time and how we all know that they get away with it because they are so clever. To start with Michael did not know how to take this and didn't seem to realize that the evening was just fun. He didn't know whether Bernie was joking or stitching him up. He was very reserved. It took him about an hour to realize that this was an evening which had nothing to do with the press. Nobody would write what was said, no pictures. He relaxed a bit and you could start to see what the fun, private person must be like.'

Michael is often perceived as lacking humour, although Eddie Irvine contends that 'you can have a laugh with him, as long as the joke's not on him. He's a bit like Nigel Mansell in that way: can't laugh at himself.'

That said, Schumacher definitely likes a good laugh. I was once with him during a lunch break at a test session when Heiner Buchinger came over with some cartoons he had cut out of an Italian magazine. One depicted Schumacher with a long body and a German First-World-War spiked army helmet on his head, goose-stepping. Behind him, a pint-sized Jean Todt was also goose-stepping. The caption read, 'Long wheelbase, Short wheelbase.' Schumacher fell about laughing.

He is not without humour and despairs at times of the impression people have of him. Because he is a superstar, this doesn't mean he isn't human.

'I'm just a normal human being. I believe I have both feet on the ground. I like to laugh and cry, although I much prefer laughing. People see me on television and reach a judgement of me, but they never have the chance to chat to me, so how can they know me?'

Damon Hill, who has a delicious, Monty Python sense of humour, despairs of Schumacher's sense of humour. In the paddock at the Austrian Grand Prix, Michael walked past wearing a green felt Tyrolean hunting hat with a feather in it. The local TV people had been handing them out to the drivers as a welcome gift. Schumacher wore his, without a trace of irony, for most of Saturday afternoon. 'That sums up his sense of humour,' sighed Damon.

Damon also tells a lovely story about a drivers' parade at the Nürburgring in 1997. Shortly before every Grand Prix the drivers are driven slowly around the track on the back of a flatbed truck to wave at the crowds. The Nürburgring crowds naturally went berserk when their hero passed and, as the German flags waved and the firecrackers went off in the grandstands, Jacques Villeneuve turned to Michael and said, 'Michael, doesn't it give you a hard on, having all these people here just for you?'

'What do you mean?' replied Schumacher.

'You know, does it give you an erection?'

Schumacher looked down at the crotch of his red Ferrari overalls and looked up again at Villeneuve.

'No.'

At this point Michael's younger brother Ralf came bowling over to see what Villeneuve and Hill were laughing about. Villeneuve repeated his question. Ralf looked at Michael's crotch.

'No,' he said blankly.

But there are plenty of examples of Michael having a good sense of humour. On one occasion Michael was being pestered by a fly. Suddenly he whipped his hand out and knocked it to the floor. He sat looking at it and I pointed out that he was clearly not a Buddhist, as they believe you should never hurt a creature because it may have been a person in a former life. Michael looked at the fly again. 'Sorry, Damon,' he shouted.

There have also been some memorable moments of self-deprecating Schumacher wit. Asked during the summer of 1998 about the possibility of him flying in for the World Cup final should Germany make it, he replied, 'Yes. But where would they play me?'

By his own admission, Schumacher doesn't make friends easily and maintains the impression of being hard to get to know. Like many very wealthy people, he is wary of others wanting to know him for what rather than who he is. But in fact, once a certain trust has been established, he is very easy-going and open.

He has a few friendships with other drivers; he often talks with David Coulthard, and Jean Alesi is a friend. Schumacher has great respect for Alesi's car control and finds his character amusing. In Adelaide in 1995, Alesi took Michael out of the lead in one of the most blatant chops of recent times. There were lots of possible motives: Schumacher was replacing Alesi at Ferrari the following year, he was also *en route* to his tenth win of the season, which would establish a new record. The rumour was that his fellow drivers had agreed not to allow him to reach that goal.

Surprisingly, Schumacher wasn't upset by the incident. He was already champion, but he forgave Alesi, who turned up after the race and said to him, 'You have to understand that this is not an accident. I cannot always pull back.' Schumacher laughed. He knew there had been plenty of incidents that year, most famously at the Nürburgring, where Michael had passed Alesi, relying on the fact that the Frenchman would give way. A highly emotional man, Alesi had been bursting with frustration, and to relieve it he had driven Michael off the road! Michael thought this was fair enough.

The relationship with his younger brother Ralf helps to keep the balance in his existence as a racing driver. Michael and Ralf look out for each other as they have throughout life.

Growing up without any money, Michael, six years the senior, always went first, broke new ground, learned the hard way. Ralf followed in his wake, having it easy, getting it all on a plate. By the time he came along there was a little more money in the family and more things were possible. Today, as top dog in Formula 1, Michael is anxious to help and protect his little brother and Ralf is always there to provide him with a reference point among the shifting loyalties of the Formula 1 paddock.

The Schumacher brothers are fundamentally old at heart. Both came into Formula 1 very young, but Michael was a trail-blazer. Adapting to the spotlight at the age of twenty-two and holding it all together to beat the top drivers required maturity beyond his years. Michael may be three years younger than his team-mate, Eddie Irvine, but he seems much older – in looks and in the way he carries himself. Ralf, perhaps because he feels he has more to prove, is even more serious than Michael and even older at heart.

On the plane to Buenos Aires in early 1998 I found myself,

by chance, seated in first class, just behind Damon and his friend Peter Boutwood. To my right was Michael and in front of him, Ralf. Michael and Ralf talked for a while to each other and then settled into their seats to eat a sensible meal and watch videos. British Airways provides first-class passengers with pyjamas and cabin socks, shaped like a child's bootees. Within ten minutes of getting airborne, Damon was cavorting around the cabin with these socks hanging down from his ears, impersonating the cartoon character Deputy Dawg. While the rest of us cried with laughter, neither Michael nor Ralf looked up from their video screens.

Michael doesn't understand Damon because he finds him moody, and in many ways he's right. Damon can greet you like a friend in the morning and walk straight past you without so much as a hello in the afternoon. It's all part of the 'focus' thing which Damon puts great store by. It is entirely genuine, but rather strange to witness. 'I don't have to live with him,' Michael said once. 'But either he's normal or he isn't. If he isn't then it's best we go our separate ways.'

As with tennis players, who from the age of three know nothing other than the racquet and the practice courts, it's hard for young drivers to get a balance in their lives; others have no problem. Damon, who despite being thirty-eight often acts like a fifteen-year-old, had a life before he became a racing driver; he played in a punk band, worked as a motorcycle courier, lived a little. Like all top drivers he is waited on hand and foot at the race track, but when he goes home he makes his own tea and sandwiches. Jacques Villeneuve too, despite his extraordinary success in the last three years, has always maintained another fulfilling, independent life away from racing. He grew up independent – travelling the world in his father's wake, living in Monaco, riding in helicopters.

Villeneuve always had the money to be able to afford an independent life. Schumacher, rather like Nigel Mansell, knew from the start that life would be what he made of it. His approach was formed early; he would always put the maximum in and expect the maximum out. So, like many top sportsmen, his adolescence and early twenties were lost in the pursuit of a higher prize, focused on the goal of improving as a driver, striving to be the best.

With success, and all the money he could ever need, has come a chance to re-evaluate. With fatherhood he has a chance to be more at peace with himself, to feel he doesn't need to be on the treadmill all the time. He has now built another life for himself away from racing and it is a world he allows hardly anyone to see.

It was perhaps appropriate that a talent as exceptional as Schumacher's should have an extraordinary introduction to the sport. The story of his first week as a Formula 1 driver is worth retelling; after his first outing in a Jordan at the Belgian Grand Prix in late 1991, he found himself a pawn in a game of deceit and double-dealing which wouldn't have been out of place in a John Le Carré novel.

Schumacher would have been happy to stay on for 1992 to learn the ropes with the Jordan team, which was enjoying an impressive first year in Formula 1. Its Ford-powered car had been very competitive, to the extent that, on occasions, it had embarrassed Benetton, the Ford works team. Benetton didn't want any repeats in 1992 and vetoed Jordan's supply of competitive customer engines for that season. Jordan was forced to look elsewhere and settled for a deal with Yamaha, despite its reputation as a very uncompetitive and unreliable package.

Throughout the Spa weekend, Schumacher's manager, Willi Weber, kept asking Jordan to confirm whether a Yamaha deal had been done, while Jordan ducked the question and tried to tie Schumacher to a long-term contract. But Benetton wanted to sign him up to drive alongside three-times champion Nelson Piquet. A middle-man from Mark McCormack's IMG group kept stalling the Jordan contract agreement, buying time in order to get Schumacher into Benetton.

Eight days after his Grand Prix début, Michael sent a fax

telling Jordan that he would not be driving for them any more. Jordan tried to take out an injunction, meetings were held until the early hours of the morning before practice at Monza. Benetton's existing driver, Roberto Moreno, was ousted and Schumacher duly made his second Grand Prix start at the wheel of a Benetton! Jordan had been taught a painful lesson about how things happen in Formula 1, and so had the twenty-two-year-old Schumacher, who wisely kept his head down and got on with the job. But he learned from the experience and, like any young man who wants to succeed, he knew he had a lot to learn.

One of Schumacher's greatest strengths as a person and as a driver is his ability to learn quickly, but his nature dictates that he doesn't want to be taught by others; he always wants to learn for himself. Martin Brundle recalls that, as team-mates at Benetton in 1992, Schumacher had 'little respect for anyone trying to offer him advice, which is all part of that incredible self-confidence he has'.

There is no question that the Jordan experience, and the many rows and controversies during his four years with Benetton forced him to develop a protective shell. Ross Brawn, then Benetton technical director and now in a similar role at Ferrari, knows him better than most people in F1. He believes that underneath the tough exterior he is still the same person.

'In 1992, when we first worked together, he was still new to Formula 1, whereas I'd done twenty-odd years. He's toughened up tremendously since then, especially mentally, because he came into it as a fresh-faced young boy and F1 is a tough, hard business – even nasty at times. He's had to come to terms with that. But underneath he is still the same person and a very nice person.

'I'll give you an example: my accountant came to the British Grand Prix with his wife. I was showing them around the Ferrari garage and, by chance, Michael came over. I introduced them and Michael took some time out to explain to them what it was like to drive an F1 car. Afterwards the wife said, "I have to admit I was wrong about him. I had an impression that he was an arrogant, stuck-up German, but he's not, is he? What a warm, generous chap!"

'And that's it really. Away from the sharp edges of F1 he is that person, but he also has to have a defence mechanism to protect himself from the difficulties.'

The accountant's wife was not alone in believing Michael to be aloof and arrogant. It's a widely held perception and one that he is aware of.

'People see me as cold, but they don't know me and I guess that's the price of fame. It's hard for me to show the real Michael Schumacher. There is so much work to do at the race track, briefings and so on, that there is no time for long chats with people. As the sport gets more popular you lose the personal side, and because people can't get close to me they get the wrong impression of me. It's sad, but there's nothing I can do about it.'

Self-confidence in a sportsman is seen as a great virtue, arrogance a shortcoming. Yet the dividing line is blurred, the leap from the one to the other is short and it's easy for outsiders to believe that leap has been made. Schumacher is perceived as being arrogant, partly because he is always so confident, partly because he is typically German – a nation often stereotyped as superior. Newspaperman Michael Schmidt sees both sides of this. 'There are some good things about the German attitude: we are good, reliable, hard workers and well organized. On the other hand we can be very narrow-minded. Some people feel Michael is arrogant and he sometimes gives that impression, but I don't think he is. I think he's sometimes not sure how to behave with people and with the public as a whole. He wants to be Mr Nice Guy to everybody, but he hasn't got the education, the worldliness that Senna had; you know, to learn how to behave like Mr Nice Guy. Having said that, I think that as he gets older he is getting more and more like Senna, particularly in the way he handles his fame. He is coming from behind because he is the typical German whereas the way Senna looked, the way he behaved, his charisma, his gestures and so on made him popular all over the world. Michael needed Ferrari to become as popular round the world as Senna.'

Schumacher's journey in life, from his humble origins to becoming Ferrari's latest hero, and drawing comparisons with Senna, has been remarkable. He is very much a working-class hero; his father was a bricklayer and his mother ran a snack bar. He did well at school in maths, English and sport. When he left school at seventeen, he continued his studies by training as a car mechanic. Indeed, if you had taken your car in for repair to Bergmeister's garage in Kerpen around 1986, the chances are it was worked on by Michael Schumacher!

Willi Bergmeister was a good boss. In addition to employing and training the young Schumacher, he also funded his motor racing. Michael saw the training through and did all the exams necessary to pass his apprenticeship, but his heart wasn't really in it. 'It helped to give me an understanding of the mechanical side, which is useful in racing, but I never wanted to be an engineer. I found it a bit boring, to be honest. I always preferred the driving.'

By then his qualification wasn't needed. Since the age of four, in parallel to his studies, he had been racing karts, and it had gradually become his life. At the age of ten, Rolf Schumacher told his son that he couldn't afford to pay for his karting any more and that he would either have to find some sponsorship or stop. Some drivers, like Niki Lauda, got involved in complicated loans to go racing, but Michael's father insisted that they spend only what they had; and they didn't have anything. Michael learned the value of money at an early age, and even though he and his family are more than secure for the future, he is still careful with his cash today. His friend Martin Brundle describes him as, 'First out of the taxi, last to the bar!'

Michael's career might have ended at the age of ten but for a local businessman called Jurgen Dilk, whose son Guido had raced against Michael in junior karts. Dilk thought Michael's talent was too good to waste and offered to help pay for his racing. Guido wasn't really interested anyway. Schumacher jumped at the opportunity.

'We had become friends, I used to help his sons out; and when it was clear that I had to stop because we had no money he said, "I'll pay, in return for your trophies." Which was a good deal for me. Later on he sponsored me in my first car races. He put up 25,000 Deutschmarks – £10,000 – and helped me find sponsors. He was very important to me.'

Schumacher won German championships, European championships and finished runner-up in the World Championship one year. By his late teens he was moving swiftly through the junior formulae of car racing, and with backing from wealthy German supporters and businessmen, drawn in by Dilk, he was able to get the best equipment in every series he entered and win. He has remained loyal and close to Dilk, and when he hit the big time he repaid him by letting him run his highly successful fan club.

Michael was picked up in 1989 by Willi Weber, a hotelier who also ran a successful Formula 3 team. Weber saw the opportunity; he put Michael in his Formula 3 car, signed him to a ten-year management contract and sold all his hotel interests. He knew he had a future superstar on his hands. Weber kept putting the deals together and Schumacher kept delivering on the track. The self-perpetuating spiral of success, always using top cars and engines, pushed him higher and higher up the ladder, so the only real surprise about his explosive Formula 1 début in 1991 is that it was such a surprise to so many other people.

Schumacher is an entirely self-made man. He was not pushed into racing by his father, unlike many young drivers, and the ambition to reach the top of the sport came entirely from within himself. His ability to attract the attention of wealthy people and to make them want to help him was crucial in his rise, and he continues to show that ability today. Ferrari's Jean Todt understood Michael's history and, recognizing his need to belong, adapted the team around him. He too looks after Michael in return for lots of trophies. The stakes may be higher but the principle is just the same. That desire to give him what he wants and to help him reach his goal is no different from the desires of men like Willi Bergmeister or Jurgen Dilk, who were only too happy in the early days to put up the money for someone else's son.

Michael's rise from penniless schoolboy to multi-millionaire household name has been very rapid. He realizes this and believes that he has taken the pressures of his position and status in his stride. 'I have come from nothing with no money. It makes me and my parents very happy about what we have achieved. Whether I have handled it well; personally I think I have, but there will be people who think the opposite. I have been successful. I have met a lot of people, won a lot of friends, I have had a great time.

'I believe that it has only worked because I wasn't closed-minded. I think that was my biggest strength. I'm not too proud of myself; I know that some people think that I don't admit my mistakes, but I believe I do. Sure there are times when I'm not sure whether I have made a mistake, but I just want to find out whether I have before committing.

'I have always been open to learning and not been too proud of myself not to listen. I've seen it often in other people – they believe in themselves so much that they don't listen to their colleagues.'

People close to Schumacher believe he is misunderstood. There are a great many demands on a man in his position and not everyone can understand the real person behind the professional. Perhaps part of the problem is that the pressure of the job forces stars like Schumacher to protect their privacy and to hide behind a public face. It is easy for a driver today to feel like a commodity. In the past the great drivers had far less outside pressure on them – they didn't have to worry about mass media, marketing, brand awareness and the like. Pino Allievi, as one of Italy's leading journalists, has known all the top drivers of the last twenty years. He believes Schumacher's attitude is symptomatic of the current age.

'I don't know the person at all, I only know the person he shows me through interviews. A lot of drivers of today show you a different person from their true selves. The driver of the past had no managers, no marketing, so they were more genuine. I feel sometimes today like the interviews I am doing are a favour to them to publicize their products. Today it could be a team, tomorrow a hat. They promote themselves. If you interview a driver today, they are all very nice, very sweet. I preferred the era of Alan Jones and Keke Rosberg. I did a lot of tough interviews with Jones and sometimes he was brutal, sometimes he did not reply, but that's the way he was. When he retired I found he was exactly the same person as during his career. I had interviewed a genuine man.

'Today sometimes I have the impression that I am interviewing actors, because close to the driver is a manager who is pushing him to say this or that about his sunglasses or some other endorsement. Maybe they are thick and don't realize that we see through this. But they use us and we use them; it's part of the game.

'But inside the driver you have a man, and inside the journalist you have a man, and each understands the other. So if you ask me what impression I have of Michael Schumacher, I would say that it is a good impression. Mostly a kind man. But from my interviews with him, and those I have read, I don't know the man at all. I only know the words that the man says.'

Pino's image of modern drivers being like actors – hiding the reality behind the appearance – is a good one, and there is no question that on one level Schumacher is acting out a role which he believes is expected of him as the leading driver of his era. He has perfected a number of roles: spokesman for Ferrari, Marlboro cigarettes and Shell Oil, ambassador for FIAT and drivers' spokesman on safety. On top of that he has his own media relations to attend to and there is a constant demand for his time from the media. None of these public masks matches the private man inside, but he plays the roles with skill and intelligence and summons up a remarkable amount of enthusiasm for each of them, considering how tiresome and distracting they must be.

Martin Brundle, who retired from Formula 1 driving to become a commentator with ITV in Britain, is amazed by the amount of time Michael gives to the press. 'Playing the press game in F1 is about accepting that some people will like you and some people won't; there's nothing you can do about it. Journalists are like a cross-section of doctors, policemen or any profession you choose – you are going to get all the characters; some are honest and some aren't, some have an axe to grind, others a chip on their shoulder. Some will champion your cause, others will nail you at every opportunity. It's hard, but you have to take the rough with the smooth.

'Michael has done all right. He has given more time to me since I switched sides than I would have expected, and I think he works really hard at giving time to the press. But I also think he's failed to understand some of the niceties and how he could have got more out of it.'

People judge their sports stars as much by their human re-actions to events as by their sporting performances. Opinions are formed about athletes not from having met them – because in most cases the public never do meet them – nor in many cases from what they are like in action. The public forms its opinions based on the sportsman's human reactions to situ-ations. Gazza bursting into tears after the World Cup knockout in 1990 said far more about him than his stunning goal against Scotland in Euro '96.

Motor racing is about heroes and villains, winning and losing, highs and lows – everything in between is dull and not newsworthy. Formula 1 at its best appeals because of the public's knowledge of the personalities, their proven skills or weaknesses, their grudges and so on. The sport is a tableau on which the enthusiast paints his or her own picture. The characters of the drivers are defined by the way they react to situations and how they match up to expectations. Opinions about them are formed on the back of that.

Nigel Mansell was always accused of play-acting, especially when it came to injuries, and certainly he milked the drama for all it was worth. But he resented the suggestion that he was a drama queen, claiming that his injuries were genuine, which in a lot of cases they were. Nevertheless, he was branded a whinger, a man who tried to make everything seem much more difficult than it really was, to show what a great effort he was making on the public's behalf. In reality his showmanship was one of his greatest strengths, but the way it was perceived undermined his greatness as a driver.

On the other hand, Benetton driver Alex Wurz's goofy smile, and his calmness as he talked after the 1998 Monaco Grand Prix, belied the severity of the accident he had just been in and the thrilling fight with Schumacher which led up to it. The public, full of admiration for this plucky young fighter, warmed to his engagingly simple but determined attitude. Likewise, Damon Hill's reaction to the intense combat with Schumacher in 1994 and 1995 revealed a lot about his own personal struggle to believe he could actually win those fights. His dark eyes took on extra depths of intensity as he reacted to questions and the mounting pressure.

Schumacher's reactions are often enigmatic, and at worst they have contributed greatly to the public's impression of an arrogant and at times inhuman racer. Jerez offered him the chance to show that he is a real human being, by admitting a mistake and saying sorry, but his flippant attitude and misjudgement of the situation led to another impression altogether, one he is still trying to shake off.

Pino Allievi believes that the key to greatness for Schumacher will hinge on his realization of this. 'Schumacher is a man with a lot of qualities, because he started from a poor family with nothing and became a multi-millionaire. So for sure he must have qualities and he must have sensibility. But he should use this sensibility in other ways than he did in Jerez. I think his greatness and his redemption will come when he realizes that what he did in Jerez was totally useless, for himself, for his image, for the respect the *tifosi* have for him. Sure, later on he said, "I made a mistake," but the moment he realizes that his action and his human reaction were wrong, that will be the moment of his glory – then people will love him and not just admire him.'

For a world-famous public figure like Schumacher –

receiving mass adulation and being feted by presidents and kings – the mark of greatness is not letting the man you really are get lost in the hero you have become. Hence Schumacher's dual existence and the haven of his home life.

'People ask me, "What's it like to be Michael Schumacher?" It means nothing. I have my family and that's what matters to me, nothing else. People on the outside may think I've changed a lot, but I haven't changed. I'm still the same guy I was when I arrived in F1. Certainly things are built up a lot by the media, but there's nothing you can do about that, you just have to take it. What is important is that when I come home to my family, then I am who I really am. It's very easy for me to do that.'

Many newspapers and magazines have tried to do the 'Schumacher at home' story; the prurient German media have tried for five years to sniff around his home life, but without success. According to his friends, the reality is quite simple and unglamorous. He and Corinna watch TV, play with the baby, walk the dogs and try to live a normal, quiet life. He has two cats called Mosley and Ecclestone and a fleet of recreational vehicles, including several Ferrari and Mercedes road cars and a fine customized Harley-Davidson motorcycle.

When he is at home in Switzerland he plays soccer for his local club and trains with the boys mid-week, even sticking around to eat with them in the clubhouse afterwards. Soccer is his escape, his main hobby. He also uses it for charitable purposes, playing frequently in fund-raising games. He took part in one such game during September 1998 and raised £200,000 for UNESCO, over half of which was money he had levied for media coverage of the event.

Time is the precious commodity that Schumacher lacks. If he could use half his personal fortune to buy himself one more day in the week, you get the impression he would agree the deal. The real Mosley and Ecclestone want Formula 1 to have less testing and more racing in future, but Schumacher would probably prefer less of both.

In many ways his life is not his own. In 1997 he spent a total of 270 days away from home, with racing, testing and other sponsor commitments. With such a punishing schedule he has little time for anything else in his life but work and family. There are many demands on his time and many tempting diversions; a lot of racers take up flying, but Michael has no interest in learning to fly his own jet plane. He has taken up Italian lessons, as a goodwill exercise towards the mechanics at Ferrari and the other important Italians in his life, but the lessons take up more valuable time.

'It is hard and obviously that's why I have my own plane because it cuts down on the time I spend in airports and gives me more time with my family. I do love to get home at night to see my little one.'

The testing routine is particularly punishing. Typically, after a Grand Prix he will return home on a Sunday night and then either Monday, or at the latest Tuesday morning, he will fly off to a test track, where he will test for three to five days. The following weekend may be spent at home, or if there is a real push, as there was throughout most of the 1998 season, he will carry on testing, doing anything from seventy to one hundred laps a day, followed by debriefs and a couple of hours in the gym before dinner. During the four-week gap between getting home from the Nürburgring and leaving for the final race in Japan, Ferrari did twenty days of testing.

It is hard for anyone to keep a balance in life with that sort of schedule, but the birth of his daughter has had a major effect on his approach. Now when he leaves the track in the evening he switches off totally as a racing driver and switches on as a family man. During pre-season testing at Mugello and Fiorano, he often managed to fly home in the evenings to Switzerland to see his family.

'When I have spare time the most important thing for me is to see my little one. I get a great pleasure from seeing her in the morning. She wakes up and walks through into our room and I have her in my arms and it's always a perfect moment. It takes you away from everything. We go for walks and play and so on. It's great, and as she gets older she understands more. Then, when I have the chance, I play football with my friends and it all helps to keep a balance. I have never had a problem keeping my feet on the ground, like some people in my position. I have a balance and can just go home and clear my head of the race just gone.'

From a paparazzi point of view he is a dead loss. He doesn't go to parties or discos, doesn't screw cocktail waitresses at the swimming pool, there's nothing of interest. Even his parents' divorce in 1997 managed to escape the media spotlight. When there is a private story, it's carefully managed by Heiner Buchinger so that there is the minimum intrusion to the family. When Gina-Maria was born the press were clamouring for pictures. Heiner arranged a photo opportunity, so that when Michael, Corinna and the baby arrived at the ski resort where Ferrari were holding a press conference, the first thing they did was pose as a family on a toboggan for ten minutes. The pictures were out in the public domain immediately, wired across the globe in a matter of hours, and there was nothing for the paparazzi to hound them about. He has been one of the most successful stars at keeping his private life private.

Does he enjoy being a superstar? Is the pleasure of driving and the glory worth all the personal sacrifice?

'There are days when I'd say yes and days when I'd say no. I suppose there are more days when I would say yes, but the bad days stay in the mind more, unfortunately. But in the end I still love the racing itself. When I'm in the car I think only about driving it and forget about all the other stuff.'

'The other stuff' is the hassle which comes with the fame. It's a double-edged sword; it's hard to be too sympathetic towards a man earning over $20 million a year for driving round and round in circles, but then if he were not so controversial and not so famous there is no doubt that he would not be earning anything like that sort of money. But does it justify people bothering him all the time, treating him like a public property? Like the Beatles before him, Schumacher has learned that there is always fear when you are the subject of public hysteria.

There is more that Schumacher hates about fame than he loves. His life is edged by unwelcome parameters over which he has no control. He cannot go out for a meal in Italy or Germany without being mobbed. Norway offers welcome respite as no-one recognizes him there, and he also enjoys the Canadian Grand Prix weekend, because he can walk and go shopping in the streets of Montreal or nearby New York quite unnoticed. By contrast, he once went to a hairdressers in Stuttgart and by the time the barber had finished there were fifty people outside peering in. Often at race meetings, when he drives into the circuit, his car is ruined, with small bumps and pen marks all over the bodywork from people trying to reach their idol. He is often followed on scooters. He gets frightened when things get out of control. Once, at Fiorano, he ran over a fan who had leapt out in front of his car.

He is also frequently disappointed by people; on a recent trip to Stuttgart he went to an old favourite restaurant with his manager, Willi Weber, for lunch. The restaurant manager rang a paparazzo to come and take a picture of Schumacher in his restaurant and within ten minutes the flashbulbs were popping as Michael ate his steak. Michael felt badly let down and was so furious he smashed a flash unit. In Italy the situation is completely impossible. He carries the hopes of the nation on his shoulders as Ferrari's great champion, so the nation feels entitled to interrupt him, whatever he is doing, to ask for an autograph or a photograph or just to shout his name. He is frequently prodded and often grabbed, like some sort of curiosity.

Having said that, he is more comfortable in a crowd than some other drivers. Jacques Villeneuve hates being penned in by hordes of fans or journalists and as soon as a pack forms he always shrinks away until his back is against a wall, or the side of a truck. Michael can handle crowds as long as they don't touch him. After Ayrton Senna won the 1991 Brazilian Grand Prix – the first time he had won on home soil – I remember seeing him emerge from a sponsor's enclosure, where he had been talking about his great victory. At the foot of the stairs, gathered around his McLaren van, was a crowd of around fifty people chanting his name. Senna was smiling as he came through the door, but in a split second his smile evaporated and a look of sheer terror passed across his face. It was the most graphic illustration I have ever seen of a superstar's fear of crowds.

Those who know him well believe that Schumacher will see out his Ferrari contract to the end of 2002, when he will be thirty-three years old, and then either retire or take a sabbatical year, as Prost did in 1992. By then he will have been at the top of the sport for a decade, amassed a fortune well in excess of £150 million and his daughter will be five – an age when there are lots of things for a family to do together. He will certainly have one, perhaps two more children by then. A break offers the chance to ventilate the mind, step off the treadmill and assess the relative values of work, family and success. And to decide whether to come back or not.

Schumacher is not in this for the records. He has no feeling for history, nor any interest in beating the records of Fangio, Prost or Senna, although he is set to eclipse most of them. He is a racing driver because he enjoys winning, seeks the satisfaction of knowing that, in a highly competitive environment, he and his team have worked to do a better job than the others. His prime motive is to be the best, and he puts more into his driving than anyone else because he wants more out.

It is quite simple: so long as the fun is there he will continue.

EIGHT THE PELE OF FORMULA 1
Buenos Aires, Argentina, April 1998

On the Thursday afternoon of the Argentine Grand Prix, McLaren-Mercedes driver Mika Hakkinen made a very foolish prediction. Sitting in a press conference with, among others, Michael Schumacher, Hakkinen said, 'It will take a miracle for anyone to catch us.'

Schumacher's ears pricked up. Certainly by the standards McLaren had set in the opening two races of the season in Melbourne, where they had lapped the entire field, and in Brazil where they had again dominated, it would indeed take a miracle to close the performance gap.

McLaren had produced one of those truly outstanding cars which appears only once or twice a decade. Almost everything about it was right – the Mercedes-Benz engine was compact, light and extremely powerful; the aerodynamics took their heritage from the economical brilliance of Adrian Newey's previous designs for Williams; the suspension, always shrouded with black cloth to maintain secrecy, was revolutionary and hugely effective. It took months for rival teams to understand how it worked, how the car could hit the kerbs without the springs rebounding, and none of them managed to copy it before the end of the season.

But perhaps the biggest advantage the McLarens held over the Ferraris in the early part of the season was the tyres. Specific chassis ideas may be worth tenths of a second here and there, but a tyre can give you a whole second's advantage over your rivals, especially over a long stint in a race. McLaren had made a dramatic pre-season switch from Goodyear to Bridgestone and the gamble had paid off handsomely; through corners and over the bumps, the McLarens had grip to spare. The Ferrari looked like a truck in comparison and even the reigning World Champions, Williams, also on Goodyear tyres, were left trailing in their wake.

Stung by their poor performances in Australia and Brazil, Ferrari had been testing hard and had found a lot of time. Much of it was in the tyres, and Goodyear and Ferrari realized they had been caught napping by Bridgestone and McLaren. A massive catch-up programme had been launched. Schumacher estimated that 70 per cent of the performance gap was in the tyres and Goodyear responded by producing a wider front tyre, which instantly made a big difference. Whatever else happened in 1998, Ferrari were not going to accept defeat.

Never a man to build expectations unnecessarily, Schumacher had nevertheless said privately before the Argentine weekend that, with the developments now on the car, he believed he could split the two McLarens in Buenos Aires. Having been over a second behind Hakkinen in qualifying in Brazil, this seemed a bold assertion. But nevertheless, in qualifying he fulfilled his promise and on Sunday afternoon he went one better, winning the race in passionate, forceful style. It had all the elements of a classic Schumacher victory: an inferior car driven to the limit with a clever and aggressive strategy; a controversial collision with a rival (David Coulthard) and that little bit of magic, a mesmerizing stint after strategist Ross Brawn had come on the radio to say, 'Michael, we need you to make up twelve seconds in five laps, please.' To illustrate the consistency of his pace, team-mate Eddie Irvine, driving the same car, was almost a minute behind him on the road at the end. 'Only Michael can do this,' said Jean Todt afterwards, sounding like a Heineken advert. But he was right. There have been plenty of very talented drivers in Formula 1 over the years, but only a handful who could win a race with a car that doesn't deserve to win. That is the definition of an ace. Senna and Prost did it many times and perhaps half of Schumacher's victories have come that way.

Argentina '98 should have been won by David Coulthard, and when he stumbled Mika Hakkinen was ideally placed to pick up the win, especially after Schumacher made a mistake near the end. Had Hakkinen kept up his pace and not already settled for second place, he would have been there to pounce, but he had forgotten the golden rule of running near the front in a Grand Prix: the race isn't over until you see the chequered flag. The McLaren team held out a pit board with the forlorn message 'PUSH' and no doubt a few people began to wonder whether that would turn out to be the defining image of the 1998 season, rather than the image of the two Mercedes Silver Arrows crossing the line in formation, which we had been treated to in Melbourne.

It was an astonishing performance by Schumacher, made all the more thrilling by a moment, five laps before the end of the race, when the Ferrari slithered off the road and into a gravel trap. Amazingly Schumacher knew the layout of this gravel trap, having watched Johnny Herbert get stuck in it during practice. Also on Sunday morning, as he toured slowly around the circuit during the drivers' parade, he had made his customary mental notes of the position of the tarmac perimeter roads around the gravel traps.

So when the Ferrari slid off the road, Schumacher kept his nerve, didn't touch the brakes and steered the car through to where he knew there was a solid landing. It sounds simple, but few people would be so well organized and even fewer could think logically at that speed. But like a great soccer player, who can make time for himself on the ball, part of his mental capacity is saved for dealing with the variables and uncertainties of the game. Perhaps this is why FIAT boss Gianni Agnelli calls Schumacher 'the Pelé of Formula 1'.

It was not the first time that Schumacher had made a mistake while pushing hard in the lead of a race and it would not be the last. According to Ross Brawn, it's just a part of Schumacher's make-up. 'Michael is only comfortable driving at a certain pace and you have to understand and respect that. He's not comfortable pootling around. He gets into his rhythm at a certain pace and that's pretty quick. Although he's going quickly he's not abusing the car; the brakes, tyres, engine and so on are not taking a hammering. I think sometimes when he makes a little error, because he knows where he's going, he lets the car go off the road rather than try to fight it and have a bigger incident. To him it's a surer way of dealing with the problem he has.

'It's very difficult with a guy like Michael to say, "I think you should drive this way." He's the best and you've got to respect that. You can discuss and analyse his driving afterwards, but you've got to let him get on with it when he's racing.

'In Monaco last year, he was leading when he hit a puddle on the pit straight and locked a wheel. It was more logical to him to go straight on down the escape road rather than try to make the corner and run the risk of going into the barrier. It was a very relaxed decision. Not many drivers would have known where the escape road was. But it's not very often that his mistakes cost us a win or a good result. Austria 1998 is a rare example, where he made a mistake, ruined his race and he put up his hand and admitted it.'

It was a great victory. Ferrari was on its way again; it had un-expectedly found glory in South America, and with it Michael Schumacher had begun to find redemption. All over the world the Ferrari flags, which had been put in the basement during the winter, were taken out again. Jerez faded from the memory. No wonder Michael was beaming.

'Well,' he said, thinking of Hakkinen's pre-race prediction, 'I guess the miracle happened.'

However much controversy may hang around Michael Schumacher, and whatever trouble he may get himself into with his reactions, there is no denying one thing: he is the best racing driver in the world. But what makes him so good? What are the key elements of his game? To start with his foundations are good; he's well organized and always learns from his experience, which means that as he gets older he has a huge reserve of experience to dip into. He also has an excellent memory and can recall details of chassis set-up, race strategy or even a random lap time from years before. On top of that he has a clear, uncluttered mind, which allows him to think very quickly and identify the root of any problem. To put it into computer language, he has an abnormally large disk space and a very good search engine. He likes to plan ahead and cover as much ground as possible, so that when the un-expected happens he can focus on it and not have to worry about the other variables. In this respect his mind is a close relative of technical director Ross Brawn's and it is one of the key reasons why they make such a formidable team.

Physically, he is extremely fit and never gets tired, no matter how gruelling or hot the conditions. He has good reflexes and the unique ability to drive every corner of every lap flat out, which is why he is so good over a full race distance. He doesn't have on days and off days, so the team know that if he is going slower it's because the car is slower, not because of anything he's doing wrong. This is a huge benefit to engineers, because it means they always have a reference point for experimenting with the car.

His style of driving is adaptable depending on conditions, so he can drive around most handling problems and keep control of a car that others would park up and call undriveable. In its basic form, his driving technique is developed from kart racing. He is, after all, still a kart racer at heart. Former Grand Prix driver Jochen Mass has watched Schumacher develop since his early days and he worked with him in his Mercedes sportscars phase.

'He's extremely focused. He's got a gift of splitting the un-important from the important. He knows what line to follow and he's very analytical in whatever he does. He has a tremen-dous feel for the car, which comes partly from his early days as a go-kart racer, because he started very young, but also I think it's instinctive. His immense will-power to learn in racing has helped him. Is he overconfident? I don't think so. He's very

111

settled within himself. He won two titles early on and that gives him a lot of additional confidence. It's a quiet confidence. One of his great assets is that he knows who he is, and if he thinks he can do it he will.'

The Schumacher driving philosophy, which can best be summed up as 'maximize everything', is born out of his philosophy of life – you only get out what you put in. Michael puts in everything, including his heart and soul. That's why he is always so close to the edge. His must-win mentality means using technology on the car that pushes the boundaries of legality as well as uncompromising racing and overtaking tactics, which are as close to the edge as is humanly possible.

Pat Symonds, now technical director at Benetton, was Michael's race engineer when he won his two World Championships. He knows the secrets of Schumacher's technique and of what makes him so special.

'He's very, very clever and always wants to maximize everything. He was the first driver of the modern era who had this incredible attention to detail, working on every single aspect of his game. It may sound trite but there are a lot of drivers who just drive around, and if they go faster they don't know why or how they did it, whereas Michael has the attention to detail so he would always know why he was faster.

'He was always trying different things. We developed the idea of splitting the circuit into segments and displaying the speeds and the segment times on the dashboard so he could see them. Say we made four segments, he would concentrate on trying different lines in the first section and then drive consistently in the other three. Once he'd found the fastest way of driving the first segment, he'd move on to the second bit and try things there, and so on.

'He has a habit of pushing like mad on the first flying lap; 100 per cent flat out. Then he'll spend the rest of the session driving at 98 per cent and go around fine-tuning the set-up of the car until he has it to the point where with him driving at 98 per cent it is going as quickly as it had earlier when he was at 100 per cent. Then he knows that he has an improvement on the car. He does this a lot in testing.

'I remember when Riccardo Patrese was with us in 1993; we were testing at Estoril and a good time around there in those days was something like 1 minute 12 seconds. On the first lap of the first day, Michael did a 1 minute 11.9 seconds and Patrese came in after his first run, having cruised around in 1 minute 13 seconds and when he saw Michael's time he said, "What the hell does that guy eat for breakfast?"'

A lot of racing drivers kid themselves that they are pushing hard, when in reality they are a long way from the limit. Each has his own limit, and at the top level of Formula 1 the margin between being a hero and hitting the wall is pretty narrow. Schumacher gets onto the limit quickly and is happiest running at a high pace: 'To me, being on the limit is very much the satisfaction of knowing that I have left out nothing which I could have done better. Most of the time in tests I drive like I do in a race. When I do a tyre test, I drive like I do in qualifying. It gives me a huge satisfaction to squeeze everything out and that I can then produce a lap time and say, "Wow, that's fantastic!"

'The satisfaction of racing is diffferent, but if you're just talking about driving a car on the limit, it's the clock that matters. I always fight against the clock. In the cockpit you can see the numbers and the lower the numbers get the more satisfaction I get. I can feel it if I have done a corner well, then I wait till I see the clock for proof.'

However much a driver may feel he knows about a situation or about the conditions in a race, there is always more he can learn which may give him the edge over a rival. Where others settle for what they already know and do the best they can in the circumstances, Schumacher tries things all the time: braking later into a corner, trying a different line. This is especially true in the rain or in changeable conditions, for example, a drying track, and this is why he's so far ahead of anyone else when the heavens open up on race day.

His drives in the wet often embarrass his rivals, some of whom drive gingerly, while others spin off trying to catch him.

Watching the races on his monitor from the Benetton pit wall, Pat Symonds has noticed that even if the safety car is sent out while the conditions are too bad to race, Schumacher's brain is always working away, looking for an edge for when the race is restarted. 'If you look closely you can see Michael moving around off line, going all over the place, slowing down and accelerating, trying to see where the grip is in the corners.'

Schumacher is always looking for ways of winning races, hopefully ways that the opposition haven't noticed. Winning against superior machinery requires something special and it is fair to say that Schumacher has never had the best car in Formula 1. Even in his first championship year in 1994, when he won the title having competed in only twelve of the sixteen races, he was powered by a Ford V8 engine against the more powerful Renault V10 in the Williams. But before we feel too sorry for him, we should remember that he chose to go to Ferrari rather than Williams, and that he chose to stay there in 1998 and 1999 rather than go to McLaren. The opportunity to be in a superior car is always open to the best driver of any era. Historically most of them have paired up. Schumacher has chosen the less-travelled path. There are two reasons for this: the first is money and the second is the desire for a challenge; the challenge of building up a team to fight against the best machinery. If it works, the satisfaction is ten times greater than just running around in front, dominating everyone. It also has the benefit of putting the spotlight on the driver's exceptional abilities, boosting his stock above all others – something Schumacher has always managed to do brilliantly.

Keke Rosberg, the 1982 World Champion and now the manager of Schumacher's rival Mika Hakkinen, is cynical about this aspect of Schumacher's reputation. 'Ferrari places its drivers on a pedestal and serenades them with violins every day, like heroes. That makes a hell of a difference. McLaren says, "We did a good race," while the whole of Italy says, "Schumacher is a saint." Of course Schumacher is good; there's no denying that. However, I think all of this super-hype about

Michael is still based on his time at Benetton and there is still some confusion as to how he is assessed as a driver. Michael should stop saying his car is no good.'

'He's always been in an inferior car,' insists Schumacher's Ferrari team-mate, Eddie Irvine. 'If you look at the statistics, I've out-qualified him three times, Johnny Herbert did him once, Martin Brundle and Riccardo Patrese never did him. Now for a guy to get out-qualified that rarely by his team-mate, and then if you look at his pole position record, which isn't very good, you'd have to conclude that he's been in an inferior car for most of his career. So he's always had to improvise to get results.'

Part of that improvisation is working on aspects of racing that others ignore, for example, starting technique. The start is one of the few places in modern Grand Prix racing in which it is possible to pass people and make up places. A good start to a race often leads to a good result, but getting off the line is more difficult than it looks. You need exactly the right amount of revs and perfect co-ordination with the clutch to get away cleanly with minimum wheelspin. Countless races have been lost through poor starts and several championships too.

In his Benetton days, Schumacher realized that by perfecting the technique he could gain a big advantage. As Pat Symonds recalls, 'It's hard to persuade the drivers to go to the windy airstrip in Northampton which Benetton use for pit-stop and start practice, but Michael would love it because he knew it was a way of winning races. He would do it over and over again.'

Ross Brawn remembers it well. 'Benetton were the first team who consciously set out to improve the drivers' starting technique and that brought its rewards. The drivers became more consistent and got a lot better at starting. When Michael left, Jean Alesi and Gerhard Berger came into the Benetton team and they said, "Oh no, we don't need to do start practice; it's not necessary, we're really good starters." And for the first few races we let it go, to see what happened. They didn't make consistently good starts. So then they had to do the practice sessions, and all of a sudden they were doing proper starts all the time. Any driver can do one stunning start a year, but why not practise it so you are able to do sixteen stunning starts?'

The trouble is, when you make perfect starts, the opposition start thinking that you've got some sort of traction-control device. This happened to Schumacher in 1997 and 1998, but the worst was in 1994, when his perfect starts were compromised by the discovery of that launch-control system in the Benetton car's software. Since then any perfect Schumacher start has been greeted with the usual innuendos. Brawn deeply regrets this. 'When you're at the back no-one's interested. As soon as you get to the front everyone starts suspecting you. At Magny Cours in 1998 there were some murmurs about Michael's second start. But his first start – the race was then stopped – had been terrible. If we had some magic system, why would we switch it on for the second start but not the first? People don't look at these things logically. The other drivers know that and they're just being a bit naughty, dropping the odd hint about our starts. But it's a real shame.'

Another aspect of Schumacher's game which is special is his talent for squeezing good lap times out of poor-handling cars. 'He might be a few tenths faster than the best of them over a given lap, but that's all,' says Martin Brundle. 'What he is able to do, however, is drive every lap of a race at or near his own personal limit, and an associated benefit of this is that he can always adapt to changing conditions. So if the car is sliding around he can cope with that, adapt his style and still drive that car on the ragged edge, whereas most drivers go into self-protect mode at that point. That's why he wins by such a large margin sometimes.'

Adaptability is a fundamental part of Schumacher's make-up and race fans still talk in awe of the time Michael finished second in the 1994 Spanish Grand Prix, despite being stuck in fifth gear for most of the race. Pat Symonds continues to be amazed by what happened. 'That was unbelievable! Lots of people don't believe it happened and I can understand that because I had to look again at all the data to convince myself. When he told us on the radio that he was stuck in fifth gear I said, "Well carry on and we'll find out what we can do." In the time it took us to investigate and realize that there was nothing we could do, he was suddenly going fast again and I thought it must have fixed itself. But when I looked at the computer screens I realized that it hadn't fixed itself and that he was still in fifth gear.

'He changed his technique massively. He used lessons he'd learned in the Mercedes sportscars in his early career where, to conserve fuel, he would minimize his energy loss going into a corner by sort of rolling it in and coming out gently.'

Schumacher's ability to drive around a problem is a strength, but from a team point of view it can also be a weakness, according to Ross Brawn. 'If the car is not working properly or is not set up properly he still manages to extract a good lap time out of it. There is never quite the disparity with Michael between a car which is perfect and one which is not so good, as you would get with most drivers. This can also be a weakness, because it makes the difference between a good car and an average car less discernible in testing and you can easily misread how competitive the car really is.

'You can go testing and the gap between Michael and Eddie when the car isn't working properly is huge, but as you get the car working that gap closes because Eddie benefits more from the car working properly. If you have a car that's not balanced, is stepping out at the back, then Eddie won't like it, but Michael will still drive it on the limit. You have to understand this and recognize when you have a problem. You might be going quickly but that could just be because Michael's driving is masking its problems.

'In fairness to Michael, he'll tell you if the car isn't right. But if your driver tells you the car isn't right when you are fastest in the test, you don't perhaps take it on board as much as when you are halfway down the field. So you have to be careful.

'Eddie is a true barometer of where we are with the car. In 1998 he has qualified quite well, because the car's been good. In 1997 he had days when he was fourteenth or even seventeenth, and that was because the car wasn't any good.

117

But Michael would still manage to be third or fourth.'

Brawn believes that Schumacher's qualifying lap in Hungary in 1998 was a perfect example of his ability to hustle a poor-handling car to a quick time.

'If you watched the car closely, he was entering every corner looking like he was going to have an accident. I was holding my breath; it would step out at the back before every corner and yet he'd manage to catch it and keep the power on. He was just going for it. There might be a few drivers in F1 who could do that for one or two corners, but I don't think that there's a driver around who could do that at every corner on a qualifying lap.

'Ayrton Senna was the same. You'd see him on a qualifying lap and the car would look very uncomfortable, but he'd get the lap time out of it.' Senna is the driver Schumacher is most often compared to. Theirs would have been an epic battle, but tragically it was cut short by the Brazilian's death in 1994.

'We started to get the battle in 1994,' says Schumacher today, 'but sadly we couldn't have it to the end. Then again, there are always different cars and so on, so to be 100 per cent sure Ayrton and I would have had to be in the same team and somehow I don't think that would ever have happened!'

Senna was fast, consistent, ruthless and heroic, just like Schumacher. He also had total self-belief and once claimed, 'I am not designed to be second or third. I am designed to win.' Neither could contemplate anyone beating them in a straight fight. It would have been fireworks every fortnight.

In 1988, at the start of Senna's epic rivalry with Alain Prost, someone observed that Senna put 100 per cent of himself into being the fastest driver, while Prost put 100 per cent of himself into winning races, and that if Senna learned to do that too he would be unstoppable. Schumacher has succeeded in marrying the two objectives. The emphasis is more on winning races than being the fastest driver, because he is the fastest anyway.

He is unlikely ever to beat Senna's record of sixty-five pole positions because, as Eddie Irvine said, he has never had the fastest car. He hasn't needed to get himself into the best car every season, as Prost and Senna used to do, because he hasn't had to race against anyone of that calibre. In his career, only Damon Hill and Jacques Villeneuve have been able to really take the fight to him, but both struggled to be consistently competitive. Mika Hakkinen raised his game in 1998 on occasions, but still looked shaky when locked in wheel-to-wheel combat with Schumacher. Had Senna survived or a new ace come along, then Schumacher admits he would surely have gone for the best car available, rather than taking on the challenge of building an underperforming team into a front runner.

'Senna and Prost always went for the best car because they had each other to race against; in those days there were four or five top drivers and you needed to have the best car to make sure you were in front of them. In my view, it counts more if you have the opportunity to work with a team which is not as good and work your way to the top and earn your victory. I get more satisfaction out of that.

'If you are in the best car, anything other than first place is losing and winning is standard. Where's the motivation in that? It's good for one or two races, but after that . . . well, it wasn't what I experienced at Benetton. I really enjoyed the satisfaction I got from those days, and it's probably the reason why I've grown to like racing that way; it gives me more satisfaction than simply winning because someone else lets you win or because you beat someone who isn't able to finish the race.

'I'll never forget the surprise I felt back in 1995 in Brazil. I had won the race ahead of Coulthard but we were both disqualified for fuel. I saw the Ferrari team, who had finished third on the road, but were now declared the winners, and they were going crazy. I thought to myself, Why the hell are you celebrating? If I had won a race in that way I would be very quiet and I would go home and know that the victory was in the books, but that it didn't mean anything to me.'

The challenge to make something of Ferrari, the perennial underperformers, is one which Senna never tried and which Prost took on and failed. To be fair to them, the management structure and personnel at Ferrari was quite different in their era and it totally lacked stability. There is little doubt that Prost would have made something of Ferrari, as Schumacher has done, under the calm, well-organized Jean Todt administration of today.

Another important task for a top Grand Prix driver, one which Senna and Prost excelled at, is getting your team to focus its attention on you alone. As a former team-mate of Schumacher's, Martin Brundle has seen his artistry in this area at first hand.

'I could never do it – very few people can in Formula 1. You've got to be as strong as hell. You've got to be able to sit down with people and, in an unemotional way, tell them what you want done and how you want it doing. You've got to be firm and be able to face people off – that's fine, any racing driver can do that. The problem then is that you've got to be right nearly all the time and be perfect on the race track! You've got to deliver. If you do, the whole team starts to fall in behind you. It happens almost automatically and the whole thing just filters in towards you.

'People like Senna and Schumacher start off with the fundamentals: I'm number-one driver, I get first call on all the new parts and the spare car and so on. Thereafter, if they want to get people around them it has to happen naturally. You can tell them which way you want to go, but you as a driver have to go out there and make sense of it on the race track. So if you are going to change something on the car, you've got to know why you're changing it. If a driver says, "Let's go this way," and he's proved to be right, then the team will automatically follow him. They want to win as well.

'People underestimate how competitive mechanics are; they'll even forgive you for trashing the car if you were on it and trying hard to win. Once they know you can win for them, they'll fall into line.'

Throughout the history of the sport, drivers have had varying levels of fitness. Some of the greats of the 1950s looked more like darts players than racers, while many past World Champions were heavy smokers or drinkers. But with the advent of aerodynamic wings, leading to much higher cornering forces, drivers had to sharpen up their act, and Schumacher was the first to reach Olympian levels of fitness.

'My resting heart beat is about forty-eight and that helps with keeping calm in a race situation. If I can keep my heart rate at around 140 for the two hours of the race, it means I will not be over the limit or too tense. It's about how you pace yourself in the car.'

In the early stages of his Grand Prix career, before the others caught up, this fitness allowed him to make up places at the end of a race, because he was still able to attack while others flagged and made mistakes. But in the last few years teams have wised up and insisted that their drivers get into the same physical shape as Schumacher. After all, why should the team spend millions of dollars trying to find something on the car worth a few tenths of a second, only for their tired driver to go and throw time away during a race?

When the young Schumacher arrived in Formula 1, many of his colleagues were amazed by his approach to fitness. According to Pat Symonds it was another key part of his fanatical desire to get an edge over his rivals.

'He didn't do what a lot of drivers do and say, "Oh well, I'm a racing driver, I suppose I should go running every day." He approached it scientifically. He used to monitor his heart rate and fluid levels in his body. Sometimes during a race simulation test, when he came in for a tyre stop, his trainer would take a blood sample and analyse it for irons and other things. The idea was that when he was training he could get his body to the same level at which it worked when he was racing.

'I think he did this not because he was afraid of leaving everything to chance. For me it was a sign of intelligence and dedication. In his early days he was much more complete than Senna was at the same stage. Senna didn't have the attention to detail in every area and he was ridiculously unfit when he came into Formula 1. But right from day one Michael really went for it.'

Schumacher has an Indian trainer, Balbir Singh, who speaks fluent German and accompanies Michael throughout the year. Their plan is to train extremely hard during the winter at his homes in Switzerland and Norway, to reach a level of what he calls 'over-fitness'. This means getting to a point *beyond* the level required, and accepting that once the season starts there isn't as much time to train, so the fitness level will slide. If you get it right, this will be the level you want. They work for up to five hours a day in the gym.

During the season, Singh oversees all of Michael's training during test sessions. He also comes to the races and looks after his diet – the food and fluids a racing driver needs to be in peak shape. Singh prepares meals which feature little meat or fat and which contain lots of fibre and carbohydrate. Before a race Schumacher usually has a small plate of pasta. Michael's one indulgence is ice-cream; Ferrari has a Mr-Whippy-style machine just inside the door of its motorhome at race meetings and Michael often sneaks a quick cone once he has finished driving for the day.

His thoroughness in all areas of his game has contributed greatly to the idea that Michael drives like a computer – an idea he detests. Some people close to him describe him as a 'digital driver', meaning that he sees everything in ones and zeros, black or white. As soon as a situation occurs he switches into the correct mode for dealing with it. Damon Hill once teased him for being 'robotic' and it's easy to see why the tag fits: his approach is structured and logical, the variables worked through as much as possible, problems analysed and solved and a clear path forwards established. But what belies the idea of him as a 'computer driver' is the way in which he is able to adapt and make decisions on the hoof.

Ross Brawn agrees with this view: 'Michael is as fast as he can go, but there's always a bit of spare mental capacity he can use for other things. If I talk to him on the radio, he'll be flat out on the track, but there's never any apparent anxiety or effort, it's just like two people talking around a table.'

Eddie Irvine drives the same car as Schumacher and so is ideally placed to assess his speed and adaptability. 'He's good at being on the limit the whole way around a lap. Sometimes there'll be a corner where I'm quicker than him, but he always tends to have the higher average speed over a lap. Sometimes he'll just be quicker everywhere and you just think, Well . . .

'If I pick up understeer – a handling problem where the car wants to go straight on rather than turn into a corner – then I'm stuffed, but he can cope with understeer very well. If there's a big difference in time between us after qualifying or a race, it'll be because I had understeer that I couldn't get rid of. He can drive a car across a wider range of handling characteristics and he's on the limit the whole way around the circuit and he's able to do that better than any other driver.'

Schumacher's style of driving involves turning into a corner earlier than most drivers and he avoids scrubbing off too much speed before the corner. 'I try to be always on the limit and use the throttle through the whole corner, not just the exit. This is different from other drivers, who use the throttle on the way out of the corner. Over a whole lap this can make quite a difference.'

Mental resilience and common sense are also key parts of Schumacher's make-up. Although he rarely has off days, he's careful not to let it show in the way he drives the car. That consistency is important for the engineers to know whether they are making progress or not. According to most engineers who have worked with him, Schumacher will work hard during the practice sessions to get the car as good as he possibly can. Come race day, he'll say to himself, 'Right, this is the car I've got, what's the best I can do with it?' The mistake of many Grand Prix drivers in uncompetitive machinery is to think that they have to try to make their car into a Williams or a McLaren or whatever is the pace-setting car of the day. This is unrealistic. A driver who understands what he's got to work with and works to get the best result he can from that car is going to do better than his team-mate, who tries to take a corner like the pace-setter. Schumacher has always understood this and, of the new generation, Alex Wurz operates in the same way.

Schumacher will never accept that a race – or championship – is lost until it's over, whereas, for example, Heinz-Harald Frentzen seems to have a sort of Islamic approach; everything is determined by kismet. So if he's in eighth place, then he's in eighth place and it's just fate which has let him down. If Schumacher is in eighth place, he could be third by the time the race finishes, who knows? So he drives flat out to see what happens.

Is he one of the greatest drivers in the sport's history? Undoubtedly. Could he go on to be *the* greatest? Unlikely. Whereas Senna's triumph is to have won so much while having to beat Prost and vice versa, Schumacher's success will always be tempered by the fact that he had no-one of his own class to beat. On top of that, the controversy and scandal which, rightly or wrongly, have surrounded him throughout his career will weigh against him in the final reckoning. Rumours stick for a reason and he will have to live with that. Then there is the human side. Schumacher is under intense scrutiny by press and public; if he blows his nose at the race track people know about it. He works hard at putting out a positive image, but when the crunch happens he often doesn't help himself. His boss at Ferrari, Jean Todt, says that it's too easy in the cold light of reason to judge a man who has had to make a decision in a fraction of a second, yet that is when a man's true colours often come out.

We should leave the final word on Schumacher the racing driver to the man who knows him best in that context – Ross Brawn. 'Michael is one of my heroes because he has this unbelievable ability. It came home to me last year. At the Nürburgring weekend he took us all to the kart track he owns in Kerpen. We all had a play around on the karts and at the end of the evening he jumped into a 125cc twin-engined thing and spent five minutes giving a demonstration around the track. It was just incredible, because the thing was never pointing straight. It was at an angle the whole time and he was flicking it in one direction and the other, even flicking it backwards down the straight. It was such an incredible display of talent. You don't always appreciate it in a racing car because he has to drive it in a certain way to get the lap time, but this was just him having fun and I've never seen anything like it. The hair was standing up on the back of my neck. He just has so much talent.

'He's pretty special and it's such a tragedy that he is misunderstood in the way he is. I won't argue that there are some things he does which don't help that, but there is always a contingent who are looking to have a go whenever they can. They should balance that against the entertainment he gives people when he gets it right. He has made some great races in both 1997 and 1998; Ferrari and Michael have been the only ones to make something of the championship. If Michael hadn't been around you would have had two really tedious years. So when people are stabbing him, they should think about what he's brought to the sport, which is a hell of a lot.

'That to me is the difference between Michael and a normal competitor.'

NINE FEAR AND LOATHING – F1 STYLE

Schumacher's win in Argentina provided a welcome boost to morale at Ferrari and gave Grand Prix fans the world over a glimmer of hope that the season might not after all be a McLaren walkover. But was it just a flash in the pan or could he mount a serious title challenge? With Michael driving, Ross Brawn strategizing and the 1998 car developing fast, it was always probable that Ferrari would win a few races, but such had been the apparent superiority of the McLaren in the first two races of the season, it seemed inconceivable that they would lose the championship.

Historically, when a truly superior car comes along, its driver gets a hat-full of pole positions, hammers home the advantage with lots of solid but dull victories and clinches the title with a few races to spare. Williams had enjoyed several years like that, and in the first two races of 1998, in Australia and Brazil, the McLaren team was shaping up to follow suit. But a series of extraordinary incidents suggested that they might make heavy going of it.

The first was when Mika Hakkinen, leading in Melbourne, came into the pits apparently to make a routine pit stop and drove straight back onto the track. The team later put up its hands and explained that there had been a miscommunication. But it was the first of many McLaren team errors in 1998, and although in this instance it didn't cost them dear, others later in the season most certainly would.

Hakkinen rejoined the race in second place, having lost almost twenty seconds, but unbeknown to the watching public there was an agreement between him and his team-mate that, at the start, whoever led into the first corner would be allowed to win the race. McLaren wanted to capitalize on its technical advantage in the early races and that meant not pushing the cars to breaking point. So a deal was struck which would ensure that once a pattern was established they would coast to victory. Hakkinen reached the corner first, but Coulthard could hardly be expected to give up his huge lead now, whatever the reasons for Hakkinen's phantom pit stop.

But the reality of the situation was quite different. Hakkinen hadn't just got to the corner first, he had got to McLaren first, had got to Ron Dennis's heart first and had stayed there. Despite strenuous denials that the team ordered Coulthard to let Hakkinen through, and frequent assertions over the following months that the two drivers were treated equally, the truth was that Hakkinen was always earmarked to go for the title and anything else was a PR illusion. Why else switch the order at Jerez, why else switch them now?

The emotional link between Hakkinen and Dennis is strong; Dennis nursed Hakkinen back to competitive form after his near-fatal accident in Adelaide in 1995 and he was the chosen man in the 1998 season, whatever Dennis may have said to deny this. Coulthard stayed at McLaren because it offered him the chance to drive the best car and establish himself once and for all as a front runner. The money wasn't great, but there was always the chance to win races and, maybe later in his career, as an established name, he would be able to hit the big payola with another team. But in two seasons with McLaren he has never truly understood Dennis's mentality and his body language has always spoken of a man trying hard to do his best, uncertain quite where he fits in and of where it's all leading him.

He knew that Dennis had talked to other drivers about the possibility of driving for McLaren before the 1998 race season started and he knew it wasn't Hakkinen they would be replacing. Some of those other drivers said that it was abundantly clear what the reality of the situation at McLaren was and who was going to come out on top in the team. Hakkinen may not be the most assertive driver in Formula 1 but, with the support he has enjoyed from the top, there was no doubt who the team was lined up behind.

After the Melbourne race there were stories of deal-making over the radio. The drivers were on substantial win-bonus deals and Coulthard wanted to be sure he would still collect if he moved over.

Coulthard moved over to let Hakkinen through and the whole tone of his season was set. The celebratory rock 'n' roll music pumping out of the Mercedes enclosure after the race was once again The Who, but this time they didn't play 'We won't get fooled again'. That would have been too ironic. In the press conference Coulthard alluded to the agreement with his team-mate and said he had felt it only right to stick to it, despite Hakkinen's pit-stop blunder. But he gave away his true feelings when he said, 'We agreed that whoever got to the first corner first would win, *if the race was normal*.' But surely Hakkinen's extra stop made it abnormal.

Afterwards McLaren asserted that Coulthard had moved over of his own accord and praised him for it, but if that were so, why did Mercedes boss, Norbert Haug, go up to the press office to talk earnestly to Coulthard and why, when they returned to the McLaren garage after the press conference, did Ron Dennis spend twenty minutes huddled in a corner talking to a miserable and slightly frustrated-looking Coulthard? If Coulthard was at peace with his decision why was Dennis 'briefing' him now?

The truth is, this was one of those hard moments in Formula 1, when appearance and reality separate. Some very tough people make some very hard decisions at all levels in Formula 1 and some very heavy things happen. Nice guys like David Coulthard get swept aside if they don't go along with the plan. He would get his reward in future for not trying to be a hero now. The public went to bed troubled that night, not quite sure what they had seen. They were disappointed by the lack of spectacle, puzzled by this astonishing show of sportsmanship. It didn't seem to fit in with the uncompromising image we have of modern Grand Prix stars. In the paddock after the race, Stirling Moss, one of the old guard, thought Coulthard's gesture was wonderful. But did it have any place in modern Formula 1? 'Of course not, but it should do,' he replied. Plenty were fooled, mainly because they wanted to be.

But there was something else about the switching of the two cars which irritated. McLaren had rubbed in their superiority, and it made them look unbearably smug. No-one begrudged McLaren and Mercedes-Benz their success; they had worked hard to achieve it and had simply done a better job than anyone else over the winter – that's motor racing. But was it really necessary to switch the lead simply because you can, while other top drivers and teams are driving flat out and still losing two seconds a lap to you? Surely that's rubbing people's noses in it. If, later on in the season, the team feels that forces beyond its control are conspiring against it, it shouldn't be too surprised if it doesn't get much sympathy.

Ron Dennis's background is that of a fighter and a man with his back to the wall. Gerald Donaldson, who wrote *Teamwork*, an official biography of the McLaren team, learned that as a young boy Dennis had determined to make something of himself, to break out of his modest background, but was ridiculed by his peers for his ambitions. He developed a life plan which hinged around the need to face up to adversity, 'whether real or perceived'. Although many who have worked with him describe him as being far more warm and human than the automaton-like image he portrays, he nevertheless seems to have something of an inferiority complex and a need not just to win, but to dominate.

Ron Dennis never speaks of 'I', only of 'we'. He talks about his 'organization' rather than his team. He never speaks of his early days as a mechanic to 1970s World Champion Jochen Rindt, preferring to ignore his humble roots rather than indulge in pride at his achievements. By all accounts he was a meticulous mechanic, obsessive about presentation and detail, who enjoyed the challenge of stripping down racing cars, but disliked the fact that it made him unclean.

There has always been the ambition to expand McLaren and to develop it into a globally recognized 'brand', manufacturing and selling goods of the highest quality, like audio systems and road cars. Ferrari is one of the world's most recognized and admired brand names, and since Luca di Montezemolo took over, it has been properly marketed around the world. Ferrari's Jean Todt believes that part of Dennis's obsession with beating Ferrari is based on his jealousy of their status and image. Tradition and charisma like Ferrari's take many years to develop.

Together with his partner, Mansour Ojjeh, who was previously Frank Williams's sponsor, he has built up the TAG McLaren company, reflecting an image of high-tech, high-profile efficiency. His 1980s masterplan was to build a better road car than Ferrari. It would be a dominant road car, the ultimate road car. In the early 1990s he began another ambitious McLaren project – a land-speed-record car.

'I'm happy to be considered obsessive about wanting to be the best. I want everyone in our organization to want that,' he says. 'I want the guy who sweeps the floors to want to be the best sweeper. You have to pay attention to even the smallest detail. It's an obsession for me. I just want absolute perfection. For years I have watched other people winning, but now we're there and it's not just the car. We have a structure in place which makes us strong.'

The reason Ron Dennis has been so successful in Formula 1 is because he pays constant attention to the details of being competitive. If there are ten elements which make up a team's package – chassis, engine, drivers, tyres, reliability, strategy and so on – Dennis is constantly tinkering with each of those individual elements to get each up to the highest level. In 1997, Williams had perhaps eight of the ten things right, but it was enough to win the title over Ferrari, who had only seven. At the start of 1998 McLaren seemed to have nine out of ten things spot on; the only question mark was the drivers. Both Hakkinen and Coulthard had come in for some stick after the 1997 season, but Dennis judged that, in the absence of Schumacher, he would be best placed to stick with the drivers he had. He considered them broadly able to win races for the team and decided not to change them.

But as the season progressed, McLaren developed a greater area of concern: reliability. They had built a fast car, but on occasions it was a fragile one too. Engine failures robbed them of two wins, a mysterious suspension failure denied them another and an equally mysterious brake problem forced Hakkinen to crawl home fourth in another race. Time and again they were unable to maintain their qualifying speed in the race. Ferrari and Schumacher picked up the pieces.

If there was a certain smugness about the way McLaren went about winning, then that quickly translated into anger when they started losing. Over the summer, Dennis accused Ferrari of running illegal systems on their car and at one point clearly implied that not only were Ferrari cheating, but that the governing body, the FIA, was turning a blind eye to it. Given Schumacher's track record with Benetton in that department, and the fact that several of the key players from that era, including Ross Brawn, were now with him at Ferrari, quite a few people were prepared to believe it.

But Dennis was not speaking without provocation. He felt that a trust had been broken, one which dated back to the start of the season. He saw both real and perceived adversity and formed the opinion that the FIA were helping Ferrari to his disadvantage. It all began before Melbourne.

The Formula 1 technical rules are notoriously vague and Ferrari wanted clarification from the FIA as to whether 'brake steer' – a system whereby the inside rear wheel is braked in a corner, thus helping both steering and traction – was legal or not. McLaren had been using the system since the middle of 1997, but such was their performance advantage in Melbourne that other teams, led by Ferrari, decided to put some pressure on. Given that the system had been in use for ten races, one can only presume they were looking for ways of slowing up McLaren, or at least destabilizing them a little. It was classic political gamesmanship, Formula 1 style.

Over the winter McLaren had shown the system to the FIA's technical delegate, Charlie Whiting, who had passed it as legal on several occasions. But the way the FIA works, only the team with the system gets confirmation from the FIA, so the others are kept in the dark about its legality and doubt and suspicion soon develop. Cynics would suggest that this vagueness is built into the rules to allow things to be manipulated once the relative competitiveness of the teams becomes clear. Formula 1 is a very complex sport and it's always possible that someone will find a big advantage which might kill the excitement of the season. As the sport is also mass-market entertainment, domination by one team is not desirable, so vagueness over the rules allows the situation to be massaged. The FIA had plenty of opportunities during the winter to clarify the legality of McLaren's brake system, but had failed to do so.

Benetton technical director, Pat Symonds, watched the drama unfold from the wings and noted that there had been a sea change in attitude in the sport over the past fifteen years. 'There's a fundamental difference nowadays from when I started in F1. In those days, if you came up with something really good, all the other engineers would say, "Great idea, wish I'd thought of that, well done." Whereas nowadays everyone thinks you're cheating. It's obvious why it's happened; there's so much more involved these days, more money and so on. The rules used to be quite clear and you knew whether you were cheating or not and you knew how far you could take things. The rules are a lot more complex these days and a lot of them are not written down. They are backed up by pages and pages of faxes that are opinions from the FIA technical delegate, and that leaves it all open to different interpretations and makes it much more difficult to deal with. Hence the implication of cheating, because it is all so much more vague.'

During the Melbourne weekend, McLaren also caught a photographer in their garage, who admitted to being the brother-in-law of a Ferrari aerodynamicist. Dennis felt aggrieved. Ferrari sporting director, Jean Todt, claimed not to know anything about the photographer, but admitted that Ferrari, like all the other teams, did have people in the pit lane, looking at what other teams were using.

In fact it's common practice for less recognizable members of a team's design department to patrol the pit lane in plain clothes, noting new developments the competition may be running. Some teams also pay a retainer to press photographers to give them access to some of their more intimate shots of cars. Teams know a reasonable amount about each others' cars and innovations, although a little knowledge is normally a dangerous thing. But Dennis claimed that this overt 'spying' had happened before at a test session and he was unambiguous in his contempt for what was going on.

'All Grand Prix teams are competitive,' he said in Melbourne. 'And when one of them has any sort of advantage, you make strenuous efforts to understand how and why. But at one time there was a code of conduct which most teams followed. There are some teams now – and specifically one – who do not seem to have a code of conduct. Different teams have different styles and some teams have no style at all.'

Before Melbourne the FIA technical delegate said that he still believed the brake-steer system was legal. But things moved on after McLaren's overt display of superiority in that first race. FIA president Max Mosley suggested to Ferrari that if they were unhappy with another team's system, they should make a formal protest to clear the matter up.

Because of the way the FIA rules are structured, a protest is judged by the stewards of the individual race meeting, not by the FIA's own technical delegate. And so it came about that in Brazil, Ferrari and several other teams made a formal protest and the stewards of that meeting agreed that the system was illegal.

Ferrari had scored a minor triumph, but they had also

seriously upset McLaren, not just in the manner of their gamesmanship, but in the way the protest was worded. They cited a rule which states that any car whose construction is deemed to be dangerous should be excluded from the meeting. Naturally, Dennis deeply resented the suggestion that his McLaren car was built to anything but the highest safety standards.

Ferrari never imagined that the loss of the brake-steer system would slow the McLarens up much, it was always designed more as a spoiling tactic. For his part Schumacher said, 'Anyone who thinks that McLaren's advantage was in that system is an idiot.' Sure enough, without the system, McLaren scored another dominant 1–2 finish in Brazil; Schumacher trailed home third after a poor start and difficulty passing slower cars. But a glance at the lap times from the race told a different story. Schumacher had set the second fastest lap of the race. The gap was closing all the time. If only he could get a decent tyre to work with, one that matched the Bridgestone's performance . . .

Agreement was reached on ways of framing rules for the following year, but the damage had been done; a full-blown cold war between Ferrari and McLaren was now underway and a summer of propaganda and suspicion was on the horizon. Ron Dennis had been outmanoeuvred for once, but worse, his pride had been offended and his beloved code of conduct violated. After all, what was his crime other than to have developed a better system than the other teams and to have checked its legality by the only means available in the rules? Now it had been thrown out for political reasons. The intrigue was just beginning. For the moment he restricted himself to a brief lament; in time he would have plenty more to say.

'People like a winner, but no-one likes a consistent winner. For years I have had to watch Frank Williams winning and I have never complained, instead I got a feeling of admiration and a desire to win again. When we dominated Australia and

Brazil, Frank congratulated us; so in Formula 1 there can be a sense of loyalty and sportsmanship. But not everyone sees it that way.

'I had a great respect for Enzo Ferrari. I liked his great dignity and the way he achieved his objectives. And my respect for him is what leads me not to want to comment about the Ferrari of today.'

Ferrari's celebrations after Argentina were short-lived. At the next race in Imola the McLaren Silver Arrows were back in control during qualifying. They blamed their defeat in Argentina on the fact that their Bridgestone tyres didn't work in the unusually cool temperatures; it had been a blip on the progress curve, a minor aberration. Ron Dennis asserted that the team had a 'steely nerve' and would not be deflected by the setback in Buenos Aires. The two drivers told every interviewer that they still had the best car in the field.

They were proved right: David Coulthard took pole position at Imola and won the race, but had to nurse the car to the finish with a gearbox problem. Schumacher finished close behind in second and set the fastest lap of the race, while Mika Hakkinen retired with terminal gearbox problems after just seventeen laps. It was McLaren's first retirement of the season.

At the following race in Spain, round five of the championship, McLaren had been expected to dominate and they did. The Barcelona circuit shows off a good chassis and McLaren had done a lot of testing there. Hakkinen out-qualified Schumacher by a second and a half and romped home, receiving the maximum ten points on the Sunday afternoon. Coulthard was out-classed by his team-mate all weekend and followed him in second place, while Schumacher trailed home third, some forty-seven seconds behind Hakkinen, after receiving a ten-second stop-and-go penalty for speeding in the pit lane.

Afterwards Schumacher repeated his claim that the tyres were accounting for 70 to 75 per cent of Ferrari's disadvantage to McLaren and urged Goodyear to dig deep and find something special. Luckily for the fans, and for the interest of the championship, they heeded his call. In the week following the Spanish Grand Prix, Schumacher tried some new tyres at Ferrari's own Fiorano test track and pronounced them a big improvement, but the good news was lost amid rumours that in the same test session he had also tried out a set of Bridgestone tyres.

It was a typical piece of Italian newspaper mischief, but like any juicy rumour in Formula 1 it caught on and spread around the world within twenty-four hours. The back-of-the-grid Minardi team, which has a contract with Bridgestone, had been given permission to test at Fiorano and representatives of Bridgestone were there to supply tyres for the test. At one point in the day, Schumacher did some laps on an unmarked set of rear tyres, prompting speculation among some of the journalists present that he was trying out a set of Bridgestones to see how much better they were than the Goodyears.

They also noticed that Bridgestone's top engineer, Hirohide Hamashima, was on site and putting two and two together they made five, quickly escalating the story to suggest that Ferrari were planning to dump Goodyear and make a dramatic mid-season switch to the same Bridgestone tyres as McLaren. There was only one problem with this theory – it was total rubbish.

First, the Goodyear technicians on site would never have allowed it; second, Hamashima was there to make sure that Ferrari *didn't* get their hands on a set of his tyres, and in any case Ferrari had no interest in doing so. From an engineering point of view the suspension would have to be modified to suit the characteristics of a different tyre and no-one in their right mind would run Goodyear fronts and Bridgestone rears. Even if the driver managed to keep the car on the road he would learn nothing at all.

On top of that, wasn't it in Bridgestone's interests for Ferrari to stay on Goodyears so that they and McLaren could beat them? That would make for a good marketing story. Having both teams on the same tyres would be of no benefit to them at all. The rear tyres in the Fiorano test were unmarked because sometimes the latest-development tyres are not branded, simple as that. But often in Formula 1 circles people don't stop to think things through logically. It makes for a less exciting story.

The story ran in the Italian papers and was picked up by the German tabloids; it even came to Britain. It gave people something to talk about for a few days but soon ran out of steam. Nevertheless, it was a classic example of the way the rumour mill in Formula 1 works. Extraordinary things happen so often in the sport that people are ready to believe anything. This particular story, although giving press officer Claudio Berro a busy couple of days, did not upset Ferrari unduly. In fact, it worked to their benefit, as it served to keep the pressure on Goodyear. Conspiracy theorists might suggest that Ferrari put the story out themselves for just that reason. And so the whole thing comes full circle.

One story which didn't emanate from Ferrari was the photograph in a British magazine, *F1 Racing*, which appeared to show Michael Schumacher's right rear brake disc glowing independently of the other three corners. The implication was that Ferrari were using a version of the same brake-steer system they had so vigorously protested about on the McLaren in the opening races of the season. Eddie Irvine claimed there was a stone in the brake calliper; Ferrari claimed the photograph was misleading, as it wasn't possible to see the other rear wheel from the angle at which the picture was taken. Ross Brawn said he had 'no idea' what had caused the brakes to behave like that. The paddock was divided into those who believed that Ferrari were cheating and those who felt the picture didn't add up.

After the furore had died down a Ferrari insider said, 'We had a delay system for opening the rear callipers, which means that when you release the brake pedal, the rear brakes release more slowly than the front ones. When that photo was published no-one knew about it and Jean Todt didn't want the explanation to come out because then the other teams would know how we were doing it. The technical solution was fairly simple: it was done with a mechanical spring on the brake cylinder of the rear wheels. Later on the technical press found out about it and it became public, but when that photo came out in *F1 Racing* no-one knew. The other teams knew we had made an application to the technical delegate about *what* the system was doing, but we didn't give details of *how* it was done.'

Ferrari had done a remarkable job of closing the gap with McLaren in a few short months and plenty of people in Formula 1 wanted to believe that it hadn't been done within the rules. Just as a swimmer or an athlete whose performance suddenly shows dramatic improvement finds himself suspected of taking banned substances, so the rumours about Schumacher and Ferrari took root, setting the scene for a summer of bitterness.

After Spain, Hakkinen had opened up a twelve-point lead in the championship and Michael went to Monaco hoping that his track record – he had won there for three of the last four years – and the fact that the driver has much more say in the lap time than the car, would help him to win again. Since Senna's death and Prost's retirement, Monaco had become Schumacher's track. The three greats had established a stranglehold on the silverware to such an extent that only one other driver, Olivier Panis, had won there since 1983.

Now Ferrari needed a little magic around the streets of Monaco.

TEN FORMULA 1 LIFE IN A DAY

Monaco, May 1998

The sun is shining, it's ten fifty-nine on a crisp Thursday morning and the first practice for the Monaco Grand Prix is about to start. Thousands of people are seated in the stands, waiting for their first sight of this year's Formula 1 field. Lots of them will be looking out for their heroes, many will be simply soaking up the spectacle and noise of the Monaco Grand Prix. Above them, the hills of Monaco are built up and overcrowded with millionaires' retreats and the villas and condominiums of tax exiles.

I'm standing on the opposite side of the track from them at the part of the circuit known as the swimming-pool complex. The armco-lined street, which snakes left and right in front of me, is empty and silent for now, but in a little over two minutes a stream of Formula 1 cars – fast, bright and deafeningly loud – will come rushing through in a colourful stampede.

Soon we will see the drivers' distinctive helmets flick from side to side, see their gloved hands wrestle with the tiny steering wheels, we'll hear the rat-tat engine note as their feet work the throttle pedal in bursts. We will once again be amazed by the sheer speed with which the cars travel through the blind, narrow corners.

Some people lament the passing of the old days, when the drivers wore open-face helmets. You could see the expressions on their oil-spattered faces as they passed by, their burly arms working away at the steering wheel. But they weren't travelling nearly as quickly then as they do now. The thrill of watching a Schumacher or an Alesi hurling their sliding cars at the walls at over 100 m.p.h., making tiny corrections of the wheel to avoid calamity, is unique to Monaco; this is the place where you can get close enough to see what racing a Grand Prix car is really all about. You can almost hear the adrenalin coursing through the drivers' veins. It certainly pumps through yours.

Eleven o'clock arrives, the pit lane opens and with it comes the whooping, wailing sound of racing engines accelerating on the other side of the track. In a built-up area like Monaco the high-pitched noise echoing off the walls sounds like ghosts, swooping and diving between buildings. The first car will be here in just over a minute. I remove my earplugs from my jacket pocket, squeeze them into tiny sausage shapes and place them carefully in my ears in anticipation of the shattering noise.

So much of the pleasure of sport is in the anticipation. The hype and build-up are rarely fulfilled – only on really great days does the event live up to, let alone surpass, expectations. Careers are the same. Sports fans savour the first flush of a new talent, like Michael Owen in soccer or Tiger Woods in golf, because they blow the established order apart and the feeling of anticipation at what they might achieve is so delicious. In reality most careers can never consistently live up to that initial promise, that's part of being human. But on the occasions when they do deliver some pure magic, it always feels really special. I know that this next hour will be special; it always is.

We hear the first cars long before we see them. They exit the tunnel and drop down towards the chicane, blasting along the waterfront to Tabac corner and then suddenly they are in view, filtering through the swimming-pool complex. The Prost looks stunning in its blue paint job, the bright-yellow Jordan, the jet-black Arrows, and the blood-red Ferrari. The Tyrrell looks like an Everton mint, all black-and-white stripes.

The pulse is racing, but it's only the installation lap, time to check that the systems are all working, that the oil is reaching all parts of the engine. Just enough time for the drivers to get that exquisite feeling, which only twenty-two people in the world will have this year, of driving flat out on the streets of Monaco. As the session goes on they will do more laps, improve the balance of their cars and get them to handle the bumps. They will tune in the sophisticated engine-mapping systems to deliver the power in the way they want it. Then they will start to blow the cobwebs away, pick up the pace and hustle their cars through the corners. When they are fully back in the rhythm, they will push harder, break a sweat and go for a good lap time.

In qualifying on Saturday afternoon, they will be travelling faster still – 110 m.p.h. into the blind entrance to this swimming-pool complex, 95 m.p.h. at the apex, letting the car dance out over the bumps towards the armco barrier. The confident ones will be on the power before the corner, catching the back end of the car as it bucks over a bump, hurling it into the apex, their right foot trailing on the throttle as they apply the power. The really confident drivers will get their rear wheels gently brushing the barriers, wiping the maker's name off the sidewall of the tyre. The less confident ones will be a few inches away from the barriers. But they will also be slow.

A quarter of an hour at the swimming pool is enough; time to walk along the harbour front, past the rows of $10-million motor yachts bobbing in the Mediterranean swell, to the chicane, where the cars rushing out of the tunnel brake down-hill from 170 m.p.h. to just 35 m.p.h., then flick-flack left and right around an absurdly slow, angular kerb. A lot of time can be made or lost here and the big trick is getting the braking right. It's a big stop and it's easy to misjudge it. Brake a fraction of a second too early and you'll be slow, possibly losing out on a front-row qualifying slot. Brake a fraction too late and you'll go straight on down the escape road, feeling like an idiot, your best lap blown. You can tell the real heroes by watching at the swimming pool, but you can tell the thinking drivers by watching at the chicane. You can also see which cars have a big technical advantage and the McLaren looks amazing through here; the car doesn't slide or buck, it seems to be stuck to the road. It arrives at immense speed, then simply slows down and turns left and right as nonchalantly as if its owner were parking outside Sainsbury's. The driver seems to be making little effort at the wheel and the back end of the car doesn't seem to slide out as he applies the power some ten metres before anyone else is able to do. It looks unspectacular, but by God it's fast. With its sinister silver-and-black colour scheme, it is almost as if the McLaren weren't a Formula 1 car at all, but some sort of top-secret military vehicle with awesome strike capabilities.

All the other drivers in the field would love to have a car like that, but they have to make do with what they've got. Some seem to be fighting the car all the way, like a stable lad struggling with a lively stallion. Others seem resigned to another weekend of making up the numbers and they drive around dolefully, two seconds off the pace.

A few drivers are trying hard though – Jean Alesi, spectacular as always, hurtles out of the tunnel and chucks his bulky Sauber at the apex of the corner. It's a very rough and ready technique, and ultimately inefficient, but the crowds in the stands love him for it. He's always been like this, and no matter how much he may look at the computer printouts telling him that smoother is faster, he will always drive his way.

You can also see the drivers who are thinking about what they're doing, trying all kinds of different approaches to get the maximum out of the car. Mika Salo looks good in the Arrows; he's trying different lines, braking in different places at different angles, really working the car to try to find the fastest way around the chicane. At one point he gets his right rear wheel up on the kerb and the whole car leaps five feet to the left. He catches it and drives away, knowing that that particular approach won't work.

Jarno Trulli in the Prost-Peugeot is also experimenting. His

142

car seems to handle like a truck in comparison with the others, but he keeps trying to coax a good lap time out of it. He comes through lap after lap and each time he's a little later on the brakes. On one lap he leaves it too late and clatters into the kerb. He drives away satisfied; now he knows what the limit is.

Michael Schumacher has been doing the same thing: trying all sorts of differerent ways through the chicane, all of them as fast or faster than anyone else, apart from McLaren. He seems to carry a higher average speed through the whole complex than anyone else and although the car doesn't seem to like it very much, he's not giving it much of a chance to argue.

Suddenly the red car appears again and this time he's flying, the engine screaming at over 17,000 r.p.m. Huge clouds of bluey-grey tyre smoke billow out from the front wheels as Schumacher leaves his braking late and locks up the front wheels. No-one else has stayed on the power so long before braking and no-one else has tried to brake with the car at such an acute angle to the direction of travel. He's braking and turning in at the same time, as if he were driving one of his childhood go-karts. The Ferrari snakes its hips reluctantly around the kerbs and slithers away. Suddenly you realize that he only lifted off the throttle for a split second and the rest of the time he was on it, urging the thing on.

Next time round he tries to go even faster, but the Ferrari has had enough of this treatment and digs its heels in. He hits the brakes impossibly late, but the back end snaps out and swings from left to right. He's not going to make the chicane so he changes tack and drives straight on, tiptoeing round the chicane and rejoining the track on the other side.

The session ends and we walk back to the paddock along the waterfront. The track announcer tells us that Schumacher is fastest with a lap of 1 minute 23.956 seconds, but it's only the first practice on a dirty track. Later that afternoon, more rubber will go down, things will speed up and the order will change.

The people on the boats settle down to lunch – lobster and

egg mayonnaise with perhaps a bottle of Chablis chilling in a silver cooler.

After his impressive speed in the first practice, things began to unravel for Schumacher. In the afternoon session he was again top of the time sheets when he lost control in the Casino Square and slammed the front of the Ferrari into the barriers. He was forced to sit out the second half of the session, while Hakkinen and Coulthard raised the ante. Schumacher stayed with the car to prevent photographers from taking pictures of its underside and draped a marshal's flag over the rear of the car.

'I wanted to try something, but it didn't work,' he said later, explaining the cause of his accident. 'I was trying to take a different line through that corner, but I guess I learned to my cost that it wasn't possible. There aren't many escape roads here . . .'

The following morning he managed just a lap and a half before a driveshaft failed, forcing him to sit out the entire morning session. This meant that he'd had no time to set up the car for qualifying with a light fuel load. In total he had lost two hours of track time. Worse still, when the mechanics finished repairing the car, they discovered another problem with a fuel pump, so Schumacher was forced to use the spare car in the afternoon.

When the qualifying hour came he looked less sharp than on Thursday morning. He tigered the spare Ferrari around the track and managed a time a full second faster than team-mate Irvine, but it was not a vintage Schumacher performance and certainly not the blast for pole-position glory he'd had in mind when he arrived in Monaco. Even he could not take the fight to McLaren in an unsorted car with so little track time, and the new Goodyear tyres he had found so good in testing at Fiorano proved a let-down when the crunch came. With fourth place on the grid behind the McLarens and Fisichella's Benetton, he and Ferrari knew they had let themselves down. There would be a lot of work to do in the race.

Before the fall. The pre-Jerez *Newsweek* cover that said it all. *Newsweek*

The crowds in the Piazza Liberta in Maranello watch the showdown of the 1997 World Championship from Jerez. Anti-Schumacher sentiment was strong after the collision with Villeneuve.

Associated Press/Mario Cassetta

A bit of bump and grind in Buenos Aires. Schumacher and David Coulthard argue over the racing line; the first of several fracas between them in 1998. *Glockner/Sutton Motorsport Images*

The two men who look after the champion's needs. Manager Willi Weber (left) handles Michael's business affairs and negotiates all his deals, while trainer Balbir Singh takes care of fitness and diet. *Sutton Motorsport Images*

Schumacher celebrates winning the 1998 Argentine Grand Prix with his mechanic Gianni Petterlini (left of Schumacher) and team-mate Eddie Irvine, who finished third. *LAT*

Close racing Monaco style – wheel-to-wheel with Alex Wurz in the Loews Hairpin. Schumacher forfeited a probable six championship points as a result. The title looked lost. *LAT*

Teamwork. Races can be won and lost through pit stops and Ferrari is one of the best-drilled teams in the game. *Action Images/Bongarts*

That's my boy. Formula-1 boss Bernie Ecclestone knows Michael's value to the sport and got his way when the FIA decided not to ban his star driver after the Jerez incident. *Associated Press/Roland Weihrauch*

Friends in high places. Michael with wife Corinna (left) chats with Argentine president Carlos Menem. *Associated Press/Jorge Vilarino*

The management drops in. FIAT boss Gianni Agnelli (left) and Ferrari president Luca di Montezemolo (centre) check on how Schumacher is earning his $20-million salary. *Associated Press/Paolo Ferrari*

With David Coulthard. They may be friends, but following their collision at Spa, where Michael missed out on ten certain championship points, it took a great deal to get them talking again.
Associated Press/Luca Bruno

On the ball. Soccer is Michael's main hobby. Here he joins the Argentine national team for a training session with their coach Daniel Passarella looking on.
Associated Press

The renaissance men (right to left): technical director Ross Brawn, driver Michael Schumacher and sporting director Jean Todt masterminded the Ferrari revival and scored fourteen wins in three seasons. But still no world title.
Darren Heath

The picture that launched a thousand suspicions. Is this the banned brake-steer system or just a misleading angle? Darren Heath's shot of the Ferrari's right rear brake disc glowing led McLaren to allege Ferrari was cheating. *Darren Heath*

The British fans at Silverstone queue up for the most desirable and hardest-to-obtain autograph of them all.
LAT

The most bizarre end to a grand prix in years. Schumacher wins the British Grand Prix in the pit lane after being handed a late stop-and-go penalty. McLaren protested in vain. *LAT*

Schumacher consoles a disappointed Hakkinen after the 1998 British Grand Prix. In the pouring rain, the Finn built up a thirty-eight-second lead over the German, only to lose it in highly controversial circumstances.
Sutton Motorsport Images

Even Schumacher can't finish a race on three wheels. The Ferrari tours in after colliding with David Coulthard at Spa. Schumacher initially thought the McLaren driver had deliberately caused the accident.
Associated Press/Peter Dejong

Getting there first. The author (right) interviews the winner of the
Hungarian Grand Prix for ITV. Such is the worldwide interest in
Schumacher that we often find ourselves in a media circus.

May the best man win. Michael shakes hands with Mika Hakkinen before the Hungarian Grand Prix. *Sutton Motorsport Images*

Chief mechanic Nigel Stepney (centre) leads the cheers beneath the podium after Ferrari's thrilling victory in Hungary. © *Speed Merchants Ltd*

Fantastico Schumi! Pure emotion on the podium at Monza as Michael celebrates his thirty-third Formula-1 victory with the Italian *tifosi*. *LAT*

Hakkinen shows his mettle. The McLaren driver kept his head and kept
Schumacher behind him for forty laps at the Nürburgring to take the title
chase down to the wire in Japan. *Action Images/Bongarts*

Back-to-back champions? Amid the hype at Suzuka, Schumacher and
Hakkinen try to forget about each other for a moment. *Action Images*

The moment of redemption? Schumacher makes up for his behaviour the year before by sportingly congratulating the 1998 World Champion, Mika Hakkinen, in Suzuka. *Action Images*

This one's for Italy! Ferrari wins at Imola for the first time since 1983 and an entire nation believes that this will be the year the world title returns to Maranello. *LAT*

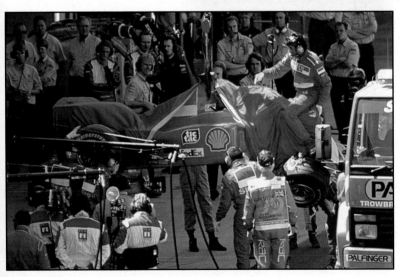

And this is where the dream ends. Schumacher's accident on the opening lap at Silverstone broke his leg and ended his 1999 challenge. Afterwards Eddie Irvine admitted he blocked his team-mate. *Action Plus*

The greatest comeback since Elvis. Schumacher dominated in Malaysia before handing the victory to Irvine, something few thought he would ever do. *Associated Press/Vincent Thian*

Suzuka 1999: Schumacher makes a bad start and settles for the constructors' championship. Afterwards he spoiled everything when he launched an unjustified attack on David Coulthard. *PA News*

The Saturday from hell had some repercussions for Ferrari's top management too. The plan had been for both Luca di Montezemolo and FIAT chairman, Gianni Agnelli, to visit the team on Saturday. But after Schumacher's breakdown in the morning di Montezemolo phoned Agnelli on his yacht in the harbour and told him not to bother coming. It wasn't going to be a glory day for Ferrari. Agnelli's non-appearance was later officially blamed on choppy waters, which in one sense was true, but it had nothing to do with boats.

In the paddock, Formula 1 life was going on as normal; in the plush motorhomes company executives tucked into exotic lunches prepared in a steamy hinterland of tiny makeshift kitchens; glamour girls in skin-tight Benetton jumpsuits pouted and squeezed their breasts together for the cameras; journalists and team members huddled in small groups, sharing information, whispering confidences.

Sylvester Stallone was making another appearance. The movie star was working on the script for a film about Formula 1, in which he planned to play a retired driver. He had struck a deal for the movie with Formula 1's commercial boss, Bernie Ecclestone, the previous autumn and had been to several races since to show how committed he was to the project. There have been a number of movie ideas floated at Bernie over the years, but none have come off. Ecclestone told one prospective director that his film must contain no drugs and no death. This posed a problem for the director as the grand finale of his screenplay called for the hero's girlfriend to take a wild cocktail of narcotics, grab a 357 magnum and shoot the hero dead on the grid!

Stallone's movie had overcome all the hurdles and it was all signed and sealed. The date for shooting to start was set for April 1999. But rumours had begun to circulate that the proposed script was so dire it had been thrown out. Another rumour said that he was struggling to raise the finance in America as the Hollywood money men questioned the box-office appeal of Formula 1. Among Formula 1 insiders there was a marked lack of enthusiasm for Stallone's movie project, which was puzzling. Many felt it would be a white elephant, Formula 1's equivalent of the Millennium Dome – an expensive but ultimately meaningless folly. Ecclestone was keen on the movie because he wanted to make ripples in America ahead of his planned flotation there of Formula 1. Enthusiasm on Wall Street would be an advantage if the float were to be successful. Stallone said he wanted to feature some real drivers in the movie. Some, like young Benetton driver Giancarlo Fisichella, thought this an excellent idea, others weren't so sure. Not surprisingly Stallone found the 'controversial German genius' character of Michael Schumacher fascinating and had himself photographed with him on many occasions. In the Monaco paddock, Michael and Sly aped the famous photo of Muhammad Ali meeting Elvis Presley, the two superstars throwing mock punches at each other.

Stallone had realized what Ecclestone and the money men in Formula 1 already knew: the box-office appeal of Formula 1 *is* Michael Schumacher. Without him the stands would be emptier, the TV ratings would be lower, the press office would be half full and the 1997 and 1998 World Championships would have been deadly dull. Everyone in the sport benefits from Schumacher's appeal, even the sponsors and partners of other teams. The more people he attracts to watch the sport, the greater coverage all the sponsors get. And of course, the more money they pour into the sport, the more the mechanics, the journalists and all the other F1 people get paid.

So would Schumacher be in the movie? His manager, Willi Weber, thought this unlikely. 'It cannot work,' was his line. 'Why make a movie about Formula 1 with artificial drama when there is so much drama in the real thing? The public understands this.'

Regardless of how the film might come out, Stallone had already provided excellent entertainment for the Formula 1 crowd, by arriving in Monaco with a posse of bodyguards, who insisted on holding back anyone who came close to the star. Unfortunately, they even held back the people Stallone was trying to talk to, causing confusion and embarrassment to the VIPs who came into contact with him. This hilarious spectacle was one of the highlights of his visits to the Formula 1 paddock.

Another familiar face making an appearance in Monaco was Flavio Briatore, the flamboyant former boss of the Benetton Formula 1 team who had been replaced by the Benetton family in late 1997. Briatore steered Benetton to its two world titles with Michael Schumacher in 1994 and 1995, but after Michael left for Ferrari he'd never quite got used to there being no crowds outside his motorhome. He had become very close to Bernie Ecclestone, but when he left the sport Ecclestone issued a statement – a rare thing for him – making it clear that although he knew Flavio as a friend, he had never done business with him. This may have had something to do with the idea that Briatore's business methods did not fit in with the image of Formula 1 Ecclestone was trying to create in the run up to the flotation of his company.

Now 'Flav' had reinvented himself. He had done a deal with Renault, who manufacture the Mecachrome engines, and announced in Monaco that he had an exclusive deal to distribute the engines, which would henceforth be known as 'Supertec Sports'. The contract would begin in 1999. Being Briatore, the word went round that the price for a season's supply, currently around $12 million, would probably rise under the new regime.

Briatore had pulled a few fast ones on Frank Williams in the past and his plans for Mecachrome greatly upset Williams, who quickly issued his own statement saying that his team had a contract with Mecachrome until the end of 2000 and that they would continue to to use Mecachrome engines. But Williams's contract also stipulated that Mecachrome could only supply one other team. It seemed that the Supertec deal was a ruse – sanctioned by Ecclestone – to get round the wording of Williams's contract and allow more teams to use the competitive Mecachrome engines. The reason for this was that a new team would be in Formula 1 in 1999: British

American Racing, a big budget operation co-owned by British American Tobacco, Jacques Villeneuve's manager, Craig Pollock, and chassis manufacturer Reynard. BAT's involvement signalled a new era in Formula 1, with the arrival of a tobacco giant as an equity holder in a team. The political climate couldn't have been hotter for such a move. The European Union was pushing for an all-out ban on tobacco sponsorship and both Ecclestone and FIA president, Max Mosley, had lobbied the British prime minister, Tony Blair, over the winter to buy the sport an extension. Blair had agreed and Formula 1 now had until 2006 to rid itself of tobacco money.

BAT, Pollock and Reynard had purchased the ailing Tyrrell team at the start of 1998 and made sure that Ecclestone had an interest in seeing this team prosper as quickly as possible. Now they had worked out a way of getting the team a supply of competitive engines. They had the money, he had found the way. This was Formula 1 wheeling and dealing at its finest and an excellent illustration of the political and financial genius of Bernie Ecclestone. He alone has made the sport what it is today, he alone had the vision, spent the money to make it happen and made himself and all his team owners very rich indeed. He is always one step ahead of them. Now aged sixty-eight, he has hinted at retirement. There are many desperate to succeed him, including Ron Dennis and Craig Pollock, but he will probably deny them all, preferring to sell out at the highest price and hand the floated business over to a professional manager to run.

While the latest intrigue develops inside the paddock, on the outside the public stands gazing through the fence which encloses this exclusive and glamorous playground. Formula 1 presents itself as a game of aspiring and belonging. At the entry level you buy into it by spending hundreds of pounds on a grandstand seat. The idea is that as you sit there watching the cars go round you don't think to yourself, Is this value for money? Instead you congratulate yourself on being able to afford to spend such a lot of money on a ticket and you brag to your friends about it. On one level you belong and it feels good.

However, you soon realize that there's another area which is a lot more interesting and glamorous to which you are not allowed access. This is the area where the teams and drivers spend all their time and where the political intrigues and multi-million-dollar deals go on. Behind the smoked glass of the luxury motorhomes, bedecked with the logos of tobacco companies, the team principals hammer out deals – whether talking about engines, sponsors or drivers; everything is a tradeable commodity. As the Mecachrome example showed, in Formula 1 a contract is worth whatever someone else is willing to pay to kill it.

The metal fences around the paddock allow the public to see the outside of these motorhomes and catch a glimpse of a driver from time to time, but they also prevent them from joining in. Exclusion creates the feeling of longing and the aspiration to belong, on which the appeal of Formula 1 is based.

The idea then is to get yourself on the next step of the ladder of belonging: the Paddock Club. This is the corporate hospitality unit, generally located above the pits, in which for $2,000 a head company high-fliers can entertain clients and loved ones and show off their involvement with the sport. Seated in a comfortable chair at a beautifully presented table with a glass of champagne in one hand and a smoked-salmon canapé in the other, the guests soon get the feeling they belong. In the sports marketing world, it is said that Formula 1 is the one corporate hospitality invitation that no-one ever turns down. Whatever the weather conditions, the punters leap at the chance to 'belong' for a day. Such opportunities are rare.

If your host sponsors a team, the drivers will normally be sent up to talk to you at lunchtime. They will stand there with a microphone and tell you about their day, how fast they drive around the circuit and what chances they have in the race.

Natural entertainers, like Nigel Mansell and Damon Hill, excel at this job and soon have the guests rolling in the aisles. Others look as though they'd prefer to have root-canal surgery done on them.

For $2,000 a Paddock Club pass gives you all of this and the opportunity to walk along the pit lane for an hour in the morning. You file along in front of the garages, which are roped off, watching the mechanics work on stripped-down cars. The biggest crowd is always gathered down one end of the pit lane, outside Ferrari. Standing there in front of the blood-red cars you get a feeling of belonging, but you still don't have access to that magic area behind the garages where you imagine the drivers are limbering up for the next session with their model girlfriends, or talking into their mobile phones ordering a new private jet.

Only a privileged few of the Paddock Club guests get the 'grand tour', in which an eager marketing executive from the team your host is involved with puts a plastic pass around your neck and takes you through the mechanical turnstiles and into the paddock. For a whirlwind thirty minutes you wander around the paddock, visit your team's garage, see the cars and hear about how the gear change is operated by paddles on the back of the steering wheel and how much a rear wing costs to make.

All around, totally undisturbed by your presence, normal F1 life goes on: drivers are interviewed by attactive female TV reporters, mechanics push trolley-loads of tyres through the well-dressed crowds, other mechanics sit in front of trucks, washing wheels with a hosepipe and keeping an eye on the pretty girls. Journalists, guests and hangers-on stand around chatting in groups outside the motorhomes. No-one seems to be doing anything. The largest group hovers around Ferrari's three red buses. Many of the crowd look Italian – tanned men in suede bomber jackets and expensive shoes, who talk animatedly, occasionally grasping each other's arms as they speak.

But there are others in the throng too: well-dressed men and women who have no obvious connection with any team, but who have cherished guest passes around their necks for the weekend. They have been drawn to the red buses because that's where the buzz seems to be, the electricity. They look confused and slightly bored, as if waiting for something to happen. Suddenly Michael Schumacher strides out of the Ferrari motorhome, his eyes set on the far distance, his lips pursed as he tries to cut through the crowds without catching anyone's eye. He's pursued by a throng of photographers and cameramen. Brushing aside a request from Slovenian TV for an interview he heads straight for the Ferrari garage, trailing a posse of the more persistent cameramen and autograph-seekers in his wake. Every day at the race track is like that for him.

As you leave after your 'grand tour' you notice the hundreds of fans looking in, their faces pressed up against the fence. Many have stood there all day hoping for an autograph or a glimpse of Schumacher or one of his colleagues. Poor bastards. You've visited the inner sanctum, you've even seen Michael Schumacher in the flesh. For a brief moment, you belonged.

It is the drivers who draw people to the sport. The cars are interesting and technically impressive and the team owners are shrewd and tough, but it's the drivers who capture the public's imagination. People are interested in other people and Formula 1 has managed to build a following around the world; there are even millions of viewers of the sport from countries with no driver in the field. If a war of words breaks out between two top rivals, the interest increases even more.

The high-speed struggle for supremacy on the track between highly competitive individuals is the box-office appeal of the sport. Yet strangely, the drivers' political influence on it is negligible. Formula 1 is an incredibly political environment, but even Michael Schumacher, the leading driver of his era, has little say in how Formula 1 is run. Ecclestone, Mosley and the team owners run the show, and they keep the drivers firmly under control. Ayrton Senna and Alain Prost – now ironically an owner himself – were the last drivers to have any influence and with their passing has come a new era of control. Drivers are employees – highly paid, highly promoted but also highly temporary. They are moved around like commodities, their time will come and go. The team owners and the powerbrokers have been around for years and will be around for many years to come.

Schumacher's star-crossed weekend deteriorated even further during the race, when he damaged his Ferrari's rear suspension in a thrilling wheel-to-wheel fight with Benetton's Alex Wurz for second place. On a two-stop strategy, Schumacher knew he had to get past Wurz, who was on a one-stop plan, or lose all chance of a big-points finish. In his desperation to get past, Michael made a lunge down the inside into the Loews Hairpin, but Wurz refused to give in and held him off. Side by side they headed through the narrowest part of the circuit. It was clear that one of them would come off worst and, given his championship situation, Schumacher had the most to lose.

Wurz had already made a name for himself with some gutsy drives in the first few races of the season. He had a lot to gain in terms of kudos and image by putting up a fight against Schumacher, and he stayed with it, forcing Schumacher to make the moves. Into the narrow Portier corner, Schumacher made another lunge, but this time his left rear wheel slammed into Wurz's right rear and he broke a link in the rear suspension. Schumacher trailed into the pits and climbed out of the car to retire. But technical director, Ross Brawn, believed the car was repairable and with such a high attrition rate at Monaco, Schumacher might still collect points even if he were a few laps down at the end. Alex Wurz continued, but a few laps later he lost control of his Benetton on the fastest part of the circuit and destroyed the car against the armco barriers. He walked away, disappointed that his race had ended so badly, but privately elated that he had put up such a defiant showing against the world number one. There would be other days.

With the suspension fixed, Schumacher leapt back into the Ferrari and roared off into the fold. He drove flat out to the finish but, sadly for him, no-one in front of him dropped out. He rolled in tenth, two laps down. To compound his misery, Hakkinen took his fifth win in seven races to open up a lead of twenty-two points in the championship.

As it turned out, this would be the biggest points lead Hakkinen would enjoy all season, because things were about to get better for Schumacher; a whole lot better.

ELEVEN PLANET MICHAEL
Montreal, Canada, June 1998

Controversy follows Michael Schumacher around like a tenacious autograph hunter.

Stirring up trouble is a major part of Michael's make-up and perhaps, when he retires, 'controversy' will be the headline in the history books for the Schumacher chapter. He is the champion with a bit of the devil in him, the man prepared to go to places in search of victory that none of his rivals even want to contemplate.

Nowhere are opinions about Michael Schumacher's driving ethics more hardened than among his fellow Formula 1 drivers. He has upset a lot of them over the past eight years and all the leading drivers of today have at least one bitter story to tell of a move Schumacher has pulled on them. Mika Hakkinen, Damon Hill, Heinz-Harald Frentzen, Jacques Villeneuve and David Coulthard all live in the shadow of Schumacher. Some of the complaints about his ethics are born out of jealousy at his tremendous gift, but they are also born of bitter experience, even fear. The late 1990s are indisputably the Schumacher era and amongst Formula 1 insiders and the public alike there is a common belief that in terms of talent and ability, he is head and shoulders above any of his rivals.

But there is another parallel belief: that he is a ruthless, dangerous hypocrite, who makes pleas for safety on behalf of the Grand Prix Drivers' Association one minute and then ram-raids his rivals off the track the next. The rough stuff is bad enough, they contend, but worse is the impression that he is allowed to 'get away with it' by the FIA, who are often inconsistent in the way they hand out penalties.

In fact this is not true: Schumacher is as heavily penalized for rule infringements as any driver and a glance at the records shows he's among the top of the list of drivers who received stop-and-go penalties in 1998. There were times in 1998 when he got away with it, but other drivers have had similar incidents at various times. Theirs have gone unnoticed. Nothing Schumacher does ever goes unnoticed because he's always at or near the front. The spotlight is always on him, and so the other drivers complain about him; he believes it's their way of bringing him down to their level and he deplores the defeatist attitude of his competitors: 'This image of me has been made out for whatever reason. I don't see myself like that. If they see me as strong then they must be weak. If they were strong then they wouldn't see me as stronger than them.

'Because I do my job precisely and because I always try hard to do my best and perhaps because I can do the job better than other people, they always try to characterize me as not normal, not human. Just because they can't do it as well as me doesn't make me inhuman.

'It's based on jealousy. It's like the fact that in Europe you don't discuss what you earn, whereas in America you are proud of what you earn. Why is that? Because in Europe people get jealous and cause you trouble. Same with this.'

There's no getting away from the fact that Michael Schumacher has been around a lot of controversy in his career and it colours the way he is judged. He may well go on to become one of the greatest drivers in the sport's history, but his regular flirtations with controversy and scandal will almost certainly prevent him from being considered *the* greatest ever.

He fights tough. In the heat of battle, Schumacher, like Ayrton Senna before him, will go for a gap which doesn't exist in the minds of others. They feel he uses the physical threat of an accident as a tactic for passing, and if the pressure is really on, they believe that he's prepared to commit a foul if it means the difference between winning and losing. Perhaps because they hold this view of him, many are beaten by him before the battle even starts.

He is unlikely to win any 'fair play awards'. Yet many people feel, as they felt about Senna, that he is too good a driver to need to resort to those kind of tactics.

'I'm not here to give presents,' Schumacher said after the 1998 Canadian Grand Prix. This was the turning point of the 1998 season in more ways than one; the race that showed the best and worst of Michael Schumacher. His pace was beyond belief, with ten consecutive laps faster than anything the other drivers could match. But he also caused a lot of trouble.

For many of his rivals in Formula 1, Canada was the final proof that Schumacher had completely lost touch with reality. And as the journalists filed their reports after the race, citing the familiar catalogue of previous Schumacher incidents, they once again reached for that dreaded word – Jerez.

Schumacher's win in Montreal was the first of three remarkable early-summer victories that turned his season around and gave him a genuine chance of beating Mika Hakkinen to the world crown. After the disappointment of Monaco, his championship charge was about to begin in earnest.

'Monaco was the only point of the year when I thought that maybe I was out of it. We had been a good second a lap off the pace on a circuit where I thought we could have done well, because if there is a technical disadvantage you can get around it by overdriving the car. But the disadvantage was so big that if something dramatic hadn't happened, there would have been no way to fight for the championship.

'The tyres from Montreal onwards made a big difference. We had made dozens of aerodynamic and chassis improvements over time, but these were detail changes, worth a maximum of a tenth or two of a second. With tyres you are talking about whole seconds.'

Montreal often provides a strange and eventful race and this time there were two major first-corner accidents, the dramatic retirements of Hakkinen and Coulthard, then two highly controversial incidents involving Schumacher – one with Heinz-Harald Frentzen and another with Damon Hill. The day ended with Frank Williams putting in a protest against Schumacher, claiming that the German was completely 'out of order'.

Schumacher had upset Frank Williams and his team by overtaking Jacques Villeneuve in the pit lane, before the race. Frank and his mechanics thought this dangerous, although there's no rule forbidding it.

But it was the incident on lap twenty, as Schumacher made his first pit stop, which caused the real upset. He rejoined the track, swerving straight out into the path of Heinz-Harald Frentzen, who was coming down the straight at around 160 m.p.h. Frentzen had nowhere to go and his car left the track at high speed. Schumacher claimed he hadn't seen Frentzen, but from the way the Ferrari lunged across the track, it looked like Schumacher was determined not to lose a place. It also looked hugely dangerous.

Ironically the drivers had discussed the possibility of this very situation in their pre-race briefing and Schumacher had argued strenuously for everyone to keep well over to the left as they rejoined the track. Yet here he was a few hours later doing exactly the opposite and taking out another car. Either he knew Frentzen was there or he didn't. If he knew, then his manoeuvre was cynical and ruthless; if he didn't, as he claimed, then why had the Ferrari team, who have always excelled at reading track positions, let Schumacher wander into such danger without any warning?

Frentzen was furious: 'Michael came out of the pits and immediately went from the left over to the right. You should be very careful doing that. What gets me is that Michael is the guy who's always telling everyone else to take care.'

He had a point: Schumacher, the head of the Grand Prix Drivers' Association, the man responsible for representing the drivers' safety concerns to the FIA, had ignored everything that had been agreed that morning and gone his own way. Frentzen later called for Schumacher to resign his position: 'I want him to give up his responsibilities as head of the GPDA. He's not worthy of it because he is not capable of applying to himself the safety measures he advises to others.'

The stewards didn't like Schumacher's move either and issued a ten-second stop-and-go penalty, which he duly served. At that point he would have realized that this had been a controversial incident, one the press would get hold of and use against him if he wasn't careful; after all, it had put Frentzen off the road and out of the race. Yet afterwards there was no sign of any contrition.

Schumacher's human reactions let him down again, as they had done so damagingly in Jerez the previous year. He acted genuinely surprised that his manoeuvre had caused such a stir. Instead he went into a tirade against Damon Hill, calling for the stewards to throw the book at him. To everyone listening it sounded like a smokescreen.

Towards the end of the race Michael had come up to his old nemesis in second place and Damon had resisted his attempts to pass. Both cars were doing close on 200 m.p.h. as Damon tried to break the slipstream by moving left, then right in front of the Ferrari. On television it looked fairly innocuous, but it frightened the life out of Schumacher.

But however hard he tried to shift the focus onto Damon, all anyone wanted to talk about was the Frentzen incident. An explanation was needed. But he ignored the opportunity to rise above the criticisms after Jerez, to redeem himself and to prove his integrity. He claimed that it was not his fault, that he hadn't seen Frentzen as he blasted out of the pit lane and that there had been no blue flag at the pit exit to warn him that a car was coming fast down the straight. But privately, Schumacher had realized the significance of the incident and, once free from the clutches of the press, he went to find Frentzen to apologize for the incident.

'If I did a mistake then I'm really sorry. I didn't see you. I saw

Diniz and Villeneuve then I thought there was a gap,' he said.

'Yeah,' said Frentzen, 'but you're the guy who always says to leave a lane open and I always do. What about you?'

'Yes, basically you're right. I'm really sorry.'

It was just like Jerez, where Luca di Montezemolo reported that he had told him the truth, only for the man himself to come out and tell the press something completely different. When he spoke publicly, Schumacher was still more concerned about Damon Hill's driving and what he saw as the unnecessary risks Hill had taken in weaving in front of him at close on 200 m.p.h.

'That was dangerous. If you want to kill someone you have to do it in a different way – not at that speed. It's all right to defend your position once, but to weave across the track three times is unacceptable.'

Strong words for an old rival. Hill and Schumacher had clashed many times during their bitter rivalry of 1994 and 1995. Some of the incidents were clearly Damon's fault, born out of desperation, others were clearly Schumacher's fault and desperation had nothing to do with them. Many of Schumacher's detractors thought that his comments about Hill in Canada were a bit rich given his own track record and his performance that afternoon. Damon too was dismissive: 'You can't put any credibility on what Michael says. He's obviously got this massive problem and overstates the case to try and defend himself. He can't claim that anybody drives badly when you look at the things he's been up to. I mean, today he took Frentzen out completely.

'We were battling and we got very close, but we were fighting for second place and I wasn't going to give it to him. I believe he is now out of touch with reality. He needs to take a long hard look at the way he conducts himself.'

What Damon failed to mention was that back in 1995 at the Belgian Grand Prix, Schumacher was given a suspended one-race ban for weaving in front of Hill on the straight to keep the Englishman behind him.

* * *

Schumacher has always aroused admiration and anger in equal quantities. But for many of the drivers, and for Frentzen's boss, Frank Williams, Montreal was the final straw. The knives came out. Williams posted his protest, not expecting any real punishment to follow; after all Schumacher had already been given a ten-second penalty. But Frank wanted to make a point on behalf of all of Schumacher's competitors:

'I was making a voice heard rather than seeking redress. I felt that Michael's behaviour was out of order on the Grand Prix track, and it's not the first time. I felt that I wanted to protest his behaviour.'

The avalanche followed; in his Tuesday-morning column in the *Daily Telegraph* newspaper, under the headline, ROOM PRECIOUS ON PLANET MICHAEL, Jacques Villeneuve laid into his old sparring partner for his 'questionable manoeuvres'.

'What planet is the guy on? On "Planet Michael" it would seem, as he believes himself to be all alone on the track. Rarely reprimanded in what many of the other drivers have concluded are driving errors, Michael thinks he is invulnerable and has become a law unto himself. It's a shame that such a talented driver has to make so many blunders in order to get placed. How is he to be stopped? That's what many of us are asking.

'He's arrogant and that makes him hard to like. Not the fact that he wins. He thinks he's on another planet, not the same one as the other drivers. He thinks he's different and sometimes he slams that in your face.'

Schumacher dismissed the criticism wearily. 'Villeneuve is becoming like a second Hill. I work very hard and not everybody likes what I do and the way I succeed, but then the world is like that. I'd rather be liked than disliked, but it's impossible to have everyone liking you.'

But this was only the start. In Germany, Frentzen was winding up his press machine, putting out stories in publications sympathetic to him which attacked Schumacher.

The German press corps in Formula 1 is split into two camps; the Schumi fan club and the Frentzen fan club. It's like something from the school classroom; the two groups of journalists dislike each other so intensely that they sit at opposite ends of the press office in the 'Schumi corner' or the 'Frentzen corner'. Loyalties are even split within newspapers, for example, *Bild* newspaper is pro-Schumacher but *Auto Bild*, its sister publication, is pro-Frentzen. Even the journalists involved admit it's childish, but it's nevertheless genuine and completely out of control.

The Frentzen lobby is smaller – there are only two or three journalists – and they are more intimate with their driver. They tell Frentzen that he is better than Schumacher but that things are slanted against him. After the incident in Canada, one of the Frentzen fan-club journalists, Christophe Schuter, went to Frentzen's home in Monaco and got him wound up, telling him that what Schumacher had done was dangerous, that it was time he was stopped and that here was a great opportunity to step out of Schumacher's shadow. Frentzen agreed to an interview, which appeared in the *Koln Express* that week.

'Michael has seen nothing once again,' Frentzen raged. 'It's like a red string through our careers from the Formula 3 days to now. Michael drives to the maximum and if he thinks it's necessary he goes over the limit. If something happens he is looking like a dog and apologizing. In Formula 3 he twice took me deliberately off the track and both times he came to me afterwards and apologized with crocodile tears. If I had not pulled back in Canada, two top teams would need two new drivers. Michael was absolutely dangerous and ruthless.'

Frentzen's complaints rumbled on until the next race at Magny Cours. Schumacher was unimpressed. He pointed to the previous year's Japanese Grand Prix, when Frentzen had come swinging out of the pit lane into the path of Irvine. Where was the difference? Nevertheless, having seen TV pictures of the incident in Montreal, Schumacher was starting to sound more contrite.

'I have to admit that I did something wrong. The next time I am in that position I will be a bit further over to make space.

But people forget that there was no blue flag there to warn me. Whether people believe me or don't believe me, I don't honestly care. I know I did everything right. But you try sitting in an F1 car with its high sides and see what I see, then maybe you can understand why I didn't see him.

'Will I change my tactics? I don't believe I'm doing anything on top of the regulations. I'm trying very hard, I'm fighting for every inch and I'm trying to do everything I can within the rules.'

If only he'd talked like that after the race in Montreal. Or, like Jerez, was that too much to expect from a young man with so much attention on him? Michael clearly knew what he'd done, hence the apology to Frentzen after the race. But something within him could not allow his public face to admit a mistake there and then. First he needed to analyse what had happened in minute detail and then park the error in the appropriate space. Only then, upon reflection, could he put his hands up and admit a mistake.

But the public draws its conclusions from reactions in the heat of the moment and this shirking of responsibility at the crunch time is a major contributing factor to the image many people have of Schumacher as a cold, arrogant, ruthless man who argues for safety then puts others at risk.

'I have to analyse and understand things and once I have understood it then it stays in my mind, so that if it ever happens again I will be able to deal with it. At the same time I think that the press plays a big part in this perception of me. If we didn't have the press then the drivers would all talk to each other, but with the press there you can't. They exaggerate everything and, when you read the stories, even if people haven't said it that way, they write it that way and the situation becomes aggravated.

'If we were all go-kart drivers we would have a crash, we would hate each other for a weekend, then we would shake hands and say, "Let's try not to do that again." That's the way it used to be. I remember when I was young and competing for German karting championships, we fought each other like mad, but then in summer we all went camping together for three weeks and had loads of fun.

'But this game has become a lot more professionalized, and in this sense it has become far harder to have proper human relationships, because the pressure is higher and the money is higher and this is difficult for some people to handle.'

Schumacher feels he handles the pressure well and conducts himself pretty well. He has learned to be philosophical about the way he's perceived. He knows that the public understands his greatness as a driver and believes that most of them will judge him on all aspects of his game, not just on the controversies.

He has had many great races, handed out many drubbings to the opposition and proved time and again that he is the only consistent performer in the sport. The other drivers know this, and occasionally some of them will admit it. Damon Hill knows Schumacher's abilities as well as anyone, and, before Canada, in one of his regular columns in *The Sunday Times*, he paid tribute to his great rival: 'No-one else can do what Schumacher does. Michael is the best not just in the way he drives, but the way he humiliates his victims. His principles are simple: possession is nine-tenths of the law, let me first win the championship and then we'll talk about whether I deserved it or not.'

Against the brilliance of his driving you have to set his controversial incidents. Every time there is a fresh one the papers and magazines remind us of past misdemeanours as sidebars to the main story, citing the 1994 Adelaide incident with Damon Hill, the black flag business at Silverstone the same year and various others. This has happened for years, but in 1998 back-references to Jerez put any fresh incident into sharper and, somehow, more critical context. Whereas previous incidents seemed to be debatable, Jerez stood out as a bald fact and inclined even the impartial observer towards the view that Schumacher is a troublemaker.

The press reaction to Canada showed that Schumacher had certainly not found redemption for Jerez. It was a stain on his career which simply would not go away. His press officer, Heine Buchinger, believed that once Michael started winning again in 1998, Jerez would be forgotten. After Argentina it had seemed that he was right, but now he was proved wrong: most reports made reference to Jerez and talked of the two sides of Schumacher's character – the brilliant and the ruthless.

In his heart he is still a go-kart driver, which might explain some of his tactics because, as every youngster learns, the only way to win in karting is through contact with opponents. Although he has moved on a long way since then in terms of wealth and fame, mentally he is still a kart racer and karting is his frame of reference. He knows and understands that the stakes are higher now in Formula 1 and that he is the leading figure in that sport, but his first recourse after an incident is to think of it in karting terms.

Senna too learned his craft in karting and there are many similarities between the two men in the way they court controversy in Formula 1. Like Senna, Schumacher believes himself to be above the other drivers and as a result he has the same blindness, believing that he makes the rules and that everyone else has to stick to them. It's not special to Formula 1; the same thing happens in the boardrooms of big companies and in the highest political offices. Successful ego-driven men have their own rules.

But look at it from their point of view and you begin to see why they feel superior. Perhaps the most significant point about the Frentzen incident in Canada is that it should never have happened at all, because Frentzen should have been three seconds further up the road when Schumacher came out of the pit lane.

As they crossed the line at the end of the previous lap, Frentzen was tucked in behind his team-mate Villeneuve, but when Mika Salo crashed heavily, the race director hung out a board saying, 'Safety Car' and static yellow flags came out all around the circuit. Neither Villeneuve nor Schumacher – who was heading for the pits at the time – slowed down in response to these signs, because the rules say they don't have to. But Frentzen backed off, giving away three seconds quite unnecessarily. This doesn't make the accident Frentzen's fault, but it does highlight the stark difference in calibre between the two drivers. It cannot have impressed Frank Williams too much either; after all he dropped Damon Hill, one of only two men able to regularly beat Schumacher, to hire Frentzen!

Bernie Ecclestone knows how special Schumacher is and realizes his value. He is never impressed with the complaints of Schumacher's beaten rivals. The continued controversy around Schumacher is good for business, keeping Formula 1 in the headlines, but as one of life's winners himself, Ecclestone knows the jealousy of others and what it feels like from Schumacher's point of view. He is always ready with a quote to support his star driver. On this occasion he was blunt:

'I get a bit fed up hearing all these complaints about Michael's driving. I don't know why people keep harping on about it. He's a racer and it's a pity there aren't a few more like him. He is in the same mould as Ayrton Senna and Nigel Mansell; they were racers, prepared to take a few risks. Whingers are losers. We don't want drivers pussyfooting around. We want them competing and going for it. He's a big boy and he'll cope with the criticism on and off the track. The sport needs him.'

One would expect those who work closely with a champion to support him at contentious moments, but the Ferrari management have raised this to an art form.

Jean Todt's relationship with Schumacher is close; both men describe the other as a friend rather than just a colleague. Todt is unusually frank about how he sees Schumacher the man and why he gets into so much trouble: 'He is much more fragile than he looks. When you look at him he doesn't seem to need to be looked after, but he does. He needs support and he needs to feel that people love him. This is a big part of why he loves being at Ferrari. Sometimes he is a mixture between a very mature person and a child. Inside his head in many ways he is still a child.

'He gets in so much trouble because he is successful, he gets more money than the others. It's difficult if you are the others to say, "He deserves it." When you see all the strong people in Formula 1, I'd like to know what they would do different from him.'

Pat Symonds, who was close to him in the Benetton days agrees: 'People are not prepared to believe that he is bloody good. There isn't much controversy surrounding Riccardo Rosset, is there, for example? Don't you think that's what the difference is? Michael is different from the others and he's very special and I think people just find that hard to take.'

Mention of Riccardo Rosset, the struggling Tyrrell driver, brings us to a little-known point in the debate on Schumacher's character. His rivals at the front of the grid, with whom he battles wheel to wheel, may complain bitterly about his tactics, but those at the back seem to have a different view. Surely a man like Schumacher would be heavy-handed and arrogant towards the backmarkers. Not so, says Rosset. 'He is always very polite. If I am sitting next to him in the drivers' briefing he always says hello and chats with me. He is also very correct on the track. If he is on a slowing-down lap in qualifying and I am coming through on a fast one, he will go off line and even get dust on his tyres to get out of my way. He has respect. Others I could mention, including one recent World Champion, stick to their line, don't care if they mess up my lap.

'I remember this, so when Schumacher comes through in a race to lap me I show him respect and get out of his way immediately. But why should I show similar respect to the other guys, who don't respect me and ruin my qualifying laps?'

Clever psychology. It just goes to show that, wherever you scratch the surface in Formula 1, you find another way in which Michael Schumacher is maximizing his chances of winning races, and that is why he's the best.

TWELVE THE COLD WAR

Budapest, Hungary, August 1998

The turnaround of Ferrari fortunes, which began in Canada in June, continued through the French and British Grands Prix, with Schumacher winning both magnificently, but again not without controversy. By now the cold war between McLaren and Ferrari was at its height and at the following races in Austria in late July and at Hockenheim in early August, McLaren boss, Ron Dennis, made some serious allegations about the legality of Schumacher's car, which put Ferrari's achievements over the summer into question and made the public feel there was a lot more going on beneath the surface of Grand Prix racing than above it.

Ferrari got involved in the war of words, but chose not to send the lawyers in to McLaren to demand proof of their damaging allegations. Instead they maintained their line that the red cars were clean and that the FIA had checked them more thoroughly than any other team. All the while they kept on improving the car, looking for the few tenths of a second that would bring them closer to the McLarens on the track. By late summer there had been over fifty detail changes on the aerodynamics, chassis and engine of the Ferrari since the start of the year – a huge programme of development in search of a few tenths of a second better performance.

There was no doubt that the tyres which Goodyear produced from Canada onwards played the biggest role in helping Ferrari close the gap; as Schumacher had said, there were whole seconds to be found in the tyres. But the paddock was split between those who believed that Ferrari had also added electronic systems to the car that didn't conform to the rules and those who didn't. Innuendo and rumour swept the paddock and no-one was quite sure who to believe, because there was no proof. And everyone is innocent until proven guilty.

The proof was lost somewhere inside the intricate maze of undetectable possibilities in the computer software. Journalists claiming to have 'cast-iron sources' asserted that the Ferrari was using illegal systems to help braking and traction and that the FIA had been turning a blind eye because they wanted Ferrari to win the title. Like an athlete who suddenly improves his personal best, the naysayers contended that it couldn't have been done naturally.

Then the tale took a twist – following a threatened protest from McLaren, the races in Austria and Hockenheim went badly for Ferrari, with Schumacher pulling in just six points to Hakkinen's twenty. The fightback seemed to have stalled, and those who suspected Ferrari had been up to something now asserted that their performance drop-off was due to the fact that they had been rumbled. But it wasn't quite as simple as that.

The controversy began at the start of the French Grand Prix in June. Hakkinen's McLaren got a good start from the front row, only to find that the race had been aborted, because Jos Verstappen's Stewart-Ford had stalled towards the back of the grid.

At the restart, Schumacher and Eddie Irvine got away better, giving Ferrari a one-two lead on the opening lap. For seventy-one dogged laps, Irvine lived up to his role as number-two driver and held Mika Hakkinen behind him, thereby allowing Schumacher to race to victory. It was clinically planned and perfectly executed and gave Ferrari its first one-two finish since 1990. Hakkinen seemed deflated in third place, unable to mount any sort of challenge to Ferrari's speed or tactical brilliance. Worse still, McLaren blew David Coulthard's chances of affecting the result with a mix-up over refuelling. Afterwards, an ecstatic Eddie Irvine taunted McLaren: 'The championship is over. That's it. McLaren has missed the boat. It had its chance to build a big lead and didn't take it. Now it's going to pay the penalty for that. Michael's going to be tough to beat and I can also give them a good fight in the coming races.'

It was typical aggressive exuberance from the man Damon Hill calls 'the number-two driver with the number-one mouth'. McLaren took it in their stride. 'His words are meaningless,' said Dennis. 'Especially as he has sold his soul as a number-two driver. We only accept criticism from qualified and competent people.' They were more concerned with the reasons given by race officials for stopping the race. It seemed a strange decision: there was no mess, Verstappen had merely stalled near the back of the grid and his car could have been pushed clear long before the leader came around.

Like the stewards' decision in Brazil which outlawed his brake-steer system, Ron Dennis found this new development 'difficult to accept'.

'You go through life and sometimes you wonder whether the playing field is level. This is one of those times. There is an inconsistency in the application of the rules. Ferrari is an environment where several people, who are not necessarily too bothered by the sporting aspect of Formula 1, would like to see them win. It is true that with Ferrari winning the World Championship, Formula 1 would benefit in terms of prestige and marketing.'

Dennis felt he was once again confronting adversity, both real and imagined. The startline confusion was blamed on a gremlin in the automatic system and TV evidence backed this up, but still Ron Dennis remained suspicious that something was going on behind the scenes and that it wasn't for his benefit.

That view hardened after the next event at Silverstone, which ended with Schumacher winning the race in the pit lane, having come in for a stop-and-go penalty *after* the chequered flag. It was the most bizarre and confusing end to a race for many years, and the catalogue of official blunders which led to this muddled finish cost the stewards their licences. In torrential rain, Schumacher had failed to see a yellow caution flag and passed Alex Wurz; an offence punishable with a ten-second penalty. But the incident happened as the officials were deciding whether the weather conditions merited sending out a safety car.

The safety car duly went out, but in the confusion Schumacher's offence was sidelined and notice of the penalty wasn't served to Ferrari within the obligatory twenty-five minutes of the offence occurring. When it was eventually served, three laps before the end of the race, the official was unable to tell the team what rule the penalty referred to. The stewards did not post the details on the official timing screens, without which any penalty is invalid.

It was a right royal mix up and no way for a multi-billion-dollar sport to conduct itself in front of a worldwide TV audience of over 300 million. Ferrari's management team of Jean Todt and Ross Brawn kept their cool and made a decision to gamble; they would bring Schumacher into the pits for a symbolic stop-and-go penalty on the last lap, so he would cross the finish line on the pit-lane side! They could all argue about it afterwards. Ferrari calculated that there were so many errors of judgement by the race officials that Ferrari would not be victimized for their handling of this bizarre situation. And so it proved.

McLaren immediately launched a protest, which was thrown out by the stewards on the grounds that the penalty had been invalid because it hadn't been published on the timing screens as the rules demanded. Ron Dennis felt that the decision not to punish Schumacher amounted to preferential treatment of Ferrari. In particular he was deeply suspicious about the reasons *why* the penalty wasn't published on the timing screens. He decided to take the matter further, to the FIA International Court of Appeal.

It was easy to feel sympathy for Dennis; McLaren had put together a winning package and seen their advantage whittled away by Ferrari. No other team had managed to get close; even the engineering wizards at Williams had floundered so badly in McLaren's wake that the World Champions had yet to score a podium in 1998. Ferrari had been the only team to take the fight to McLaren and Schumacher had taken advantage of every opportunity.

After the startline mix up in France, McLaren believed they saw an unpleasant pattern emerging, and they weren't alone. Around the Silverstone paddock that Sunday evening there were mutterings that McLaren were victims of a conspiracy between the FIA and Ferrari, something the FIA president, Max Mosley, denied vigorously. 'Anyone who looks at all the races this year would realize that there is no conspiracy. Take the Canadian Grand Prix, where the race was stopped and restarted. You could say that Ferrari was disadvantaged as Schumacher was second at the first start and third at the second start, but it is just not the case.'

It sounded hollow. But Mosley was well aware of the suspicions. There had been a belief for some time that there was one rule for Ferrari and another for all the other teams.

Ferrari had not been singled out for special treatment in the past so it was difficult to see why they would be now. Schumacher had hardly been the FIA's darling when he was at Benetton and he had been on the wrong end of a lot of politics during that time. Yet the suspicions of favouritism had begun around the time of Schumacher's arrival at Maranello. It seemed strange that the governing body would seek to help one of its competitors at a time when the sport as a whole was coming under increasing scrutiny. More and more TV viewers were tuning in to the races and ever greater sums of money were pouring into the sport. So much more was at stake now. On top of that, Bernie Ecclestone's plans for the flotation of Formula 1 called for the sport to be 'transparent', open and understandable to the mandarins of the world's financial markets, with no hidden agendas. Nevertheless, the combination of Schumacher and Ferrari was one of the main reasons for Formula 1's surge of popularity and the conspiracy theorists concluded that the FIA wanted them to win because it would help the $2-billion flotation that hovered on the horizon.

A glance around at other sports shows that greater financial stakes have not always been a good thing for competition: match-fixing in soccer, drugs in athletics and cycling, result-rigging in horse racing. Motor racing, the most complex and sophisticated sport of all, is perhaps also the most open to sharp practices and there is far more money at stake in Formula 1 than in other sports. But the FIA has improved its detection process greatly in recent years and, despite all the rumours and suspicions, there was no proof at any time in 1998 of any wrongdoing by Ferrari. But the suspicion continued.

Part of the problem is that the rules are vague. Teams are obliged to submit details of any new electonic systems to the FIA for approval, but as the FIA only have to notify the other teams of *what* the system does, not *how* it does it, an atmosphere of doubt is created. Electronic 'driver aids' are banned in the rules, but it's terribly difficult to define what constitutes a driver aid. This disparity was largely responsible for McLaren's suspicions about Ferrari in 1998. There was just one problem: there was no proof.

Ross Brawn explained the difficulty of trying to prove your innocence: 'We've had twenty visits from the FIA to approve our software in the factory and at the race track in 1998. But there is a nasty malicious process some teams are taking. How do you defend yourself against the allegation that you're using traction control but it's not detectable because it's so clever? Nobody's applying any logic here.'

Schumacher was also troubled by the trend and by people's willingness to believe that he would bend the rules, but privately he believed that his track record spoke louder than any paddock gossip. 'I am paid to win and to make Ferrari win, and to get the title for the first time in many years. As for McLaren's insinuations, we are not cheats. I have never cheated. It's all down to jealousy. We made progress and we started winning, people automatically think we are cheating. I'm disappointed but it's politics. People read the stories and believe them because it's all technical and it's unfair on someone else. Gossips are always around and they create politics, but I don't mind, it'll sort itself out in the end. People will judge me on my races, regardless of what stories are around.

'I've done too many great races, people must believe that it's not because there was something special in the car, it was because everything comes together and because I worked for it.'

Things came to a head in Austria in July. Ron Dennis's unhappiness with Ferrari was fuelled that weekend by information reaching him from his engineers about the way the Ferrari chassis was behaving out on the track.

The McLaren people had noticed that the Ferrari tended to lock its outside wheel when braking, which is unusual. Normally the inside wheel, which is not bearing the load, locks up. They suspected that Ferrari had some sort of device which affected the braking and steering of the car; a programmable brake-balance system.

On top of that they had also noticed at a recent test session in Monza that, although the McLaren had the higher straight-line speed and its speed in each sector was better, the Ferrari had the better overall lap time. Most of the top teams had sophisticated electronic engine mapping, but the suspicion now was that Ferrari's system worked rather like the outlawed traction-control systems. But again these were only suspicions; there was no proof.

In Austria, Dennis decided to do something about this. At ten o'clock on the Saturday morning, before qualifying, he and his team manager, Davey Ryan, went to the Ferrari motorhome. The purpose of the visit was to tell Jean Todt that McLaren intended to protest the Ferrari's braking system. At the start of the year the two teams had set up a 'gentlemen's agreement' to inform the other side ahead of any proposed protest. No details were given of what McLaren thought was wrong with the system, but Todt told them that, if they had suspicions, it would be a good idea to protest. A protest would clear the air of suspicion and Todt admitted that he was keen to put an end to this atmosphere of doubt.

After the meeting, Todt went to the FIA technical delegate, Charlie Whiting, and asked for clarification on the Ferrari's legality. The FIA posted one of its scrutineers in the Ferrari garage during qualifying to observe. Alan Prudhomme, the FIA's software expert, checked the Ferrari's computer and after qualifying he went through the software.

The Ferrari was declared legal. But something troubled Todt – Dennis had not yet put in his protest. Only he knew the reason why: perhaps he had never intended to protest but merely wanted Ferrari to know he was keeping an eye on them. Perhaps he was just stirring up trouble, frustrated at the way Ferrari had closed the gap on his once-dominant team, or perhaps he thought his visit would scare them into removing whatever systems he thought they were using. Either way Todt, exasperated by the lingering impression of doubt created by Dennis's visit, went to the press, explaining Dennis's intention to protest. This infuriated the McLaren boss who felt that Todt had violated their 'gentlemen's agreement' by going public: 'We agreed that it would be correct if we had a code of conduct in respect of each team's intentions. I'm a bit disappointed, having followed that code, that the management of Ferrari choose to immediately share it with the media.'

Jean Todt was unimpressed. 'Some people say that our cars are very close to what is illegal, but if that is the case then they are legal. There is a fine line, but we respect it, and those who accuse us of cheating have not exactly been whiter than white themselves. If anyone questions our legality then my advice to them is to lodge a protest.'

Four weeks later, in Hungary, Dennis was adamant that his plan had worked and claimed that Ferrari had removed the braking system in question for the Austrian and German Grands Prix. It was tempting to believe him because Ferrari had just suffered two of its worst performances of the year, allowing McLaren to regain the championship initiative. Hakkinen now led the championship by sixteen points with five races to go. The only bright spot from Ferrari's point of view was that it won the Silverstone appeal. Alex Wurz, whom Schumacher had passed under the caution flags, said conditions had been so bad that he hadn't seen the yellow flag, so how could Schumacher, who could see nothing but spray from Wurz's car, be expected to see it?

Schumacher kept his ten points. Ron Dennis, who felt that Schumacher should have been penalized, was greatly upset by what he saw as further evidence of the FIA's desire to help Ferrari. He gave vent to his feelings of frustration and anger: 'Sometimes we don't feel we're just racing against Michael Schumacher in a Ferrari, and that's tough. This is not a sport for the faint-hearted but there's a new focus we've had to build around the team in recent races; a sort of resilience to the constant propaganda and psychological warfare that's coming from our principal competition.'

Schumacher was off the pace all weekend in Germany and lost all track time on Saturday morning when he crashed on his first lap out of the pits. He struggled to finish fifth in the race. The conspiracy theorists felt that this was proof that systems had been removed from the car. The software from his car was checked again by the FIA after the race so thoroughly that it delayed the announcement of the official results. It was found to be legal. Ferrari said that nothing had been taken off the car in Austria or Germany and claimed that it was vicious rumour-mongering to suggest it had. Schumacher deeply resented the way his achievements were being undermined: 'I have always maintained that my car is correct and now everyone knows it. I have never cheated and would leave a team if I felt they were.'

On the face of it Ferrari lost momentum and performed badly at the Austrian and German races, after Ron Dennis had threatened to protest them. But according to Ross Brawn there is nothing suspicious about the explanation. 'One of the problems with Germany is that we overstepped ourselves. We put some things on the car at Hockenheim which made the car worse not better. We created our own problem. Those who took care to look will have noticed that we used a new front wing on Friday and Saturday which wasn't on the car in the race because of all the problems we had. When it first came out at a test before Hockenheim, Eddie crashed and destroyed it, so we got no information there. We then used it in a test at Fiorano and it looked quite good there. So we took it to Hockenheim and Michael was going to do a test with it on Saturday morning, but we all know he only did two laps on Saturday morning. So you see?

'When you design a Formula 1 car you have to decide on your parameters because even with all the resources in the world you can't design a car which is perfect on all types of track. On the calendar in Formula 1 today you have two very high downforce circuits, Monaco and Budapest, and two very low downforce circuits, Monza and Hockenheim, so it's logical that you concentrate your development on the rest, the medium downforce area. That's what we've done at Ferrari and maybe we should question that, because both last year and this year we were poor on the low downforce tracks.

'In Austria our plan involved Michael being able to get past Hakkinen. Although he had a good chance, he just couldn't do it. So we had to use plan B, but that didn't happen because Michael then made a mistake and lost control of the car, knocking the front wing off. After that we were into plan C, which was a recovery plan, not an attack plan.'

The heart of the problem was the ability of the FIA to police electronic devices. Many engineers voiced their concern during the 1998 season that the FIA was unable to spot traction-control devices in the cars' computer software. But at the same time, the engine-mapping systems were now so sophisticated that they were able to duplicate the effect of traction control, whilst staying within the rules. Some team owners wanted traction control to be made legal because it was hard to police. One thing was for sure, it had cast an unpleasant shadow of doubt over what had otherwise been a fantastic season of racing.

McLaren had stunned the opposition with a revolutionary car which exploited many loopholes in the rules, and they had the superior Bridgestone tyres. With an advantage like that, they should have had the title wrapped up by late summer. Instead, Ferrari, Schumacher and Goodyear staged one of the most remarkable and controversial catch-ups in the history of the sport and took the championship down to the wire. The team had to sail close to the wind to close up such a massive gap so quickly. They say they did it within the rules and the FIA checks agreed with them. But McLaren felt that Ferrari had cut some corners, crossed the line into illegality, and voiced its suspicions. It was an impossible situation and one which caused both Ferrari and McLaren intense pain for very different reasons.

Shortly before the Hungarian Grand Prix, FIA president, Max Mosley, intervened in the debate once again, aware that the McLaren/Ferrari cold war – and all the official blunders surrounding it – threatened the credibility of the sport at a critical time. Unbeknown to most people in the paddock, Formula 1 was planning to launch a £1.2-billion bond issue the following month; a preliminary step prior to a full flotation of Formula 1.

'There are interesting things at Ferrari,' he said, 'yet nothing illegal. I believe McLaren has understood that now and is well on the way to finding an equivalent system.'

Ross Brawn is used to allegations. As one of the brightest engineering heads in the sport he has had tremendous success and that has often meant sailing close to the wind. He started his career in winning form at Williams in the late 1970s and hasn't looked back. He has been involved in controversy – back in 1994 with Benetton when a few things didn't add up and he, like Schumacher, found himself on the wrong side of the FIA. He believes that suspicion often follows success and regrets that his success with Ferrari has been tarnished by the suspicions of other teams: 'It's the unfortunate nature of the business. What can you do to defend yourself except ask, "Where's the evidence?" People look for easy answers all the time and there aren't any easy answers.

'Unfortunately I can't do anything about it. I've just had to come to terms with it. I've had to come to terms with 1994 and 1995. It's very hard to reverse people's opinions; it takes a lot of effort and I've got other, more important things to put my effort into. My family know what I'm like and the people I work with know what I'm like.

'I don't think anyone has ever left an organization I've been in, Benetton or Ferrari, and said, "Well I know what was going on." Surely if anything funny had been going on, something would have come out by now, because to do that kind of thing people would have to know it wasn't correct. For example, in 1994 we worked with Ford, Cosworth and Benetton. If there was anything hookey happening, all three would have to have been involved, and the way this business works someone would have said something by now.

'When mechanics and technicians change teams they tell their new team what they know about their old team, but we've never had anyone come to us and tell us that another team's been cheating and I know for a fact that no-one has ever left us and told their new team that we were cheating. Simply because it didn't happen. There are so many logical things which people ignore because it doesn't fit the story.

'There was one guy who left Benetton in 1994 to work in motorcycle Grand Prix racing. He was the person who, in 1993, had developed our traction-control system, when it was legal. When it was banned in F1, he applied that system to GP bikes. During 1994 someone approached him and said, "Spill the beans on what Benetton are doing," and he said, "I can't tell you because I'm not there any more. I don't know what they're up to." He called us and warned us that there was some guy offering him money to induce him to spill the beans, and that's the nature of this business. But there were no beans to spill.

'It's disappointing, but I know in my heart and my head what we have done and I have nothing to be ashamed of. I'm proud of what I've achieved and if other people don't chose to see that, it's a shame.

'We've got some great people here at Ferrari and they proved last year, and again this year, that they're prepared to get stuck in. I could take you through our car and show you probably forty or fifty changes we've made this year, all of which have given us a bit of performance. If there was a simple solution, like a piece of funny software we could put in, why would we spend all the time and money and effort we have made to improve the details?'

Brawn's reasoning seems persuasive, and his views on the Benetton controversy are backed up by Pat Symonds, who worked alongside him in the Benetton days. He believes that the seeds of suspicion were sown quite deliberately by the racing establishment and that he, Brawn and Schumacher have all been suffering for it since. 'The fact was that we were the new kids on the block and we were shaking the establishment a little bit and that didn't go down too well. Also we were very naive and left ourselves open to suspicion. I learned a lesson from it. Loads of people have come up to me this year and said, "Ferrari are cheating, McLaren are cheating," in other words, whoever is at the front is cheating. I always say, "They're not, they're just doing a better job," because I know that if you do a better job you dominate. We did it in 1994 and McLaren are doing it this year.'

Martin Brundle, who worked with Benetton and Schumacher in 1992, believes that Schumacher and Brawn push everything to the limit, which is why they are so successful, but also why there has been so much controversy around them. 'Michael has been around a lot of controversy and that's not by chance. I'm afraid he'll have to live with that. He has worked with some very imaginative people and he attracts the top engineers because they want their skills to be reflected on the race track through his driving. You could debate it, is it unfair advantage, is it cheating, or is it just maximizing what's available to you? It's always gone on. But it's more under control now by the FIA than it's ever been.

'Stories in Formula 1 are always wilder than the reality on the inside. In my experience, usually the people behind the scenes who are supposed to be doing all these things are saying, "Mmm really? Are we doing that?" But the stories get out of control and bear no relation to the facts.

'In this game, everyone reads the regulations once to understand them and then a second time to find a way around them – that's standard behaviour. And that's the wonderful thing about competition: you have to look at every single angle. All these suggestions that Ferrari switched off the system in Germany, I don't believe a word of it. I cannot believe anyone risks out and out cheating these days.'

Brawn is a big factor in Schumacher's success. The pair have worked together for all but one of the German's nine seasons in the sport, which means that he has been the strategic brains behind thirty-two of Schumacher's thirty-five victories. In 1998 their slick teamwork bought Ferrari some fine wins. Nowhere was their telepathic understanding more in evidence than in the Hungarian Grand Prix.

McLaren should have won the race in Budapest, instead it was snatched from under their noses by an audacious change of strategy by Ross Brawn and intense, consistent flat-out driving from Schumacher.

The start worked to McLaren's advantage, the two Silver Arrows running comfortably at the front for the first twenty-five laps. Brawn's original strategy called for Schumacher to stop twice, but after Michael's first stop he found himself caught up behind Jacques Villeneuve's Williams for six laps, losing vital time to the leaders. Brawn looked at the computer predictions and started thinking. Once Schumacher had got clear of Villeneuve, he started lapping half a second quicker than anything the McLarens had managed all day. He chased and caught Coulthard in second place. Hakkinen was three seconds further ahead. At this point Brawn dramatically changed the plan.

He had worked out that Schumacher would not have the speed or enough laps to beat the McLarens if he stuck to the same two-stop plan as them. He decided on a switch to three stops, which would require Schumacher to drive absolutely flat-out for the whole race – exactly the sort of challenge he loves. The McLaren strategists watched in surprise as Schumacher blasted into the pits very early for his second stop, took on a light fuel load and shot out again past them. Then McLaren took a snap decision which would ultimately cost them the race; they called in David Coulthard.

It was like a finely balanced game of chess and McLaren moved the wrong piece. Had they brought Hakkinen in first he would easily have been able to rejoin ahead of Schumacher and Ferrari's bold plan would have been in tatters. Instead, by bringing in Coulthard, they moved Schumacher into second place. When Hakkinen came in shortly afterwards Schumacher took the lead and put in a burst of laps as intense as any he had ever done in qualifying. On his light fuel load he sailed off into the distance, buying himself enough of a gap to make his third stop safely and rejoin in the lead.

Over the radio, Brawn asked him to find twenty-five seconds in nineteen laps, which meant finding the time within himself, maintaining a consistent pace far faster than anything the others could manage. Schumacher responded quite brilliantly, and with Hakkinen struggling home in sixth place, having developed a mysterious suspension problem, it blew the World Championship wide open again.

Afterwards Schumacher and Brawn hugged each other like lovers who have been separated for years, and Brawn paid tribute to the trust the two have in each other: 'Sometimes I have to think very quickly. Other times it's best to just slow things down and think about them properly. I know some people say it's better to have some decision rather than no decision at all. But I'd rather it was the right decision, even if it's a lap late. Sometimes you have to make a quick decision and it's great working with Michael because there's no problem. He trusts what I can see from the pit wall and I trust what he can see from the track.

'Because we put our faith in each other. If you say you need something out of him, he's on the limit to do it, because he knows that our judgement is going to be close to what's needed.

'My philosophy is to get everything you can organized and then, when the unanswered questions come along, you can cope with them. I like to get all the variables out of the way so we can be ready for whatever happens. If you have a feeling about how a race may pan out, then you plan for that. It's like all good military operations. There's a plan A, but always a plan B and C, so if it all goes wrong you have other solutions. You get all your plans laid out and then the decisions you make are not complicated by things going on around you.

'It also helps a lot that Eddie accepts the number-two role. There are occasions when I have to think only about Michael and give him priority treatment on the track. I always keep as close as I can to Eddie's race effort, but if there's suddenly a drama, like it pours with rain, Michael gets the service first. In some ways it makes my job easier.'

Brawn first noticed Schumacher when they were adversaries in the 1991 world sportscar championship. Brawn, taking a brief sabbatical from Formula 1, was with Jaguar, while Schumacher was learning his craft with Mercedes-Benz. 'He was our arch enemy because he was the only driver at Mercedes who could make our life difficult. There were two drivers in each car and we always dreaded it when he got in the car because we knew he was going to give us a hard time.

'I've only had one year in the last six where I wasn't working with Michael, so we really understand each other, which is a very valuable and powerful element of our race strategy.'

Brawn and Schumacher's logical step-by-step approach was something of a revolution at Ferrari, who had tended in the past to try to find a half a second improvement in one glorious blast rather than chip away at it steadily. This was partly motivated by the intense politics which existed at Maranello and by the constant pressure from the Italian media for results. Now, with Jean Todt at the helm and Ross Brawn in charge of the technical side, the team has sorted out its fundamentals and works steadily towards its goals. Schumacher's consistent pace gives them the benchmark to move forward. Race craft, strategy and pit stops are all subject to the same methodical approach.

Every Thursday afternoon of a Grand Prix weekend at around 5 p.m. you will find Ross Brawn, Nigel Stepney, the chief mechanic, and the entire Ferrari crew in the pit lane practising pit stops. Standing in front of the car with a stop-watch around his neck, Brawn will shout instructions to the mechanics in Italian about what kind of situation they will practice next. 'Gomme' he yells, the car rolls in and the mechanics whip off the tyres and fit a new set. 'Muso,' comes the cry from the massive Englishman and the mechanics skilfully rip the nose from the car and replace it with a fresh one. Brawn clicks the watch, his owlish eyes note the time and he writes it neatly in the appropriate column in his file. Quiet and unspectacular, but with the respect of everyone around him, he is like an avuncular headmaster taking a crowd of sixteen-year-old boys for games.

'It's a great challenge to build something up together. That's what Michael is in it for too and that's why he's committed to Ferrari because he wants to achieve it here. It means much more than just driving the best car to win a championship. He's not really interested in that. He's achieved two World Championships with Benetton, now his ambition is to win two championships with Ferrari. If he had jumped into a McLaren everyone would expect him to win. I'm sure he would win, but is that as rewarding as making it work at Ferrari?

'I guess if one was completely truthful from an engineering and team point of view it would be wonderful if you had such a dominant car that you could take any driver and win the World Championship with him, that would be a fantastic achievement. I guess Williams maybe feel they took drivers and made them champions. But there are always two drivers in a team and you always have to ask, why was Villeneuve champion and Frentzen not? They're still very good drivers.

'Michael is a key part of the Ferrari package in more ways than driving. He is very involved in the way the team functions and maybe some drivers aren't. Michael is the added ingredient.

'He has strong opinions. But if he can see that you have a firm conviction about something, then he'll go with your view. I think a lot of time he's strong just to make sure you've thought through your side as well. He doesn't want to run the car. He knows that the engineers and myself will run it. He wants to concentrate on driving it. There are some occasions during practice where he'll say "I think we should try this," and I'll say, "No, Michael, if you think about it we need to do such and such," and he'll accept it. I've never known him to get petulant and say, "Let's do it my way." He's always willing to listen to sensible reason on what we should do. He's always been very easy to work with in that respect.'

Expectations are always high at Ferrari and before the season started much was made of Luca di Montezemolo's confident assertion that 1998 would be the year Ferrari would win the title. In any other year they probably would have done, but McLaren and their new technical director, Adrian Newey, came up with something special. It was a case of 'our Newey is better than your Shuey'. Newey is a more hands-on technical director than Brawn, who doesn't design any pieces these days. Jean Todt had tried to get Newey on board in 1997, but persuading him to move to Italy wasn't easy, and in any case, at $3 million the price was too high for an engineer. So McLaren got him and Ferrari played catch-up. Brawn is full of praise for his main rival: 'Adrian is a very strong engineer and there's no doubt that he's contributed a lot to McLaren's success. I also think that there are a load of good people at McLaren who had got 95 per cent of the way there before Adrian arrived. Maybe Adrian has brought something to finish the job off. It's a very strong organization. It will be interesting to see what happens in the next few years.

'They've done a fantastic job this year and I wouldn't take anything away from them, despite what they've been saying about us! If they hadn't done a fantastic job we would have won the championship for sure this year. It always depends on how good a job other people do in this business. We've done a good job, but not good enough.

'Most people who have experienced winning have high expectations. When you've tasted it you want it again. I've got a lot of personal high expectations, so I don't feel that Ferrari expect too much because we have the best driver in the world, a good budget – not the best budget, whatever people say, but a good budget – and we do the engine ourselves, which is an advantage. So our expectation should be to win the championship.'

The challenge of making Ferrari great again would be of interest to any racing romantic, but there are practical considerations as well. Brawn had to move from his long-established home in Oxfordshire to Maranello, which, with its countless ceramics factories and industrial estates, is hardly the most attractive part of Italy. Part of the problem with Ferrari's previous technical chief, John Barnard, was that he refused to leave his home in Surrey, so the technical department was split between England and Italy.

One of Brawn's first tasks was to restructure the whole technical department under one roof. The upheaval was quite a sacrifice: 'I took the chance to come here because it is the ultimate challenge. There have been concessions, particularly with my family life. I used to live in England with my family and was forty minutes from work. I don't see as much of my daughters now as I would like. My wife, Jean, manages to travel to Italy between races, so that's not so bad. I have made sacrifices in the short term, but in the long term it will pay off. Now I'm looking at a more permanent base in Italy. I've been living in an apartment, now I'm getting a house and getting into the Italian way of life. So once we've adjusted it'll be OK. Once my second daughter gets off to university next year, she'll have flown the coop and life will get a bit simpler for Jean and me in Italy.

'The Italians are lovely people, the food's good, the weather's great and it offers things you cannot get in England. There are some sides to it which are very nice. The Italian people are very passionate about Formula 1 and quite know-ledgeable. When you go to a function or a restaurant, the fact that you are involved with Ferrari means something to people. It is very special. It's much more than you'd have at McLaren or Williams or Benetton. When you go to a circuit there are masses of Ferrari flags; it's the best-supported team in F1 and there is a romance to that side that we all feel.

'If you can give them a good result they're in heaven. I think that they can see that we are closer than Ferrari have been for many years. While they passionately want us to win the championship, they're very supportive.'

THIRTEEN MADE IN ITALY

Maranello, Italy, July 1998

As the battle for the World Championship hotted up on the track and the bruising propaganda campaign between the two rival teams rumbled on in parallel, quietly and with the minimum of fuss, Michael Schumacher put an end to a third, invisible battle which had been raging between McLaren and Ferrari all year – the fight to get his signature on a contract.

Schumacher signed a deal to stay with Ferrari for four years, and in so doing he became the highest-paid driver in the history of motor racing. He and his manager, Willi Weber, had been working on the new deal all summer and its announcement put to an end all the speculation that McLaren-Mercedes were going to tempt him away.

Schumacher's future as a racing driver was entrusted to the Italian team and Ferrari meant to keep him until the end of his career. It was a massive commitment on both sides, Schumacher pledging to keep Ferrari on the cutting edge of competition into the twenty-first century, in return for an income of almost £100 million. Add to that his revenue from endorsements like Nike and his prosperous merchandising business, which sold over 300,000 baseball caps in 1998, and estimates of a four-year yield in the region of £175 million would not be far wrong.

When he announced the deal, which made him the second highest-paid sportsman in the world after basketball star Michael Jordan, Schumacher pointed out that money had not been his primary motive. There had been a higher offer, and it had indeed come from McLaren-Mercedes. It was the human factor that had persuaded him to stay put.

Schumacher's main objective was to finish the job he had set out to achieve. Like Jean Todt and Ross Brawn he held the burning ambition to win the World Championship for Ferrari, and until he succeeded he could not possibly leave; that would be an admission of defeat. On top of that Ferrari had spent three years building a team of people around him and he had made a great personal investment in the team. To leave that emotional life-support system behind now would make no sense, unless the car was competely uncompetitive, which it clearly wasn't. Ferrari, with its long tradition, its charisma and the unique enthusiasm of its fans, made him feel part of something more than just a team and gave him the support he needed to do his job.

'The human relationships here at Ferrari are fantastic. From the top down, from Montezemolo, Todt, Ross and so on, it is such a stable situation, such good relationships that we have inside the team, nobody wants to hurt anybody, just to support each other in any way that they can, and that's a feeling that I get every day. They look after me so well.'

Looking around Maranello it's easy to see what he means. At Fiorano, the team's private test track behind the factory, they have turned Enzo Ferrari's old office building into a villa for Schumacher to live in when he's testing or visiting the factory. It's a home away from home. Enzo's office is preserved as it was when the great man died in 1988, and his presence hangs in the air. The charisma and strength of the *commendatore* is everywhere and it must be quite an experience to sleep there; Michael can be under no illusions about which team he is driving for.

On the top floor there's a room full of photographs and memorabilia from Ferrari's racing past. The smiling, oil-covered faces of long-dead racing heroes cover the walls, along with the constantly evolving Ferrari racing cars through the decades: the bulbous, open, cigar tubes of the Fifties;

the slinky, skinny torpedoes of the Sixties; the funky, angular, fat-tyred monsters of the Seventies; and the sleek, aerodynamic jet fighters of the Nineties.

The rest of the house is fitted out for Michael's needs, with a state-of-the-art gym and all the facilities for a short stay. Being located in the middle of the test track, the place is secured by guards on the gate, and if he's testing he has only the shortest of walks to work in the morning – the pit garage is 100 metres from his front door. His trainer, Balbir Singh, stays with him and makes him breakfast and lunch each day. In the evenings they work in the gym.

The atmosphere at Fiorano is special. Michael walks out of his door every morning into a courtyard which reeks of history and motor racing. On the left is an old-fashioned garage area used by Goodyear for storing tyres. On the right is a large salon, kitted out for press conferences and for feeding the mechanics. Food is very important to the Italians, and on test days a lady arrives on the dot of noon in a small white van to drop off a tasty lunch of pasta, salad, veal scaloppine and vegetables, not to mention a huge bowl of grated Parmesan cheese.

Near by there are two Ferrari restaurants: the Cavallino and the Montana. Both serve straightforward delicious Italian food with a warm welcome. Of the two, Montana is favoured by the race team and most evenings there are a good number of mechanics and management eating there. The place is run by a lady called Rosella, who greets all her regulars with giant enthusiasm and whom Schumacher calls 'my second mother', because of the way she looks after him. 'Italy is fantastic in human terms,' he says. 'The Italians have a way of life which is so warm and which makes you feel so welcome. On the other side, they respect each other a lot. This is a tough job, but in a family atmosphere, like this, it is made a whole lot easier.'

There is no menu at Montana, just a selection of specials each day. The restaurant has a small wood-panelled side room, which has become like a family dining room for the many dis-placed people in the Ferrari team. Formula 1 expertise is hard to find in Italy, and over the past six years Todt has had to persuade a lot of foreigners to leave their homes and come to live in Maranello to share his dream. Todt himself lives in a plush suite at a nearby golf club from Monday to Friday and commutes to his home in Paris at weekends.

Cut off from their roots but thrown together by a shared goal, the team has bonded well. Perhaps working on the principle that 'the family that eats together stays together', Todt and his recruits often dine together, and when Schumacher is in town he joins them. The relationship which has developed between Todt and his star driver goes beyond a mere working relationship, as Schumacher acknowledges: 'There is a blind understanding between us. We are more than colleagues, we are friends, and that's rare in this business. Todt leads by example. Wherever you go in this team you will find everybody doing 100 per cent in their job, which is a good sign to every employee. Everyone is pushing, it's not just the mechanics. The boss himself is there from morning to midnight and that gives a big motivation.'

After Enzo Ferrari died, the team went into decline. There was a brief hiatus when Alain Prost and designer John Barnard clicked in 1990 and almost won the championship with six victories in the season. They failed to give Prost the support he needed and in disgust he fumed, 'Ferrari doesn't deserve to win the championship.' He went and the team slid back into decline. It was a difficult time, with a high management turnover as FIAT-appointed executives came and went in the highly political atmosphere of Maranello. The team totally lacked stability; an area where their English rivals Williams and McLaren were especially strong. It was also locked in the past. As Gerhard Berger once said, 'Stand outside the Ferrari factory and you wonder why Ferrari doesn't win every race, stand inside and you wonder how they manage to win any.'

The problem was there was no plan; it was hard to attract the best technical people to Maranello, so Ferrari decided simply to throw money at the problem. The disparate foreign engineers who passed through the team in those days regarded a stint at Ferrari merely as a way of building a pension fund, a big pay day, not a team-building exercise. There was talent, but it lacked any focus, and the politics undermined everything. Having filled their pockets, the engineers left. To make matters worse every internal matter at Maranello was reported in the Italian press, who held tremendous influence over the team. The old guard leaked stories like a sieve. Ferrari was like a reed in the wind of press criticism and many wrong decisions were taken because of this.

Prost's departure was the final straw for FIAT patriarch Gianni Agnelli, who called in his reliable lieutenant Luca di Montezemolo as president, to put some vision back into the road car operation and to get the race team back to winning form. Montezemolo recognized the worldwide marketing value of Ferrari, with its immense prestige and tradition, and he persuaded FIAT and tobacco giant Philip Morris to increase the budget. He then hired Jean Todt to bring first stability, then success to Maranello. On his shoulders lay the responsibility for staging one of the great comebacks of sporting history.

Todt arrived at Ferrari in 1993, from Peugeot Sport, with whom he had won Le Mans, and countless rallies, including the Paris-Dakar. A small man with fair hair, a hooked nose and small, piercing blue eyes, he is very calm, with a thoughtful, pragmatic streak. He always likes to know what's going on and keeps his ear very close to the ground.

Within his team he commands tremendous respect. Like several famous small Frenchmen before him, he is a man of immense ambition, and he recognized straight away that restoring success to Ferrari was the greatest challenge in motor sport. The team had the history and the marketability; all it needed was the winning formula and the platform on which to build its global appeal.

Todt's first problem was that the team was split in two. Acting on the advice of his old friend Niki Lauda, di Montezemolo had re-hired John Barnard, who had once again established a design and development base in England, while the cars were built in Italy. Todt knew this arrangement could never get Ferrari back to the top, but it took him longer to unravel di Montezemolo's whim than he hoped.

He knew that it wasn't going to happen overnight and he decided to ignore the backstabbers and old guard, all of whom had an opinion on how the team should be run. He wanted to take the politics out of Ferrari and replace them with stability, but it was an uphill task. 'At Ferrari you have lots of people who have been around for fifty years and they have their way of seeing things. They say things like, "The engine is not good, if they were still with twelve cylinders they would win." There are lots of rumours, and inside the team there are still a few people who are living in the past and who are not happy about the way the structure is working now. And then the stories come out. Ferrari is more in the spotlight than any other team.

'But I'm pleased with how things have moved forwards. When you arrive in a team like Ferrari it is like a beautiful castle, but you see that there are leaks everywhere and repairs to do, otherwise it will fall down. So you have to make a plan and then repair. What I did took time because it is not easy to find the best people at all levels. It's not just about finding two or three people. Ferrari has a workforce of about 500, between the engine and chassis and so on. So you cannot think that because you change one guy things will go better. You have to consider the whole structure and modify all that has to be changed. It's a long-term job and it's never finished because things move all the time.

'The market for expertise is not in Italy, neither for engines nor for the chassis. So you have to call in people from outside and you have to make sure that they fit in. So even if someone is the best guy in his field, he may destroy it. I like the image of an orchestra; my job is not to play the piano or the guitar, my job is to find the right people to play those instruments. And I must make sure that the pianist and the guitarist work well together. It's a team.

'Then you've got to find the drivers. It's too easy to say that Ferrari have got the best driver because they pay the most money. That's not true. Others have more money than us. You have to deal with nasty people from other teams saying, "Well, of course Schumacher is at Ferrari because they let him run the team, and we don't have him because that's what he wanted." There is a lot of unfairness in Formula 1.'

By 1995 Todt had raised the team to a sufficient level to be able, realistically, to go after the best driver in the world. He and Schumacher both knew that Ferrari was still in the second division, but it now had the knowledge and the resources to get to the top. As Oscar Wilde said, 'We are all in the gutter, but some of us are looking at the stars.'

Schumacher saw the opportunity to do something far more rewarding than merely win races. He joined Ferrari in 1996 first because the money was right and second because the charisma and tradition of the Scuderia offered him something he could find with no other team. When he arrived he also discoved that the family atmosphere and the human relations in the team were stronger than he had imagined possible in a racing organization.

He found something that reminded him of his early days, when family friends like Jurgen Dilk had clubbed together to pay for his racing because his own father couldn't afford it.

Although the stage he was playing on now was in a different league and Ferrari's budget was tens of millions of pounds, Todt had build around Michael an atmosphere uncannily similar to that of his karting days or the days at Willi Bergmeister's garage in Kerpen, where he got his hands dirty and they all went racing together. Schumacher felt the continuity: 'They look after me so well.'

Ferrari offered him the chance to build something on a world stage together with a special group of people, and after three years with many highs and just as many lows the job was not yet done. This is why he decided to stay. Of course, if the car had been totally uncompetitive he would have gone elsewhere, but it wasn't. By turning down McLaren he was once again opting to race *against* the best car rather than with it.

* * *

Todt's office at Maranello is spacious and modern. The walls are decorated with photographs of podium celebrations from his seven-year reign at Ferrari. After a lot of hard work restructuring the team, it has been a successful period. 'Each of these photos is a win. I don't have time to be satisfied or proud. I am always thinking of the present or the future. There are always problems to solve. Having said that, the days following a result like Budapest are easier than after a result like Germany. Results help a lot, especially in an environment which is such a storm. It's important that you are well balanced, have a thick skin and just move forwards.'

Todt's quiet office is a refuge from the bruising encounters at the race tracks during the 1998 season. Keeping a balanced head is very difficult in a highly competitive environment like Formula 1. Todt was on the receiving end of a great deal of antagonistic rhetoric from his opposite number at McLaren during the 1998 season and often he handed it back. Both sides were desperate to succeed and both were angered by the way the campaign had been fought by the opposition, above and below the surface. '1998 has been a big fight and the fight on the track was interesting. The team we've been racing against did not have the attitude I would have appreciated. I mean I don't feel part of the same world as the boss of McLaren!

'It could have been a good fight with a different atmosphere. I give credit when they deserve it, but they never give us credit. I think we deserved it sometimes, but every time we did well they just put suspicion out about us. That's a very bad thing to do in Formula 1. Believe me, Ferrari is such a clean team.'

Todt's huge desk is dotted with small, neat piles of letters and faxes. He has an array of telephones in front of him. The bookshelves are stacked with memorabilia; Schumacher and Irvine's helmets, a steering wheel in a perspex case and in the centre a black-and-white photograph of the man whose team he's running – Enzo Ferrari. 'I have a big respect for the man, he achieved something truly great which is still living. If Ferrari is something special, it's thanks to what he did. But when I arrived it was in a bad situation. The challenge is even greater, because when you do something for Ferrari, it's different from any other team. He is one of very few people who did something great in the sport. It's a phenomenon.'

The two most successful periods of Ferrari's history were the 1950s, when Alberto Ascari and Juan Manuel Fangio were racing for the team, and the 1970s, the Niki Lauda era. Lauda was Ferrari's most successful driver with fifteen wins, but in three years Schumacher had caught him up. In 1999, barring misfortune, he would surely become their most successful driver. But these days, after a nineteen-year drought, a World Championship would be a more precious measure of success.

With guaranteed finance from its backers, four more years of Schumacher driving them on and a restructured technical department, the Todt era looked set to be the most successful in Ferrari's seventy-year history.

Todt is one of the new breed of managers who take care of their people and work on their problems. After Ayrton Senna's death during the San Marino Grand Prix in 1994, his close friend Gerhard Berger decided to race on, but he was clearly working out his grief by overdriving the Ferrari. When he came in for a pit stop, Todt walked over and quietly said, 'Get out of the car.' He had done the unthinkable: advising a Ferrari driver to park a healthy car in the team's 'home' race.

His management philosophy follows that of former US President Truman, whose motto was, 'Talk quietly and carry a big stick.' A key part of the new structure was getting control of the press relations. Given the background, Todt thought this area was so important that he installed his right-hand man, Claudio Berro, in the job. Berro has done well; he has managed to make Ferrari more open, while at the same time keeping a lid on the wild stories which ruined things in the early Nineties. Whereas before Ferrari had been economical with the truth, telling the press a car had suffered a 'small electrical problem' when in fact the engine had blown-up, now what they tell the press is true, even if they don't tell the full story.

Berro works closely with Heiner Buchinger, Schumacher's press officer, and they, together with the inner sanctum of Todt, Brawn, Schumacher and Irvine, hold regular meetings to make sure they all sing from the same hymn sheet. Todt's management style is very much about being united with his team, being open and straightforward. 'I aim to be available for the others. I give a lot of time in the office. Lots of people say, "He's always away," but it's not true, I'm always here. I go to the races and I'm away from my desk just the Thursday and Friday. I'm back here on Monday morning. If there's a meeting in England or in Switzerland I always go just for the day. People can see me when they want. I need to be close to the problems and it's very important to give credit to what others do. It's not good to take the credit yourself. It's good to give credit when things go well and to cover your people when things go badly. I have strong views and make sure that things happen. I like us to be an educated family, without being too bothered by what's going on around.'

Todt's rapport with Schumacher is central to Ferrari's success. Great drivers will lift a team, but only if they are given the right environment. 'You may be a great champion, but if you haven't got a good car you will be beaten by a lot of other drivers. From a driver's point of view that is the most frustrating thing. On another level, if you hire a driver like Senna, Prost or Schumacher without giving him a good car, then you are making a big mistake.

'I'm very close to him. He's a very mature and clever guy and he has good common sense. The thing I most like about him as a colleague is that he's a hard worker. He wants to know and he wants to understand. He's not lazy. He's close to the team, win or lose. If he goes out of a race he is very much affected because he feels he has not delivered the success the team was expecting, which is true. But sometimes it happens the other way around as well. We are a team – we win together and we lose together. Very often racing drivers are there for the best but not

196

for the worst. In other words, they are happy to take the credit when they win, but they are not happy when the team loses. Michael has been very good, very consistent.

'Consistency in motor racing is very difficult – on the driving level, especially. If you look back over the last five years he has been the most consistent driver, but he never had the best car. He had a good enough package to allow him to deliver the best from himself.'

The announcement of Schumacher's long commitment to the national team was well received in Italy. Pino Allievi, writing in *La Gazzetta dello Sport*, said, 'The news is beautiful and important. Schumacher is the guiding force of Ferrari, the man who has constructed around him the family team.

'Ferrari is a prisoner of Schumacher, but Schumacher is a prisoner of Ferrari, which pays him well and gives him the freedom of action which he would not find in any other team. This is yet another act of faith in Ferrari and in the *tifosi* – Agnelli most of all.'

Gianni Agnelli, the great patriarch of FIAT and Ferrari and the man who ultimately pays the bills, has such faith in Schumacher that, back in 1996 when Schumacher arrived, he announced that if Ferrari failed to win with the German as their driver, it would be Ferrari's fault, not Schumacher's.

Agnelli was delighted to have held on to Schumacher and to have built into the new contract terms whereby he would become an ambassador for FIAT cars and take part in TV commercials for their latest models. 'Schumacher is a great champion but also an investment for "Made in Italy". As a driver he is without doubt the best. He's one of those people of whom Enzo Ferrari would have said, "He has three, four, five or six extra horsepower under his foot." I personally believe that if you take all the tracks into account, he is between half a second and a second faster every lap.'

That view was shared by some very important people in another company, one with a racing tradition almost as long as

Ferrari's – Mercedes-Benz. Although McLaren's Ron Dennis would not be publicly drawn on the subject of Schumacher, the Mercedes-Benz management were not so coy. Mercedes put out messages through board members like Jurgen Hubbert that Schumacher was the man they wanted. Now they had lost him for sure and it was a bigger surprise to them than they were letting on.

Schumacher was spotted as a youngster by Mercedes competitions director, Norbert Haug. Mercedes started a junior team to allow Schumacher, along with Heinz-Harald Frentzen and Karl Wendlinger, to grow. The trio learned their craft in the mighty Mercedes sportscars and received funding for other racing programmes. Whatever the mythology about the other two being quicker in Formula 3 days, Schumacher was clearly the class of the field, and Haug knew that this youngster from a poor northern family was going to turn the sport on its head one day.

Their relationship has always been strong. When Schumacher made his Grand Prix début with Jordan in 1991, Mercedes were not involved in Grand Prix racing, despite Haug's insistence that they should be. Mercedes paid Jordan £150,000 for the outing at Spa-Francorchamps, where Schumacher fulfilled Haug's prediction. When he moved to Benetton, many believed that his contract contained a clause whereby Mercedes could claim him back if ever it found itself in a strong position in Formula 1.

Mercedes re-entered Grand Prix racing in 1994 with the Sauber team but initially struggled to find competitiveness. By then Schumacher was already established as the world's leading driver and there was no suggestion of any move. Mercedes joined forces with McLaren in 1995, but the chassis was miles off the pace and that summer Schumacher decided to make his move to Ferrari.

So 1998 represented the first real chance Mercedes had had to fulfil the master plan and get their protégé into one of their own Formula 1 cars. Schumacher listened to their offers. In the paddock one April evening in Argentina he had a long, very public discussion with Haug and Dennis. Mercedes had just extended their deal with McLaren to the end of 2002 and Schumacher was the final piece of the jigsaw. Mercedes's great rival BMW would be entering the sport in 2000 with Williams, and having Schumacher on board would be vital for Mercedes's image.

But there were question marks about how Schumacher would fit into the team structure. At Ferrari he was clear number one, but at McLaren he would have to accept equal number one with Mika Hakkinen. Also, since Senna left, McLaren has kept its drivers under strict control and they are obliged to play the corporate game. They are encouraged to be team players, not individual megastars. No personal sponsorship deals are allowed, which would present serious problems for Schumacher with his huge Nike and Dekra deals.

In the end Michael had chosen Ferrari, and it looked like he was there for good. 'Why change a winning team?' he had said with a smile.

The day after the announcement, the German newspaper *Bild* ran a headline saying, I'LL SHOW YOU WHAT HAPPENS WHEN YOU SAY YOU DON'T NEED ME, above a story which claimed that Schumacher was angry with Mercedes-Benz president, Jurgen Schrempp, who had muddied the waters back in May when he declared, 'We don't need Schumacher.'

This was a little bit of tabloid mischief, designed to set Schumacher and Mercedes against each other, and Norbert Haug issued a firm denial: 'We kept in touch constantly, but we soon realized that the marriage of the century was not going to happen.'

The German tabloid newspaper suggested that the deal had not come about because Schumacher had asked for too much money. Schumacher himself denied this, saying that Mercedes had made a higher offer than the one he'd accepted from Ferrari. It was the human relationship he had gone for.

* * *

The link between the German race fans and Mercedes-Benz is closer than any similar relationship with a manufacturer, apart from the Italians with Ferrari. When Mercedes started winning regularly in 1998, the Germans had a new story to interest them: national hero races against German company. The fans' enthusiasm for Mercedes grew rapidly, which was their objective, as it was good for business. In Germany, Schumacher was the number-one draw, but Mercedes now moved into second place, ahead of the two other German drivers, Heinz-Harald Frentzen and Ralf Schumacher.

The marketing was well conceived. They played on the Silver Arrows theme, recalling the great tradition of Mercedes race cars before the war and in the 1950s, which had utterly dominated Grand Prix racing. Mercedes had come and gone from Formula 1 over the years, as the company's objectives had changed. Theirs was an image that wasn't dependent on a glamorous racing association, like Ferrari.

The McLaren team too had a tradition of excellence, but theirs stretched back only two decades. Although they were working hard to build a recognizable brand name of their own, they couldn't compete with the traditions of Mercedes or Ferrari, hence the attraction to Mercedes executives of calling the cars 'Silver Arrows'. Ron Dennis was not a great fan of the idea, but reluctantly accepted that many people would see them that way, especially in Germany.

McLaren's drivers, Mika Hakkinen and David Coulthard, were considered to be among the fastest in the sport and Hakkinen appeared to have come of age as a racing driver. Yet opinion polls showed that his popularity in Germany was less than that of Norbert Haug!

Hakkinen drove some dynamic races during the 1998 season and his qualifying performances were beyond reproach. He also proved that he could handle the pressure and was able to deliver when the chips were down. And yet the public sensed that he was only winning now because his car gave him the opportunity. He had been a McLaren driver since 1993, but where had he finished in the seasons when he didn't have the benchmark car? Senna had won plenty of races in uncompetitive McLarens and Schumacher had scored most of his wins against better machinery. Perhaps this was why Hakkinen's success now failed to inspire the public.

One important Mercedes tradition was always to employ the best drivers of the day: in the mid-1950s they had both Juan Manuel Fangio and Stirling Moss – still considered two of the best drivers ever – on their books. In the normal scheme of things, Michael Schumacher was their natural successor in the 1990s and all the correct preparations had been meticulously made in his youth. But now the well-oiled chain had slipped off the cog.

Some within the company believed that Mercedes was better off without Michael Schumacher for two reasons: first because it was better for Mercedes's image of engineering excellence if it won the championship by *beating* the best driver in the world rather than because of him; secondly because Schumacher winning in a Mercedes would have the journalists, particularly in Britain and France, reaching for unfavourable but evocative images of German tanks steam-rollering to victory.

But others on the Mercedes board were not so sure; they were looking at the newspaper headlines which had been built up through the season. It had started with his stunning victory in Argentina, described in one paper as, 'A red scratch on the silver paintwork.' The story continued, 'Schumi has stopped the Silver Arrows. He gave Ferrari supporters cause to celebrate with an aggressive drive. Formula 1 is exciting again.' Fourteen million Germans saw the race on television and probably drew the same conclusion.

Hans Stuck, writing in the daily *Bild* said, 'Only Schumi wins like that against the Silver Arrows.' *Bild on Sunday* was even more direct: 'Michael Schumacher, with his sensational win in Argentina, saved F1 from deadly boredom by stopping the dominance of the Silver Arrows.' One Mercedes board member, perhaps echoing the feelings of many of his colleagues, had optimistically said in an interview with

Stuttgarter Zeitung in April, 'Michael would be very welcome as he is at present undoubtedly the best driver.'

But it hadn't worked out that way. The only ray of hope for Mercedes was the possibility that Ferrari would provide a poor car in 1999 and that Schumacher would be able to walk away. But even here there was to be no joy. Although Schumacher's original contract with Ferrari had stipulated that if he did not finish in the top three places in the World Championship he was entitled to leave, in the new 1998 contract that clause had been removed. 'We didn't need it,' said Schumacher, 'because I'm sure we're going to have plenty of success.'

FOURTEEN THE EXQUISITE AGONY

Monza, Italy, August 1998

Motor racing is about real highs and lows and there isn't much in between.

Schumacher and Ferrari visited both extremes as the 1998 season moved towards a thrilling climax. At Spa in late August, Schumacher erupted with fury as McLaren driver David Coulthard, in very mysterious circumstances, caused him to crash out of the lead, with the loss of ten vital points.

Then, two weeks later at Monza, Schumacher won against the odds, in front of almost 120,000 ecstatic fans, to level the championship with two races to go.

The collision at Spa was by far the most controversial on-track incident of the 1998 season. By that stage the championship had developed into a tense battle between Schumacher and Hakkinen. Only seven points separated them and a mistake by either driver would hand the initiative to the other.

Having built up a thirty-seven-second lead in heavy rain, Schumacher came up to lap Coulthard's McLaren. For corner after corner, Coulthard held Schumacher up. He had several opportunities to let the Ferrari past in safety, the best coming at the 30 m.p.h. La Source hairpin, where he ran wide and, seeing Schumacher on the inside of him, he could easily have delayed picking up the throttle, thus allowing the leader to pass. But he chose not to do that and instead Schumacher stared into a ball of spray at over 100 m.p.h. and wondered what Coulthard was up to. In the context of the cold war between McLaren and Ferrari, anything could be behind it.

It had been another virtuoso performance in the wet. Like the previous year at Spa, Schumacher had given his competitors a driving lesson. After a massive pile-up involving thirteen cars at the first start, which he had avoided, he got away well at the second start and attacked Hakkinen in the first corner. The Finn tried to push him out wide, but spun as he hit the throttle. He was hit hard by Johnny Herbert's Sauber and his race was over. Schumacher soon passed Damon Hill's Jordan for the lead, and with a clear track in front of him he set about building on it. By lap twenty-five he was over half a minute clear and in a class of his own.

A distinct opportunity had opened up before him. With Hakkinen out of the race, a win here at Spa would mean Michael would take the lead in the World Championship for the first time this season, with just three races to go. After the dominance of McLaren in the early part of the season, with Hakkinen winning five of the first seven races, Michael would have turned the whole thing around and set himself up with a great chance of winning the title. It was almost too good to be true.

And so it proved. The two cars came out of a left-hander and onto the short downhill straight which led to the challenging Pouhon corner. But something was wrong. Coulthard did not pick up the throttle as he shifted up from second to third gear. In fact he was using just 56 per cent of the throttle compared to Schumacher, who was accelerating hard with his foot flat on the throttle, as was the norm. Now suddenly the McLaren was travelling at just 160 km/h compared to the 220 km/h of the Ferrari.

This was Coulthard's way of letting Schumacher past and it made no sense at all. Although he was well over to the right of the track, he hadn't moved off the racing line, which is why Schumacher didn't read the situation. Driving into a ball of spray, Michael suddenly sensed that something was wrong and instinctively swerved to the left, but everything happened too fast. He hammered into the back of Coulthard's car, removing its rear wing, while his own right front wheel was ripped off, flailing uselessly over the barrier, landing in the forest near by.

With the wheel had gone a cast-iron ten points and the psychological comfort of a championship lead going into Ferrari's home race at Monza. The Ferrari crew were speechless, Schumacher toured in on three wheels and thought about what had just happened. Coulthard's actions made no sense to him at all and he wondered, just wondered, whether Coulthard had been acting under orders from his McLaren team. He parked the car in the garage, sprang out of it and set off up the pit lane to McLaren, pursued by Jean Todt and the team manager, Stefano Domenicalli, whose attempts to restrain his driver were shrugged off.

He burst into the McLaren area and shouted, 'You tried to fucking kill me!' at an astonished Coulthard, before being pushed away by McLaren mechanics. Schumacher, by now convinced that McLaren had instructed Coulthard to take him out, went directly to the stewards, accompanied by Todt, to make a strenuous protest. For over three-quarters of an hour he sat in the stewards' room, still highly animated, gesturing vigorously as he made his point. Outside everyone held their breath and wondered what would happen next in this amazing Formula 1 season.

Against the backdrop of the strange decisions taken already that year in stewards' rooms in Brazil, Montreal and Silverstone, anything could happen. Conspiracy theorists began speculating that the entire McLaren team would be banned for two races, but they were dreaming. The stewards studied the computer data of both cars and decided that Coulthard had not 'backed off', he had simply not accelerated. They saw nothing untoward in Coulthard's actions and described it as a racing incident. A huge posse of press and TV gathered outside the Ferrari motorhome in scenes reminiscent of Jerez the previous year. Schumacher emerged to make a brief statement, maintaining his line that 'one could think it had been done deliberately. We think that there may be something more behind it because we are fighting for the World Championship.'

People close to Coulthard admitted privately that he had made a terrible mess of it, but strenuously denied that he had done it deliberately. There are very few drivers in Formula 1 who would take such a risk to help their own championship hopes and even fewer who would do it for their team-mate. One of the fairest and most gentlemanly drivers in the field, Coulthard does not fit into either group and he bitterly resented Schumacher's suggestion that he might. 'I saw the blue flag, the team informed me that Michael was behind me and that I should let him past. I maintained my speed to allow him to get past me into Pouhon corner, but he ran into the back of me. It's a regrettable incident, there's no way I wanted to get involved in his race. But his behaviour in coming into the garage and accusing me of trying to "Fucking kill him" is unacceptable. I've had incidents with Michael in the past and I've waited until afterwards to talk to him man to man, face to face. I take it very badly; it's disgusting behaviour from some-one who's got such a fantastic record for driving in this sport. He needs to get some sort of help for controlling his anger.

'It's total paranoia to suggest I did it deliberately. All the radio conversations between me and the team are recorded and available. It's ridiculous to accuse us of trying to do such a thing.'

In his heart, Schumacher knew that Coulthard was right. The mild-mannered Scot was not capable of a deliberate foul. Michael was angry because it could have been avoided and because ten points had been lost in the stupidest way imagin-able. After things had calmed down a little, and once they'd had time to study the incident, Ferrari technical director, Ross Brawn, put his own rational spin on it: 'I don't believe that Coulthard did it deliberately. It was a misjudgement which was compounded by the fact that he had a chance to let Michael by in far safer positions. So it's very unfortunate because we feel aggrieved not by what happened there and then, but because there were other places on the track where he had ample opportunity to let Michael through – that's the added bit of the incident which is unpleasant to us.

'You could argue that Michael was too close and that with a thirty-seven-second lead he should have held back. But it's not in Michael's make-up, and there are certain things about the guy you just won't change. Ninety-nine per cent of the time that's what you want out of him. He has this total belief in his own ability and a total confidence in what he's doing. That's what makes him the driver he is. So if you try to compromise that, even in a situation like Spa, that might change him. Maybe it's an aspect of his game that could be strengthened, but when a guy is at the front all the time, challenging for wins, they are right in the public eye. This was so important, it got all the media attention.'

Reaction in the press and among former drivers was largely critical of Schumacher. *La Gazzetta dello Sport* ran the headline PAZZO SCHUMI (Crazy Schumi) above a photo of the scuffle in the McLaren garage. The paper's sense of frustration was as great as its driver's but the editorial view was that Schumacher had brought the incident on himself by running so close to the back of the McLaren. Candido Cannavo turned Luca di Montezemolo's jibe about a World Championship of taxi drivers back onto Schumacher: 'With the race already won, what were you doing running risks? Your rivals were out of the race or beaten by your brilliance, all you needed to do was go like a taxi driver, clicking off the kilometres to the finish line. That's all, with no hurry and no supplementary tariffs. Lauda would have done it, icy cool and precise as he was. But you, dear Schumi, are different.'

In Britain, Schumacher was painted as the villain of the piece. The *Sun* ran a headline, CRAZY SCHU ATTACKS 'KILLER' COUL, while the *Independent* claimed that the German 'seemed too close to Coulthard when he knew that he didn't need to take any risks'.

In Germany, ex-Grand Prix star Hans Joachim Stuck wrote in *Bild*, 'My honest opinion: Schumacher lost his nerve for a second. If you are leading the race by thirty-seven seconds you don't need to run three metres behind your opponent. Not at that speed and not at that time.'

Former driver Keke Rosberg, now manager of Hakkinen, was clearly delighted at Schumacher's stumble and said, 'I don't know who he's trying to please to overdrive that way. He's brilliant and he's very quick, but to be honest, by now you'd expect him also to slow down. Maybe he's the type of guy who never will.'

Clay Regazzoni, who drove for Ferrari in the 1970s and became a darling of the *tifosi*, was highly critical: 'He drives with arrogance and thinks he is a demi-god. He wants to humiliate his rivals, not just beat them. He could have avoided the scene in the McLaren pit. His behaviour was not worthy of a champion.'

Jackie Stewart said, 'Michael is the best driver, but he has something I don't think is healthy. He has something I hope I never had. Real champions don't have to bully.'

While Stirling Moss said, 'He's head and shoulders above the opposition. It's the attitude of the other drivers I find depressing. They seem very defeatist. If you are a real fighter, as Schumacher is, that makes it a greater challenge.'

Spa was one of the defining incidents of the year. In some ways it summed up the 1998 season: a bitter row between Ferrari and McLaren, a race decided in the stewards' room and the thwarted impetuous brilliance of Schumacher, who had risen above the restrictions of his machinery and the conditions only to end up with controversy.

The day after Spa, Mercedes director Norbert Haug said that the incident was clearly Schumacher's fault and called for him to make an apology to Coulthard: 'There is too much tension in the whole thing with Monza coming up. We want a sporting challenge not a war, and the best way is for Michael to apologize.' It was a surprising misjudgement of Schumacher's character from someone who knows him well. In Michael's mind he was not the one who needed to apologize: 'I over-reacted by saying what I did, but David did make a mistake.'

However, he did know that he and Coulthard needed to talk. But after Haug's demands for an apology, how could Schumacher start the dialogue? It would look like he was doing it on request from the opposition. The facts required a different solution. As Michael saw it, a McLaren driver who wasn't in the race with him had robbed him of ten points and the lead in the World Championship. Sure he had gone down and yelled at him, but wouldn't anyone have done the same?

Many people were critical of Schumacher for the incident, but Jean Todt believes that people who rush to judgement in such situations are making an error: 'It is easy to judge when you are behind a TV screen with all the coldness of being removed. Often you have to judge facts which happen in one-hundredth of a second and that's a lot more difficult.

'I think that the emphasis was on it far more because it was Ferrari and Schumacher. Can you imagine what the reaction would have been like if it was Hakkinen who had hit Irvine while lapping him? I'm not persecuted, I'm not paranoid, but don't you think that the reaction would have been rather different? It would have been a disaster.'

Schumacher himself feels that it's difficult for anyone who hasn't been in a similar situation to judge his actions. 'People tend to judge things from the outside and characterize me, but they don't really understand. You have to see it from the inside. Even former drivers think they know what it's like on the inside, but as the years go by things change and they don't know 100 per cent what the situation is today. Hans Joachim Stuck criticized me for what happened in Spa with Coulthard, but then I found out that, years ago, he had exactly the same accident with Jochen Mass at the Nürburgring!

'The fact is that Coulthard had the chance to let me past at La Source hairpin, when I was alongside him. If he really wanted to let me through, then he made a mess of it and did it too late. In the previous corners he was accelerating out of them normally. What do I know of it if suddenly he doesn't accelerate? He cannot do that, not there on the straight. If you had seen the TV shots from a helicopter you would have seen that, before the incident, the distance between us was normal. But the speed at which we hit was not; he was going too slowly.

'I have lost many races and I've always offered my hand to the winner. And I have apologized too, when I made a mistake, as I did to Frentzen in Canada. But in this sport there are episodes which divide opinion. One sees it one way and the other sees it another way. For me the incident is 100 per cent David's fault.'

Coulthard and Schumacher went through a Mexican stand-off in the week following Spa. Two days after the incident, both found themselves at Monza for a major test session. The newpaper headlines in Italy shouted to Michael to give Coulthard his hand. The pair had many opportunities during the week to talk and the press turned out in force to see it. So did the *tifosi* – over 8,000 of them sat in the grandstands each day, a few crazies bringing anti-Coulthard banners with messages like 'Coulthard killer'. Every time the Scotsman's silver car pulled out of the garage they whistled their contempt.

But no meeting took place. With Monza being the next race on the calendar many shared Norbert Haug's fear that the hooligan element of the *tifosi* would turn nasty on McLaren if the situation wasn't resolved. In the paranoid atmosphere that existed beween the two teams, many in the McLaren camp felt that Michael was keeping the conflict on the boil for just that reason.

Schumacher calmed down, and although he had no intention of making the first move, he did claim to want to discuss the matter with Coulthard. Ironically, Schumacher has always liked the Scotsman: 'You can talk to David. He's not a prima donna that you can't discuss things with afterwards. He's a very stable person. After the collision in Argentina we took the video and watched it together on my plane, and at first he was angry with me, but when we watched it through together he agreed that it was a racing accident.'

That was Argentina, but attempts to get them together now proved more difficult. Max Mosley, the FIA president, and

Ferrari boss, Luca di Montezemolo, entered the debate. Both were mindful of the possibility that the confrontation could spark off violence among the more lunatic fringe of the *tifosi* and they urged the two sides to shake hands and forget the matter. What made the situation worse was that Coulthard and Schumacher were both directors of the Grand Prix Drivers' Association, which didn't need a public feud between two senior members. The other director, Benetton's Alex Wurz, spent time that week trying shuttle diplomacy between the McLaren and Ferrari garages to no avail.

Eventually, Michael's press officer, Heiner Buchinger, attempted to get them together in the Sauber motorhome on the Friday afternoon, the final day of the test. Coulthard turned up at 4 p.m., as scheduled, but there was no sign of Schumacher. Buchinger arrived with some bad news. Michael had to leave because he needed to get his brother and father to Cologne airport and then fly on to Geneva before that airport closed at 10 p.m. This would not leave enough time to have a proper discussion. Coulthard accepted this, although he later learned that at around 4 p.m. Schumacher had been in the Ferrari motorhome eating an ice cream. He could have told David himself.

Eventually they met on the Thursday of the Monza race weekend in the neutral motorhome of Winfield, Williams's main sponsor, which is run by the genial Austrian host, Karl-Heinz Zimmerman. They talked for seventy-five minutes and not just about Spa; they revisited the Argentina incident and talked about the problems of visibility in the rain. They came out afterwards to shake hands for the cameras. As they walked away, Coulthard looked the less pleased of the two: 'We've cleared the air a bit. It was a calm discussion. We agreed that it was a regrettable incident and that we should talk to our fellow drivers, because there were problems with blue flags – which warn a driver he is about to be lapped. In these conditions it was almost impossible to see them.

'Basically we are once again ready to challenge each other on the track, wheel to wheel, as before. As for the accusations, we are not children. Some things hurt, but you get over them. My conscience is clear; it wasn't my fault.'

Schumacher seemed cheerful and claimed that his mind was now at rest. He was sure that Coulthard had not taken him out deliberately. 'It was good to talk and there are no more problems. The important thing is that there are no suspicions between us. I was very unhappy about the situation which had developed between us. Now that's the end of it, what has happened has happened. The important thing now is I know that David did not deliberately try to take me out. To be honest, I realized that even before we spoke. I didn't think so immediately after the incident because there were a lot of factors which led me to believe otherwise. But having analysed everything properly, I saw that it was a situation which, although unfortunate for me, was not caused on purpose.

'I've never lost my temper like that before and I never will again. Never. It was just an exceptional reaction in an extraordinary situation; people will understand or not understand, that doesn't matter to me. I know what I was feeling at the time, but I didn't go to see David to hit him. I just went to express my view on what had happened. I've never punched anyone in my life; it's not in my way. There is no reason to hurt anyone, but every reason to say what you feel. So I just did what I felt like doing at the time.'

The two were alone in the small room throughout the meeting, not wishing to have any witnesses. Zimmerman later revealed that he stuck his head around the door at one point to see if either of them wanted to buy the other a glass of grappa, 'But as neither of them had any money in their wallets I didn't serve them one!'

It had not been a real war between the two, there was too much friendship in place beforehand, but there was a palpable air of sadness on both sides about what had happened. Jean Todt rallied his troops. 'With Michael we are now stronger and more united than ever before,' he said. But the truth was that a golden opportunity had been lost.

Schumacher had seen ten points disappear, points he had

already worked hard for. With them he would have gone into the Monza weekend three points ahead in the championship, an almost unbelievable prospect after Melbourne. From a position like that, he and Ferrari would have fancied their chances to grab the title from Hakkinen in the last three races.

As it was, he still trailed Hakkinen by seven points. The test the previous week had shown that Ferrari would be more competitive at the high-speed Monza track than it had been at Hockenheim, but the McLarens still looked like the favourites. A precious chance had slipped through Michael's fingers and the whole team knew it. Now the championship, although still open, seemed a more distant possibility.

Coulthard went away disappointed in Schumacher and in the way he had drawn out their reconciliation by avoiding him at the Monza test. In a revealing interview with Hugh McIllvaney for a *Sunday Times* profile of Schumacher, headlined BULLY BOY ON WHEELS, he gave voice to his doubts about Michael's character: 'I believe strongly that Mika deserves to win the title because his sportsmanship has never been open to question, whereas there have been many occasions when Michael has got involved with other drivers during a race – and everybody knows I'm one of them – where he has severely bent the rules. And bending the rules is, in most people's language, the same as cheating. He has been guilty of the equivalent of low blows in boxing.

'I know I'll be accused of envy and sour grapes, but I don't feel either. People will applaud Michael for some of the things he has got away with, for being prepared to go to extremes to win. But there is nothing soft about adherence to the rules. Without it any sport risks anarchy.'

It rained on qualifying day at Monza and, as the track dried out, Schumacher claimed the most dramatic pole position of his career, with Jacques Villeneuve's Williams qualifying alongside him on the front row. The two McLarens, caught out by the changing track conditions, timed their runs badly and wound up disappointed on the second row of the grid.

The following morning the *tifosi*, old and young, those with tickets and those without, poured into Monza. Security is a relative term at Grand Prix circuits. Some venues are guarded like Colditz, often by black-shirted, jack-booted skinheads, who discourage entry without the proper credentials.

At Monza on race day, with a Ferrari on pole, the concept of 'no entry' becomes meaningless. The unofficial ways into the circuit are a time-honoured secret, but one shared by thousands. They came under fences, through forests, climbed out of car boots, laughing and excited. The *autodromo* filled with noise and colour and expectation. By the time the warm-up began at 9.30 a.m., the place was packed, airhorns blasting around the circuit as the cars poured out onto the track for their final half-hour preparation.

A giant diamond-vision screen above the pits transmitted TV pictures to the thousands in the grandstands. When a shot of Schumacher came on screen, sharing a joke with his mechanics as he put on his crash helmet, the place erupted. Men and women, children and pensioners leapt to their feet and waved their caps above their heads. When a similar shot of Coulthard came on they whistled and jeered, but mercifully it was more the reaction of a pantomime crowd than a football terrace.

Ferrari is not just about cars and motor racing, it is part of Italian culture. Frank Williams and Ron Dennis, though deserving of great respect, are not part of Britain's history. But Enzo Ferrari is very much part of Italy's. Motor racing has played a more important role in Italian twentieth-century history than many foreigners realize.

The Mille Miglia, a 1,000-mile flat-out race on Italian public roads, captured the imagination of the public the first time it was run in 1927 and developed into a key part of Italian life, until common sense prevailed in the mid-1950s. Cars and racing became part of the culture. When the Second World War ended in 1945 there were bridges all over Italy which had been destroyed by bombing. These were rebuilt in a hurry because the Mille Miglia had to pass through.

For the 1946 race, the bridge on the River Po, which used to be the link between the two halves of Italy, was still down, and Italy remained a divided nation. The bridge was rebuilt so that the race could go ahead and it symbolically reunited Italy.

Enzo Ferrari raced in the 1920s and started up his own team in 1929. He took as his logo the *cavallino* or Prancing Horse, a black stallion on a yellow shield, formerly the emblem of the heroic First-World-War fighter pilot Count Barraca. It has been Ferrari's symbol of racing and victory ever since.

Ferrari created and managed Enzo's myth with ruthless precision and his name became synonymous with cars, speed, racing, passion and enthusiasm. His name spans four generations and the tradition is strong because Ferrari has always been what it is today: a car builder with a well-supported race team. If you are a forty-year-old Italian, you will have seen the best years of Williams, but your grandfather will know nothing about the team, because it didn't exist in his day. But he will know that Ferrari used to have the great Tazio Nuvolari driving his cars in the 1930s.

Throughout the 1930s, the Italian Grand Prix at Monza attracted over 200,000 spectators, far more than today. Enzo Ferrari became an icon in Italy because he lived through the different eras of twentieth-century history and played a role in them. He was around when Mussolini and his Fascists controlled Italy. The dictator used the sport to build his short-term popularity, but Enzo Ferrari outlasted him.

There is a very wide base of enthusiasts who make up the *tifosi*. A tiny number, probably less than 1 per cent, are the football-hooligan element, but the great majority are genuine enthusiasts, who know a great deal about the sport. They are kept informed by the four national daily sports papers, including *La Gazzetta dello Sport*, which runs a story every single day about the team, even when there is no story to tell.

The *tifosi* love racing, and they love Ferrari because it's the common thread through the generations. It's a family thing as well, in much the same way that support for a soccer club is passed down through the generations. But there are many soccer clubs and only one Ferrari. That's why there are so many *tifosi*.

Many of them had forgiven Schumacher for what happened in Jerez the previous year, because now he once again offered them the dream of the world title. But they hadn't forgotten it. One fan summed up his mixed feelings about the character of Ferrari's champion: 'I think Schumi needs to examine his conscience and admit that to become a great champion he needs to be more calm and rational. World Championships are won by great driving, I won't deny that, but you also need a little maturity, which he still lacks.'

He had offered them some thrilling moments through the season and some magical and emotional victories. There was also a great sympathy for the man after what had happened at Spa. Now they had come to see him do it again on home turf on the tenth anniversary of Enzo Ferrari's death.

He got the worst start imaginable. The wheels spun, the car bogged down and all his hard-won advantage in pole position was lost. When it mattered most he had made a real mess of the start – no accusations of Ferrari having illegal traction systems on the car that day!

Hakkinen was past him before he'd gone 100 metres and Coulthard went by as well. Irvine and Villeneuve also out-dragged him on the run down to the first chicane. He had gone from first place to fifth in ten seconds. But he was on the attack immediately and soon found himself back up in third place. At the front, Hakkinen was struggling with a lack of grip from his tyres and he allowed Coulthard past into the lead. After sixteen laps the Scot had a margin of almost ten seconds and Schumacher had caught Hakkinen.

Suddenly Coulthard's Mercedes engine blew up massively: huge billows of white, oily smoke filled the track at the Roggia chicane. Hakkinen's car slid while braking and Schumacher lined up to pass. Hakkinen scrabbled to recover, but he'd lost momentum, and as they blasted out of the corner Schumacher eased past. The two championship rivals were wheel to wheel for what seemed like an eternity, before Schumacher cut across the McLaren and into the lead. This was Grand Prix racing at its very finest.

The *tifosi* lifted the roof of the grandstands. Schumacher pulled away steadily and the race settled down a bit. As the laps ticked by, the *tifosi* crossed and uncrossed their fingers, the exquisite agony too much to take. Schumacher had suffered mechanical failure only once that season, in the very first race. Would fate intervene now, or was Ferrari's reliability as good as it appeared?

The tension was eased greatly when Hakkinen momentarily lost control of his car in the Roggia chicane, the car spinning backwards across the kerbs, bouncing through the sand, before landing back on the track. The McLaren rolled backwards in an arc, and Hakkinen managed to engage first gear and rejoin the race. But there was no question that he was in trouble. McLaren's Achilles heel – their reliability – had let them down again and Hakkinen's front brakes were playing up. The crowd cheered wildly as first Irvine, then Ralf Schumacher, passed the slow-moving Silver Arrow.

Whereas before the finish line couldn't come soon enough, now the *tifosi* wanted the race to last another twenty laps as Hakkinen slipped down the field. But he kept going and crossed the line in fourth place, which meant that he and Schumacher were now tied with eighty points each. There were just two races to go.

That night Coulthard and Schumacher met again at the Winfield motorhome, this time by chance and with no waiting media. Schumacher was celebrating his win with a glass of beer, when Coulthard walked in and sportingly offered his congratulations. At this point Karl-Heinz Zimmerman appeared and shouted, 'You are a pair of idiots, now drink a toast to lasting peace with a glass of my grappa!'

Schumacher threw one down his throat but, seeing his astonished expression, Coulthard decided not to bother. Eventually, under pressure, he took a sip to the applause of all present.

The weekend had come full circle.

FIFTEEN THE SPRINT FINISH

Nürburgring, Germany, September 1998

Everything was looking good as Schumacher peeled off into the pit lane for his first fuel and tyre stop of the race. He had started from pole and for the first fourteen laps his team-mate, Eddie Irvine, had acted as a buffer between himself and Hakkinen. But then Hakkinen had passed the second Ferrari – far too easily for his liking – and had closed to within five seconds of the lead. The game was on.

Drivers who find themselves in a straight fight with Michael Schumacher for the World Championship tend to raise their game in the closing stages of the season. It happened with Damon Hill in 1994 and with Jacques Villeneuve in 1997: both dug deep to find previously unseen levels of speed and consistency to take on the German. Now it was Hakkinen's turn. He had led the championship all season, but his wins had all been down to superior machinery. Three poor results in a row had put the pressure squarely on his shoulders going into the Nürburgring race. Schumacher had said before the start that Mika would not be able to take the pressure, that he would crack, but instead the Finn was steadily taking control of the race, taming Ferrari.

As Schumacher made his pit stop, the McLaren flashed past into the lead. With a clear track in front of him Hakkinen pushed harder than ever. He was taking Schumacher on at his own game. Many times Ross Brawn had adopted the same tactic of running Schumacher a few laps longer than the

218

opposition, building a cushion in order to retain a lead after the pit stops. Now McLaren was doing it back to them.

Brawn and Schumacher read McLaren's tactic well: Michael pushed as hard as he could, but the low track temperatures caused by the cold weather meant that his Goodyear tyres were not working as well as they might. It was beginning to look as though Hakkinen had the measure of him. Sure enough, when the McLaren team called him in after four blisteringly fast laps, he was able to rejoin just in front of the Ferrari. Not many people make up five seconds on Michael Schumacher in the middle of a race; Hakkinen had managed it, but now the Ferrari was crowding him, pushing him, making life difficult.

As he looked in his mirrors, Hakkinen realized that Schumacher wasn't looking for a way past him, he was simply trying to force him into a mistake. The Ferrari didn't have the speed to make a pass. There were still nearly forty laps to go and he had a lead of no more than a few car lengths. The pressure would be immense, but then this was the World Championship they were fighting for.

Not many racers would welcome a pit board which read, 'Forty laps to go' with the world's best driver just four-tenths of a second behind them. But Hakkinen kept his nerve and the McLaren held together. Forty agonizing laps later he crossed the finish line just two seconds ahead of the Ferrari to take a four-point lead into the final race in Suzuka, Japan.

Much was made afterwards of Schumacher being 'devastated' by having lost in a straight fight at the Nürburgring, but in reality he was easily able to understand how the race had got away from him and knew that he had nothing to reproach himself for. McLaren had been off-form in qualifying and it was always likely that they would discover their missing speed before the race. The reality was that both drivers had pushed to the limit with no mistakes, but the Ferrari just wasn't quite fast enough on the day. Far from being 'devastated', Schumacher was able to accept this.

'He drove a very good race. On the other side, to be fair his best lap was only half a second faster than mine. If I had a car which was half a second faster, well . . . for sure he had eight seconds disadvantage in the early stages and to get that back and make an advantage over me after the first pit stop, he had to push very hard. He used his car to the maximum over five or six laps and that's why he's there and fighting to the maximum. He is not at all a bad racing driver. He knows his job and he does it quite well.'

There followed five weeks of the sort of madness only Formula 1 can create. Five weeks in which two well-funded teams, staffed by highly motivated and competitive individuals, threw everything they had into their preparations for a single race and played psychological games with each other to pass the time. By the end of it, Ferrari had done seventeen days and over 5,000 miles of testing. McLaren covered less ground but still had parallel test teams running in Spain, France and England, looking for the vital technical edge that would give them the championship.

Schumacher's pole positions at Monza and Nürburgring showed that Ferrari's technical package was now equal to McLaren's. Having lost so much ground in the early part of the year it had come on song when it most needed to be. Both teams knew that, in a development race like this, chassis improvements would probably cancel each other out on either side. Only by finding something in the tyres could one side get any decisive edge over the other at Suzuka. McLaren had one sure advantage: the four-point gap which meant that victory would not be enough for Schumacher, he would need Irvine to finish second to win the crown.

In that weird inverted logic for which Formula 1 is famous, Irvine was now under more pressure than Schumacher or Hakkinen. His half-hearted attempt to keep the Finn behind him at the Nürburgring had won him no friends in the Ferrari team. Most felt he should have held up the McLaren driver for longer, as he'd done in the French Grand Prix. But Eddie had been off-form, largely due to a back injury, which was aggravated by an ill-fitting seat. Every time he pressed the brake pedal hard, he got shooting pains in his back. If he was to play his part at Suzuka, he would need to be comfortable in the car, so a new seat was developed with small airbags for him to inflate in key areas to give him more support. Nothing would be left to chance in the run up to Suzuka.

Eddie needed support of a different kind from the team as the Italian press went to town on the rumours that Ferrari were thinking of replacing him with Jean Alesi. One paper, *Tuttosport*, suggested that the switch would be made before the race in Suzuka. There was nothing new in this; ever since he'd joined Ferrari there had been a section of the Italian media which thought Irvine a good-for-nothing and sought to replace him. But this time the suggestion was backed by rumours that Schumacher had become disillusioned with his team-mate.

Irvine had made a lot of fuss about being allowed to win races when he renewed his contract for 1999, having spent three years in the number-two role. On top of that, after Schumacher's controversial collision at Spa, Irvine had been the first driver to publicly support Coulthard in the dispute over blame. Schumacher's acknowledged friendship with Alesi and the Frenchman's burning desire to drive for Ferrari again one day added strength to the story.

Jean Todt was aware of the rumours and had his own thoughts on Irvine's standing with Schumacher: 'Eddie and Michael have a fantastic relationship, but you always have to be careful because it's like a couple. If you get on well, it doesn't mean that you will always get on well. Enough little things and it will go wrong. So it's a daily job to make sure that things don't go wrong.'

Schumacher himself admitted to feeling a mild concern about Irvine's ability to help him win the title: 'Eddie is well known to be very fast at Suzuka. I hope we are going to see that this year. He has struggled a bit recently with back problems and I hope he gets them under control, because if you have back problems then you struggle a bit to concentrate on the main issue, which is the racing.

'It's still open. It's a more difficult mission now, but not an impossible one. I'm still looking forward to it.'

Luca di Montezemolo, who had criticized Irvine immediately after Nüburgring and who, some felt, had planted the Alesi story in the press to encourage Irvine to do his utmost in Suzuka, publicly backed his man: 'You may as well talk about things that happen on the moon. I am expecting great things of our drivers, especially from Eddie, who drove an exceptional race on that track last year.'

Irvine himself was sanguine. It was not the first time he'd had to rebut such a rumour and if he felt anger at the way the story had got out of control, he didn't show it: 'It's like water off a duck's back to me, I'm used to it. Perhaps I've just got a thick skin. The Italian press are always calling for my head. They just need to fill the pages. They have been saying for two and a half years now that I shouldn't be driving for Ferrari. Last year, after Suzuka, they were calling me a hero, but the race before they had been calling for my head. Nothing had changed except that we had a new front wing in Suzuka!

'So how can you take anything these people write about you seriously? You've got to have a strong head and know what you're doing and don't believe the press. I don't listen to adulation or criticism. I work things out for myself.

'Some guy has made up a story for a few bob and my problem is that he's flogged it around the world. Anyone who knows anything can see it would be ridiculous to sack me. If anyone can do anything at Suzuka it's me.'

But Irvine had another, more pressing reason for wanting Schumacher to clinch the title. He believed from his contract negotiations with Jean Todt and Luca di Montezemolo that if he played his part in helping Ferrari to win the title this time he would be allowed to race Schumacher the following year and, if circumstances permitted, he would be allowed to win races and fight for the title himself. Winless after eighty-one starts in Formula 1, he desperately needed a fresh start in 1999.

If Irvine was one of Ferrari's secret weapons in Japan, another was the '*supermotore*', a special 800-horsepower qualifying engine, which Ferrari had been perfecting for several months. It had almost 500 more revs than the normal engine and gave anything up to 20 horsepower more. It was too risky to use it in the race, but for qualifying it might give Ferrari the boost it needed to get both Irvine and Schumacher onto the front row of the grid, from where they could control the race.

The long weeks of waiting dragged on. Ferrari tested tyres, chassis modifications and the *supermotore* at its Fiorano and Mugello test facilities. Day after day, lap after lap they worked with a single goal in mind. On one day Schumacher did over 170 laps of Fiorano, trying different tyre compounds. Some days the track was flooded with water to simulate wet race conditions. Suzuka would be Goodyear's last race before quitting the sport and they desperately wanted to go out as champions.

The cheating stories had died down after those difficult summer months. The two teams were now engaged in a development race and the cold war became a phoney war as rumours and propaganda poured out from both camps: McLaren had found a Bridgestone dry tyre which was worth a second a lap, Goodyear had a secret wet tyre worth four seconds a lap, Irvine had gone to a Paris clinic to get his back seen to, Hakkinen had turned down all media obligations claiming he was ill, Irvine was ready to take Hakkinen out if a situation like Nüburgring happened again . . .

Some stories are just too wild to pass without comment. 'I'm many things, but I'm not stupid,' said Irvine, when this theory was put to him. 'The guy who's fighting for the championship has a bit more to lose than the guy who's not. But I wouldn't want to take Mika off so that Michael could win the championship, because I wouldn't want somebody to do it to me.'

It was only a routine denial of a rumour, and a wild one at that, but it had the effect of once again bringing Jerez to mind. As the long wait for the final race came to an end, Formula 1 was plunged back into memories of the unsatisfactory way in which the last championship had ended and all reflected on Schumacher's tarnished reputation. Everyone hoped that, despite all the bitterness beneath the surface in the 1998 title chase, this time there would at least be a sporting conclusion.

Schumacher had been in title deciders before, but had never been behind on points. This time he had nothing to lose. If he came away from Suzuka empty-handed he could point to Spa and to the early races of the season as the places where the championship had got away from him. Twenty-two points behind Hakkinen after Monaco, he had put up a magnificent fight in an inferior car to take the championship this far. The title had been tantalizingly close at times and seemingly lost at others. It had been Ferrari's most successful season ever in terms of points and wins, but someone else had done better still. What would be would be.

Schumacher seemed relaxed as the weekend got underway. He had spent a few days in Tokyo with his brother Ralf and Willi Weber, and as he arrived at Suzuka, he talked of having slept better on this visit to Japan than ever before. He had been taking it easy, keeping his mind clear. 'I've had a rest, walked around the city, trying to distract myself as much as possible. I think I've succeeded. I'm very optimistic and surprised by just how much of an improvement we've been able to make on the car in all areas. I just have a feeling that something will happen to allow me to win the championship. I don't know where this feeling comes from but I keep feeling it. Something keeps telling me that on Sunday I will be the champion.'

With a four-point disadvantage to make up, Michael was clearly bent on using the psychological weapons in his armoury. In an interview with *Bild*, conducted before the weekend and earmarked for publication the day before the race, Michael said that Suzuka would determine who was the World Champion, but it would not establish who was the fastest driver in the world. 'For a challenge like that we would need to swap cars,' he said. 'Then we would see where we were.' It was quite a curved ball, but when he heard about it, Hakkinen made no response.

For a man who twelve months ago had yet to win his first Grand Prix and now found himself in a championship dogfight with Schumacher, Hakkinen too was calm; calm enough not to take the bait. He claimed to have his own special techniques for handling pressure: 'At a Grand Prix it's no use just to keep thinking about the same things. You've got to keep your mind clear, otherwise you'd go crazy. I do it by playing some sport or spending time with friends, keeping my life simple. In the days before any race I keep myself to myself and just think about other things. Before coming here I spent a few days in China. I went to the old part of Shanghai; absolutely fascinating. It's amazing to see how enthusiastic the Chinese are for Formula 1. I couldn't believe how many people recognized me.

'I'm relaxed. All year we have been competitive and have made few mistakes. When I first came into Formula 1, I thought I was the best driver. And now I am.'

The most obviously angst-ridden figure in either camp was Luca di Montezemolo. Having missed Jerez the previous year he had decided at short notice to be with the team in Suzuka. 'If we had been ahead on points I would not have come. But in this thrilling, even desperate challenge I want to be in the front line, putting my face about.'

Many in the team wished he hadn't come. As the big boss, who rarely comes to races, he was the focus of much media interest, but no-one in the team could tell him what to say or do; he was just a loose cannon. And his nervousness was infectious. His presence among the team was a substantial distraction. His children, Matteo and Clementina, were also with him, getting in the way by trying to keep out of it. Matteo wore a Ferrari shirt and clearly felt at home, even sidling up to Schumacher for a chat just as he was putting on his helmet for practice.

In the pits during practice, Luca was dressed in chic pale-blue Levi jeans and a denim shirt, a chilled-out Nineties version of his Seventies look. He paced up and down the garage, clearly locked in some sort of frantic inner dialogue, his smile interrupted only by the occasional nervous twitch. From time to time his left arm shot up involuntarily and he reacted by making it look as though he was waving to someone.

Clementina had a green Formula 1 guest pass around her neck, which allows access to the pit garage but not the pit lane. She seemed slightly bored hanging around the Ferrari garage, so Luca sent her off for a wander down the pit lane. At some point she must have run into one of the F1 security people, who no doubt left her alone having ascertained whose daughter she was. Such is the way of the world.

His inner dialogue satisfactorily concluded, Luca crossed the wide pit lane to the Ferrari timing stand and turned to look back at the garage. Suddenly ten photographers appeared, with huge howitzer lenses trained on the president. Drivers learn to ignore the camera; being so focused on the job they don't even see them. Luca had seen them and held his head high, perhaps imagining the caption beneath the picture in the following day's paper. If they won on Sunday it would be THE MAN WHO BROUGHT GLORY BACK TO FERRARI. If they failed again, it would be DI MONTEZEMOLO: NEXT YEAR WE *WILL* BE CHAMPIONS.

Friday afternoon and the second practice session. The drivers work on getting their cars set up for the race, perfecting the balance with a full fuel load. It's not the all-out banzai of the qualifying hour, but fast enough nevertheless. Suzuka is a demanding track, one corner follows another and there are lots of places where time can be gained and lost.

Schumacher is visibly quicker than anyone else, quicker than the McLarens, which seem rather ill at ease on their tyres. Through the flat-out 130R corner the Ferrari is extended to the very limit, the engine screaming, the tyres scuffing up dust as the driver uses all the road and more on the exit.

After finishing the first day with the fastest time,

Schumacher quipped that he had 'provisional pole position' – a throwback to the days when there were two qualifying sessions, on Friday and Saturday. Things were looking good for Ferrari; Irvine too was very fast in race trim, while the McLarens seemed to be struggling a bit, as they had in the pre-race practices at the Nürburgring. The difference, once again, seemed to be the tyres. The Goodyears looked to have the edge, and some in the Bridgestone camp were muttering that the company had been too conservative in their choice of tyre, not wishing to embarrass their Japanese bosses at such an important race. Inside McLaren there was concern, but they were not about to lose their nerve. Nevertheless the management was a little prickly.

When Ron Dennis heard about Schumacher's quip he dismissed it petulantly. 'There is no such thing as a provisional pole any more and it shouldn't be reported as such,' he barked at a small group of journalists. He had seen enough of Schumacher's psychotricks over the years to know that his team and driver needed protecting. He had done well to keep Hakkinen insulated from outside pressures, fulfilling a minimum of press and sponsor commitments in the run up to the weekend, keeping his mind fresh and clear. Now Dennis turned the tables on Schumacher.

'If you analyse the season you see that Michael has made more mistakes than Mika. As for Ferrari, I have no comment to make on our competitor. I have now found myself fighting with them for the title three times and McLaren has always won.'

Those at the highest levels in Formula 1 have no need of New-Labour-style spin doctors. Spinning is part of their own armoury of skills. Dennis is fascinated by mind games. One theory emanating from the McLaren camp suggested that Dennis had treated Coulthard as he had in 1998 because he felt the young Scot needed toughening up. He believed that Coulthard had had it too easy in his rise up the ladder to the top seat in Formula 1 and that he needed to experience a bit of adversity to make him a better fighter. Like some sort of

Ninja training school, only once he'd proved himself to have the inner strength would he be given the chance to fight for the title.

To anyone who knows Dennis this theory makes a lot of sense. This is why he admires and favours Hakkinen; not only had the Finn sat out most of the 1993 season as McLaren's test driver, but he had come back from the dead following the Adelaide shunt in 1995. He knew the meaning of life and death and he knew how to struggle to succeed. He had been cocooned in the chrysalis of Dennis's care and attention since his accident, and with his drive under pressure from Schumacher at the Nürburgring he seemed finally to have emerged as the driver McLaren had been looking for since Senna left in 1993. The word was out that Dennis had offered Hakkinen a Schumacher-style multi-year contract and had asked him to stay with McLaren until the end of his career.

Dennis, clearly in the mood to fire back a few more psychotricks at Schumacher, once again brought up the spectre of Jerez. 'We want to win, but in the right way. How you win is sometimes more important than the victory. I am comfortable with our style and the way we race.'

The press loved every second of it, scribbling down the quotes and then taking them to Schumacher for a reaction. The spotlight once again fell on Michael's reputation and he was forced to reflect on Jerez, to trawl back through the negative memories he hoped he had parked once and for all in the recesses of his mind.

'That was a bad moment for me. But I don't feel it has added to the pressure. Sure I'm four points behind, and that is obviously a disadvantage for this race, but I am not feeling pressure because of that.

'Last year, I was criticized because I made a mistake. I am realistic enough to accept that, to say that I failed and to know why. But all the people who know me will say that I am not the sort of guy who goes out and makes the same mistake twice.'

* * *

As the sun set on Saturday evening a crowd of about 2,000 people sat in the grandstands watching the activity in the pit lane. The Japanese are patiently obsessive about Formula 1. In the era of their greatest hero, Ayrton Senna, when applications for tickets to Suzuka outstripped capacity by ten times, mechanics used to arrive at the circuit in darkness at 6.30 a.m. to begin work on the cars. The light would come up around 7 a.m. to reveal the stands already packed with Japanese fans, who had been watching them in silence.

On this sunny Saturday evening there were many banners in the stands, most cheering on Hakkinen, who is a big favourite with the Japanese fans. 'Go, Go, Go Mika', read one. There were plenty of Ferrari flags and Finnish flags fluttering in the breeze. It was a tranquil scene. Soft rock played out over the PA system and Japanese track marshals in orange uniforms with white hard hats wandered up the main straight chattering excitedly about the day's events.

After a thrilling qualifying session in which, as expected, the two championship rivals had raised themselves a full notch above the rest, Schumacher had taken pole position ahead of Hakkinen and Coulthard, with Irvine fourth. McLaren were disappointed, but nevertheless satisfied to be second and third. If they could just hold on to those positions in the race tomorrow, Hakkinen would be champion.

In the garage, the McLaren mechanics seemed relaxed. Many of them had been with the team when Senna and Prost were around, and had remained loyal team members throughout the bad times in the mid-1990s. They were all excited about the big day ahead and about the stunning season they had enjoyed.

A slow, gentle ticking sound could be heard as an air jack lifted up the rear of Hakkinen's car onto trestles. The garage looked immaculate. Silver-clad mechanics moved with a fluid motion, almost choreographed. Knowing Dennis's obsession with precision and discipline it was tempting to imagine he had invited some time-and-motion experts in to give his team a plan to work to! With the gentle ticking in the background, the garage scene looked like a human Swiss watch.

Both teams had brought four cars, and Ferrari had no less than sixty people on site. They looked tired after a long, hard seventeen-race season and five weeks of flat-out testing.

Twelve months on from Jerez, the Ferrari boys seemed a lot more relaxed on the eve of this title decider. Perhaps in the interim they had become more used to success. There had been some fantastic days to be a Ferrari mechanic in 1998 and they all felt they had a lot to show for the year. They wanted to win tomorrow but, if they failed, they knew that it had been a great season.

Gianni Petterlini, Schumacher's chief mechanic, tied a red apron around his neck and set to work on the back end of his boss's car. Gently he pulled away the 800-horsepower *supermotore*, which that afternoon had powered Schumacher to his extraordinary pole position. What a fantastic performance he had put on. Surely he would win again tomorrow, but wasn't it a shame that this race wouldn't be a straight fight for victory like last year, that Schumacher needed Irvine in second place to become champion? The Irishman had struggled badly with the handling of his car in qualifying trim and had been lucky to achieve fourth place on the grid, almost two seconds slower than Schumacher. The consolation was that in race conditions he was a lot more comfortable. Tomorrow all would be revealed.

The five red startline lights went on, the revs rose and then suddenly the yellow abort lights came on. Jarno Trulli had stalled the Prost on the seventh row of the grid. After the steady build-up of tension to the race, it was a massive anti-climax. But what happened in the next three minutes decided the world title.

Within twelve seconds of the start being aborted, ten of Hakkinen's McLaren mechanics were back on the grid with all their pit equipment, fussing around the car, plugging in laptops, stuffing dry ice into the radiator ducts to cool the engine and hydraulics. Schumacher sat alone at the front. A full minute later the first of his Ferrari mechanics arrived. Ten seconds after that another mechanic arrived and put a tyre cover on one of the wheels. Ten seconds later – now one and a half minutes after the aborted start – the rest of Schumacher's mechanics arrived and went through the same procedures the McLaren team had started ninety seconds earlier. It was only a short delay, which on a cooler day would probably have meant nothing, but the thoroughness of the McLaren mechanics was to pay massive dividends.

The restart signal was given a couple of minutes later, but as the cars set off on their second parade lap, Schumacher was concerned about the temperatures. He was right to worry. Normally the hydraulic fluids operate at around 140 degrees, but after the long hold on the grid and the aborted start, his Ferrari's temperatures were closer to 180 degrees. There hadn't been time to cool the car properly.

Formula 1 cars carry the minimum of cooling equipment on board and are designed to run at speed, not to be stationary. Schumacher knew that at this stage the only answer was to drive quickly around the parade lap, allowing air into the radiators to cool down the engine and gearbox. But as he approached the grid he was forced to slow right down to allow the others to catch him up. The engine revs dropped and, crucially, so did the hydraulic pressure, which controls gear selection. He sat on the grid waiting for the rest of the field to line up. He then pulled the clutch in, but as he selected first gear the car lurched forward and stalled. The rules dictate that a stalled car must go back to the back of the grid. Five weeks of work and a whole season of hard labour by Ferrari had come to an end.

We have all stalled our car at the traffic lights in the middle of rush hour and heard the horn blasts of impatient commuters behind us. But imagine doing it with the world title at stake, in front of hundreds of millions of television viewers around the world, after almost 3,000 miles of competitive racing during the season, and 5,000 miles of testing for this one event.

Afterwards the Ferrari management stood behind Schumacher, as they had all season, saying that the failure was technical and not the fault of the driver. Many weren't so sure, and some in the press reported it as Schumacher's mistake. Ross Brawn denied this vigorously: 'Michael was in neutral when he came to the grid, but when he engaged first gear with the clutch down, the mechanism failed somewhere and the power was transmitted. There is no way it could have occurred because of driver error.'

The revs had been allowed to drop and the fluid temperatures were too high. His detractors claimed it was nervousness on the driver's part and implied that once again he was refusing to accept his mistakes. After the weekend, stories emerged of a 'Ferrari source' complaining that Michael failed to follow the correct procedure after the first aborted start and stalled the car himself.

Starting from the back of the grid, Michael drove like a man possessed. Already twelfth by the end of the first lap, by lap five he was up with Damon Hill in sixth place, and here his progress slowed for some time. The Jordan team got on the radio to tell Hill that Schumacher was behind him. Earlier they had told Ralf Schumacher that his brother was behind him and Ralf had immediately let him through. Hill wasn't so eager to yield and with good reason.

Jordan were locked in a constructors' championship battle with Williams and Benetton and needed all the points they could get. On the face of it the battle was for third place, but in reality each team was desperately trying to avoid the stigma of finishing fifth.

Ralf, who was leaving Jordan after this race to join Williams, might think nothing of giving a place away. But Damon, who was staying, was not going to give in so easily. He was committed to Jordan's struggle and, battling with Villeneuve, he had no intention of letting Schumacher through. 'There was a championship position at stake. I couldn't let him through without costing myself a lot of time,' said Damon afterwards.

Ralf criticized Damon for it, but Michael knew what Damon was up to. 'He watched his mirrors more than in front of him, and it's not like it's the first time. His Schumacher complex becomes more and more evident over the years. But I can't complain about Damon. He did nothing unfair. He just didn't make it easy for me.'

So the gap opened up. When he caught up with Hill on lap five he was just twelve seconds behind Hakkinen. By lap thirteen the margin was thirty-two seconds. When Hill made his first pit stop, Schumacher flew past Villeneuve, and after making his own first stop he found himself in third place, just twenty-two laps after starting from the back of the grid! He was now only twenty-five seconds behind Hakkinen, with Irvine trailing the McLaren in second place and over half the race still left to run.

His driving was sublime to watch. The Ferrari was sliding through the corners in full-blooded power slides. He was chucking the car about like a go-kart, deftly controlling the back end as he pushed the car beyond the limit. Inside the cockpit he was loving every second of it. Resigned after the startline disaster to the fact that the title was more or less gone, he revelled in the chance to drive flat out with nothing to lose.

Schumacher's chances of winning the championship had been dealt a hefty blow by what had happened on the grid, and by Irvine's inability to get in front of Hakkinen and hold him up. But they were destroyed on lap thirty-two when his rear tyre exploded.

His tyre had been punctured by debris from an accident between Esteban Tuero and Tora Takagi at the chicane. Tuero had made a highly optimistic move down the inside, the two cars had collided and one of them had come to rest in a dangerous place atop the chicane. If the conspiracy theorists were right and the FIA really had wanted to help Ferrari win the title, they would surely have deployed the safety car at this point while the mess was cleared up. This would have allowed Schumacher and Irvine to catch Hakkinen with twenty laps to go. But there was no sign of a safety car.

As the cars filtered past, a furious Takagi rushed over to Tuero and began shoving him. It was a far stronger reaction than Schumacher's to Coulthard in Spa, but because it was between back-of-the-grid drivers, no-one paid the slightest attention.

Some debris from the shunt lay on the track, shards of carbon fibre which both Hakkinen and Irvine passed through unscathed. But Schumacher managed to pick some up. As he flew into another highly-charged lap the right rear tyre exploded. Ferrari's World Championship jinx had stretched to twenty years.

Schumacher fought to bring the car under control and parked it by the side of the track. He had given it his best shot, but it wasn't to be. Once again he had lost, but this time there would be no sourness about the manner of his losing. After a few minutes' reflection, he made his way back to the pits to face the music.

In the Ferrari garage, Luca di Montezemolo went up to each of the mechanics and sadly shook hands. Schumacher returned shortly afterwards and did the same, apologizing to them all individually for not making their dream come true once again.

He disappeared into the Ferrari office in the paddock, where he talked through the defeat with Willi Weber. He took just ten minutes to compose his thoughts before emerging from the office to talk to the massive scrum of media, many of whom had waited three hours for him in Jerez.

'It's a great disappointment for sure, but I am not distraught like on other occasions in the past. The problem at the start was a huge blow. When I put the car into first gear the engine died because the clutch had closed by itself, I think maybe there was a drop in hydraulic pressure. I knew right then that the championship was lost. It's a real shame, but the world will continue to turn.

'The championship was not lost here it was lost at the start of the season, when we took a long time to catch up to McLaren. Here we had a great car and we could have made the miracle happen. I had believed it, especially after the qualifying and my pole position. We would have needed favourable circumstances, but in the end they all went against us. It's incredible, even before the race had started the whole thing was ruined; so much work destroyed by one little problem. I had done dozens of practice starts at Fiorano and Mugello and never had a problem. When I found myself at the back of the grid I thought I would go mad with rage.

'What could I do? As I came up through the field I was pursuing a mirage; it was just a way of giving an outlet to my anger. In the first two laps I really enjoyed myself, the other drivers were all very polite and gave me no problems in passing them. I knew that the only chance I might have would be if Hakkinen had a problem. But it was me who had the problem. I don't really know how it happened. I didn't see any debris in my path and I didn't think I had picked any up. It just wasn't our day.

'I'm most sorry for the Ferrari fans and for the team, which has worked so hard. I think we can all be proud of our season.'

The new World Champion steers his McLaren-Mercedes Silver Arrow into the *parc fermé*. The visor on his helmet is raised and it's clear that he has been crying. He stops the car and cuts the engine as Schumacher approaches. The beaten man has changed out of his race overalls into a Ferrari sweater and jeans. He reaches down into the cockpit of the McLaren and takes the new champion's hand. Hakkinen looks up and sees a man at peace with himself, beaten but upbeat, making a genuine expression of sporting congratulation to his conqueror.

As he looks into the eyes of Michael Schumacher, Hakkinen realizes the significance of his achievement. To be World Champion is a great feat in any year, but to be champion by beating one of the finest drivers in history is what really counts.

It was a very sporting end to what had been, at times, a very unsporting year, and his gesture sent out all the right signals to the watching world; he had done what he should have done twelve months before. It had been a great year for Michael Schumacher; he had underlined his greatness as a driver with some magnificent performances and he and Ferrari had kept worldwide interest in the sport alive by taking the fight to McLaren.

He had lost again, but this time he had lost gracefully. He had accepted defeat, and perhaps in that handshake in the *parc fermé* he had begun to find the redemption he had been searching for since Jerez.

As he walked away from the fervent McLaren celebrations he was smiling. 'Mika deserved it. He and his team were the best this year. But next season, I hope, will be a different story.'

SIXTEEN THE UNDERSTUDY

Eddie Irvine is lying on the deck of his twenty-six-metre motor yacht *Anaconda S*, moored in a marina near Genoa on the west coast of Italy. It is early February, the sea air is cool and the sky a deep blue. Eddie is lying back with his hands behind his head, the ever-present Oakley sunglasses clamped down over his eyes. Across from him is Sarah Edworthy, a journalist from the *Daily Telegraph*, who always gets the best out of Irvine and with whom Irvine has enjoyed flirting over the years. But this time he is not fluttering his eyelashes – Irvine is talking tough and honest. As the interview progresses it becomes clear that Irvine is delivering a manifesto for the season ahead. And there are some highly controversial new promises.

'I didn't come into Formula 1 to help Michael Schumacher,' he says bluntly. 'Every driver is in Formula 1 for themselves. Japan woke me up to how bad I feel about having to do the job for Michael. As soon as he went to the back of the grid, the switch flicked inside my head and I was surprised it did. All of a sudden Ferrari were relying on me and as opposed to me think-ing, oh well they don't give a fuck about me, I felt important. I responded to it. I was surprised it made so much difference.

'I got out of Jordan because I didn't feel they were going places fast enough and I had the option of Ferrari which got me to the next level. Now the level above that is to be consistently challenging for victories. That's where I've got to look.'

Now thirty-four years old with the unenviable record of having the most podium finishes without winning a race, Irvine was growing restless with his situation at Ferrari. He had joined the team as the number-two driver, obliged to follow team orders which Ferrari believed was the best way to win the championship. For the tough, pragmatic Irvine it was a means to an end. Driving a Ferrari meant having the chance to be at the front, to make a name for himself and to notch up all those podium finishes. The downside of his Faustian deal was clear all along; he was the number-two driver to the best driver in the business, with a contractual obligation to let his boss pass, should he find himself in front during a race.

Irvine had been honest in admitting he was outclassed by Schumacher – he never really expected it to be any other way. But by working alongside the fastest driver in the game, he had learned a great deal about how to be successful in Formula 1 and raised his stock on the driver market. His objective all along was to find a team willing to hire him as leader, with a salary to match. Ideally, that would be Ferrari because Irvine enjoyed being a Ferrari driver and was seduced by the allure and image of the team. But Schumacher's new long-term contract put paid to any illusions Irvine may have had about his own long-term future with the team. The coming season, driving a car he knew would give him plenty of opportunity to mix it at the front, was the moment he had decided to stake his claim. He wanted to draw attention to himself, to make gentle barbs about his enforced subservience throughout his three years at Ferrari and get taken seriously as a big name.

It can't be easy to play second fiddle, but Irvine was honest enough with himself to know that he had never looked like being faster than Schumacher. In their three seasons together he had outqualified him only three times. But during the 1998 season Irvine had been asked by the team to let Michael through on five separate occasions, sometimes following a mistake of Michael's, like in Austria, sometimes when Michael was cutting through the field, acting out one of Ross Brawn's more aggressive strategies. Each time he knew what he had to do and he moved over, something which is anathema to a naturally selfish and competitive individual such as a Formula 1 driver.

Jean Todt had taken a chance hiring Irvine back in 1995 and the Italian press had given him a hard time for it ever since. Irvine was not a real Ferrari driver in their eyes, he was not good enough to wear the red overalls and on top of that he was rude and awkward to deal with. Todt and di Montezemolo had lost count of the number of times the Italian press had called for them to get rid of the Irishman, but they had always resisted. Irvine and Michael worked well together. They had a disciplined partnership, working in tandem during race weekends and tests to develop the car and pull the team forwards. Schumacher would not have enjoyed the success he had without Irvine's contribution and he knew it. Irvine was on a fraction of the money they paid to Schumacher, but then their expectations of him were different.

The signs now as the 1999 season drew closer were that he was growing restless with his subservient role. He had kept his side of the bargain in Suzuka, finishing second in the race. It was Michael who had let the side down and now, knowing that he would be sitting on the best car he had ever had in Formula 1, Irvine was lobbying for better working conditions and a chance to race for the win himself. But even as he spoke he knew he was clutching at straws.

'Michael's not moving, why should he? He has the whole team focused around him.'

So did that mean that Irvine would have to move elsewhere?

'I don't know. Michael could end up driving into a wall, God forbid. Look at Damon Hill, what was he? A lackey, until Senna drove into a wall?'

The interview was published in the *Telegraph* the day before Valentine's Day. It did not go unnoticed.

At the launch of the new Ferrari, codenamed F399, back in January 1999, the Ferrari team had been, as ever, full of optimism. With Goodyear having withdrawn from Formula 1, Ferrari would be using the same tyres as McLaren and with steady technical progress for the past two years, the new car was touted as one which would allow Ferrari to be competitive from the start of the season, not the middle as had happened the previous year. Schumacher was relaxed and rested after another long winter break in Norway with his family. Initially only one F399 car was available and it would be some time before a second chassis was ready. Schumacher would begin the test programme on the car; Irvine would get his chance to try it later in the month.

'I start with the objective of winning races,' Irvine said rather acidly at the launch, 'seeing as I cannot win the title.'

In another corner of the room, Todt was heading off any speculation about a change in Irvine's role. 'History teaches us that Schumacher is the stronger and it is right that Ferrari points towards him as the lead driver,' he said flatly.

As ever, the mood of optimism among the Ferrari management was considerable, but for once a touch of reality crept into the otherwise rose-tinted presentation. Gianni Agnelli spoke of Ferrari's challenge, adding poignantly, 'It's been twenty years that Ferrari has not won the title. It would be a shame if that figure were to increase.'

Meanwhile, in England McLaren were finishing off their new car which featured many radical new ideas. Controversially, Adrian Newey had built on only a few of the strengths of the 1998 car, and had decided to break even further away from the opposition rather than settle for a refinement of tried and proven ideas. But when testing began it was clear that the car was far from reliable. They had scored a one-two in Melbourne the previous year but they would struggle to get both drivers to the finish with this car. There was a brief debate within the team about how to play the start of the season. Some pointed to the reliability of the Ferraris and the way in which they had dramatically improved their performance towards the end of 1998. They were sure to have a fast, reliable car in Melbourne and without any tyre advantages on McLaren's side they were running a risk by taking the new car. Surely it made more sense to run the 1998 cars while putting plenty of test miles on the new model. Newey had a short answer to this. 'We move forwards, not backwards,' he said.

For both Ferrari and McLaren their worst fears were realized in Melbourne: Hakkinen put the Silver Arrow on pole, 1.3 seconds faster than Schumacher's Ferrari; a bigger gap than the year before! After three months of hard work by the Ferrari team, again mostly out of view of the opposition at Mugello and Fiorano, the new car was simply not fast enough. But disaster struck McLaren too, both cars failing within the first twenty-two laps. Ron Dennis said he stood by the decision to bring the new car, as it had allowed them to assess its competitiveness, but it also emerged that it had been a very hard-fought call; the team had adapted the 1998 cars to the 1999 specifications before finally shipping the new ones out to Australia.

For once it was not Schumacher who benefited from the McLarens' demise, but Irvine. Schumacher began the new season the same way he ended the old, by stalling on the start line. Once again he was sent to the back of the grid and forced to race through the field, but he could not make the same progress as he had at Suzuka and scored no points in eighth place. Meanwhile Irvine, who had been given just two days of testing in the car before Melbourne, controlled the race from the front and came through strongly to claim his first Grand Prix victory. The Ferrari mechanics were ecstatic. Neither McLaren had finished so the title campaign would start from zero in Brazil; meanwhile the understudy finally had a piece of the glory.

'I'm really pleased,' said Ross Brawn after the race. 'Once or twice it's been a difficult decision to take his first win away, like at Suzuka a couple of years ago. He has in some ways an unfortunate attitude and some people don't treat him seriously because he has this playboy image. But he's a very serious racing driver and it has been fantastic to have got in behind him.'

Irvine was away and running, he had broken his duck far earlier than expected, and was leading the World Championship for the first time in his career with a full five weeks to enjoy it and milk the attention before the next race in Brazil. Now it was time to live up to his manifesto. 'Michael did a lot of pre-season testing for me,' he said, tongue-in-cheek, 'which made the car reliable. Hats off to him, he did a good job! Last year I did all the tyre testing which helped close the gap to McLaren and he got all the victories, so this year the roles are being reversed. It would be nice if he didn't finish the next one and I won again. It would be difficult to cry.

'I can't beat Michael on sheer speed,' he added, more serious now, 'but I'm better in other areas. It's just that I can't use those other areas because I have to move over for him in any case. If I can qualify alongside him I will be ahead of him into the first corner. I'm confident of that. He knows that and I know that. If that was a team-mate with equal status alongside me instead I could beat him because I'd get into the first corner first. Then he's got to overtake me and he could only do that in the pits.

'Michael has his weaknesses. . .'

A couple of weeks later stories began to emerge in the German newspapers suggesting that the relationship between Irvine and Schumacher was unravelling. The Irishman had certainly been crowing after his maiden victory, doing a lot of press interviews, always making the same tongue-in-cheek comments about the roles being reversed but always leaving the reader in no doubt that there was a grain of truth in what he was saying. In interviews with, among others, *Autosport* and *Bunte* magazine in Germany he emphasized that Ferrari now had two drivers capable of winning. It became clear that his agenda was to change his circumstances at Ferrari, to threaten the established order from his new-found position of strength.

He told *Bild* newspaper, 'We are not friends, we're too different. Michael is all about work and family, I love my freedom.' *Bild* ran the story under a headline which read, 'When will the quarrel at Ferrari explode?' and concluded that

Irvine had learned nothing from his years alongside Schumacher. It asked whether a war was threatening to break out within the team.

Perhaps under pressure from Jean Todt, or more likely from Luca di Montezemolo to cool this growing debate, Irvine was in a conciliatory mood a few days later when he told *La Gazzetta dello Sport*, 'Do you think I'm stupid enough to put myself in conflict with Michael just because I've won my first Grand Prix? Between him and me there is a great relationship, we are friends, we work well together. Then at night he goes home to his wife and kids and I go out and amuse myself.'

On the subject of the stories in Germany, which contradicted what he was now saying, he replied, 'They translate badly into German what I have said in English, distorting the meaning of my words. Perhaps in the euphoria of my win in Melbourne I might have said that now it is important for Ferrari to have two drivers capable of winning, but this doesn't mean that I'm putting myself up in antagonism with Michael.'

Schumacher, meanwhile, kept out of the discussions for the moment. He had bigger things to think about. First the lack of pace of the new Ferrari. There was no doubt that it was the best-balanced car Ferrari had produced for him, but it lacked outright speed compared to the McLarens. Part of the reason for the gulf in qualifying in Australia had been the Bridgestone tyres, which McLaren had used to greater effect. They had learned that by using the same set of tyres for several timed laps the performance improves as the tyre wears down. In Melbourne both drivers had used just one set of tyres for all twelve of their qualifying laps, whereas Ferrari had used four sets per driver. In the five weeks between Melbourne and Brazil the team launched a huge testing programme, two days in Barcelona, two days in Jerez, five days in Fiorano and three days in Mugello. After the Fiorano test Schumacher was particularly upbeat about the car's progress. 'I still believe I can win the World Championship in this car,' he said.

At the same time Corinna Schumacher was due to give birth to their second child. The date they had been given clashed with the proposed Argentine Grand Prix, but that event was cancelled at short notice, so Michael was at home for the birth of his son, Mick. In the days leading up to the birth, Michael commuted from the team's test headquarters at Jerez to Switzerland and Irvine was drafted in to take up the lion's share of the work. This time the Schumachers managed to keep the birth secret and it was not until two days afterwards that the stories began to appear in the papers. This was in marked contrast to the birth of Gina-Maria in a clinic with a hundred journalists and photographers waiting outside.

'It was nice of him to wait until I got back from Spain,' said Michael. 'It was also fortunate that the Argentine GP was cancelled otherwise I would have been far away when it happened.'

Schumacher finished second to Hakkinen in Brazil, while Irvine was fifth, which meant that he was still in the lead of the championship going into the race at Imola and Ferrari were on top in the constructors' table. But the plain fact was that Ferrari was still not on the pace of the McLarens and it was only reliability which stood between McLaren and a clean sweep of points. Hakkinen's gearbox had played up in Brazil, and he only managed to finish the race because the car's computer had a safety programme which took over. He had to nurse the car home, but still had enough pace to beat the Ferrari by four seconds at the finish.

But all was not well during the Brazil weekend. After qualifying Schumacher was despondent, his car still a full second slower than the McLaren, despite twenty days and almost 3,000 miles of testing in the five weeks since Melbourne. It was a real blow to morale and in his press briefing after the session he came as close as he ever had, in his three years with Ferrari, to criticizing the team.

'I'm very deeply disappointed, not so much about where I am on the grid, but about the time differential,' he said. 'Before we came here I expected to be half a second behind, but it's a whole second. We cannot gain that in a couple of days, it will take time. The deficits of the car are very small, but they are in every area. Our goal was to be competitive from the first race and we obviously did not achieve that.'

After a more competitive showing in the race, where his fastest race lap was just two-tenths of a second slower than Hakkinen's, Schumacher backed away from these comments but remained in a prickly mood. When one journalist asked him about Irvine's championship aspirations, Schumacher was dismissive. 'After winning one Grand Prix it is a bit early to talk about winning the title. If the situation has continued after half the season, then it would be time to ask the question.

'The situation between us is the same as it was before the first race and I would be very surprised if it had changed. I have the upper hand so far and I haven't seen a sign that I do not have it any more. It would need a lot of bad luck for me and Ferrari for that to happen and I don't see myself being that unlucky . . .'

Schumacher's comments in the heat of the moment after qualifying inevitably provoked a flurry of rumours that he was disillusioned with Ferrari and would switch teams. After all, went the logic, he had gone there in 1996 and found the John Barnard-designed car much further off the pace of Adrian Newey's Williams than he had imagined. The following year, even with the ex-Benetton dream team of Rory Byrne and Ross Brawn at Ferrari, the team was still playing catch up to Williams. In 1998 Ferrari made real progress, but once again Newey outsmarted them with a superior McLaren design. This year Schumacher had high hopes and Ferrari had delivered their best effort, but again it had fallen short of Newey's work of genius. Schumacher's outburst in Brazil indicated to many that his patience with Ferrari was running out, the dream of the world title was as far away as it had ever been and he was now questioning his long-term commitment to the team.

Willi Weber appeared to endorse this view when he told the Cologne newspaper *Express*, 'Second place is not good enough. We must be able to win by ourselves and not because McLaren retire. Ferrari are the champions at coming back, but we are getting tired of saying, "Next year will be better".'

The private relationship between Schumacher and his team principals did not fully match the emerging public picture. The bond which links him with Jean Todt and Ross Brawn is strong, so strong that they are linked by contract to each other. If either Todt or Brawn leaves the team, Schumacher can terminate his contract. Ferrari is petrified of losing him and had staked its short-term future on the Todt/Brawn/Schumacher package. Michael was not going anywhere, but the episode did show that the harmonized press relations were slipping. Things said in Germany were being reported back in Italy, something which was to prove an increasing problem for the team as the year wore on.

This was supposed to be the season when things fell into place. Without the excuse of having different tyres, with the Byrne/Brawn team in position, the new state of the art wind tunnel up and running, bigger budgets and the continuity of drivers for three years, there would be no excuse for failing this time. Comparisons were drawn with Ayrton Senna, who, after three world titles with McLaren-Honda, spent only two seasons with the team after Honda left, before giving up and joining Williams, then clearly the best team in Formula 1.

But if Schumacher had been interested only in winning races and being in the best car, he would have joined Williams, instead of Ferrari, in 1996, and won at least two more titles before signing for McLaren when Newey joined them for 1998. He would be equal with Juan Manuel Fangio with five world titles. Schumacher's motivation was to earn a large salary and to be the one who resurrected Ferrari. If things had worked out slightly differently, if he had judged Villeneuve's lunge at Jerez better and not hit Coulthard at Spa, he would have been World Champion in both 1997 and 1998 and no-one would be questioning his desire to stay with Ferrari.

Bernie Ecclestone added his voice to the discussion when he told *Autosport* magazine that Schumacher's goal was to win the championship for Ferrari and that he would not leave until he had achieved that. 'He would be much better known for winning the title for Ferrari after whatever length of time it turns out to be than winning it in a McLaren. He's a Ferrari man and that's where he's going to be.'

The reality, of course, was that Schumacher had committed to Ferrari and would stay there until at least 2002, hoping that he would perhaps win one more championship in that time. The frustration of the 1999 car not being as fast as everyone at Maranello had hoped was quickly replaced with the team buckling down to improve the car. More intensive testing followed; six days at Jerez and two at Fiorano. By the time the cars arrived at Imola in late April the F399 had covered over 8,500 miles since its launch in January!

At the same time as the debate about Schumacher's future was raging in the press, Ferrari's nemesis, Adrian Newey, quietly committed himself to McLaren for a similar, slightly longer, period. The pattern of Formula 1 for the foreseeable future was set.

Imola came and went in a blur. Schumacher was third behind the two McLarens in both the practice sessions and in qualifying, but the gap was down to just two-tenths of a second. The McLarens looked strong. A record crowd of 187,000 turned out on the Sunday hoping to see the first Ferrari victory for sixteen years on the track named after Enzo and Dino Ferrari, and they got it, thanks to some brilliant tactical thinking by Ross Brawn and a catastrophic mistake by Mika Hakkinen, who took the early lead from pole and seemed to be pulling away comfortably from Coulthard and Schumacher. The Finn was on a different race strategy, a two-stop plan, which showed a little nervousness on the part of McLaren. They gambled that Schumacher would opt to make just one stop, and by putting Coulthard on the same plan hoped that he would hold Schumacher up while Hakkinen got away. In fact, Hakkinen would have been fast enough to carry the extra fuel of a one-stop plan but in his eagerness to capitalize on his light fuel load he pushed a little too hard, hooked a rear wheel over the kerb in the chicane and slammed his car into the wall. The *tifosi* cheered deliriously, for it had seemed as though McLaren had started to gain the upper hand. Now only Coulthard stood between them and a Ferrari victory.

Having only to beat Coulthard and not McLaren's point man Hakkinen, Brawn played the aggressive tactical game. Although he had enough fuel to run past the mid point in the race, Schumacher was called in at half-distance on lap thirty-one, Brawn having noticed that his driver would soon be coming up to some slower traffic. At the Nürburgring the previous year, Hakkinen had won the race by staying out a few laps longer than the Ferrari and McLaren tried to do the same thing again. But the plan required Coulthard to be forceful in traffic and he failed, losing ten seconds in five laps, rather than making ten seconds. Like a lamb to the slaughter he pitted on lap thirty-five and as he rejoined the track from the pit lane, Schumacher sailed past, egged on by the roars of the crowd. Ferrari were leading at Imola and Schumacher had a clear track ahead. Unfazed by the lapped traffic he pressed his advantage, while Coulthard got mired in a melee of Benettons and Prosts. Five seconds became fifteen seconds as the Scot dragged his heels behind the slower cars.

On lap forty-six Irvine's engine blew up while he was running in third place, quite a surprise given Ferrari's reputation for reliability, and an unlucky Heinz-Harald Frentzen spun on the oil which spewed from the Ferrari. Meanwhile, at the front, Coulthard pushed hard to catch Schumacher, shaving the odd tenth of a second off the margin each lap. He closed to within five seconds, but ran out of laps as the chequered flag fell on another great Ferrari victory in Italy; one which put Schumacher and Irvine into the top two places in the championship table and Ferrari top in the constructors' chase.

Afterwards, Coulthard was angry with the backmarkers. 'Today I lost a race I should have won,' he fumed, 'but because of factors other than the performance of the car and my driving. We had the correct strategy and a quick enough package to have won.'

But Ferrari had a better strategy and had won the race with a slower car once again. 'We are right with them,' said Schumacher enthusiastically. 'In Brazil we were half a second slower than McLaren, but we've gained between three- and five-tenths.' He was asked how he felt about overtaking Irvine in the championship table. 'Does that mean I can return to being number one again now?' he laughed. 'Well thank you very much!'

Schumacher was smiling, relieved to be back in the hunt and to know that the F399 was not going to prove another disappointment. Of course he knew that one swallow doesn't make a summer and the result would have been quite different if Hakkinen had not made his error, but at least the effort put into developing the car had made a measurable difference and once again they had been able to capitalize on McLaren's errors.

He had never felt particularly embarrassed about being behind Irvine in the points table, but it was also a relief to be in front at last and hopefully that would put an end to all the talk about number ones and number twos. In fact, there had been a moment of friction between them on the Friday in the newly convened drivers' briefing. Irvine was the only driver who objected to the new time for the briefing, preferring to meet at the traditional time on the Sunday morning three hours before the race. Irvine got up and said his piece and, as he sat down, Schumacher stated quite publicly, 'Eddie, you're an idiot.'

Irvine had been careful to mind his words all weekend. Quizzed by the Italian press on the state of his relationship with Schumi he said, 'We have different views but between the two of us there is a great professional respect.' If anything the one at fault in Imola was Schumacher for having let his guard down in the drivers' briefing, calling his team-mate an idiot in front of the other drivers. Luca di Montezemolo, beside himself with joy at the Imola result and the way the championship tables looked, delivered his verdict on the state of play between his two drivers. 'Michael is the best driver in the world but his greatest strength is the way he pulls together the different forces which make up the team. Eddie has had his best season with us and he has been an ideal team-mate for

Michael, bringing important points to the team. But it's the track which establishes the hierarchy; if he were faster than Schumacher he would be able to win.'

Victory again in Monaco two weeks later put Ferrari in the driving seat of the World Championship. Imola had allowed them to believe that this might be their year, and a one-two finish in Monte Carlo with Irvine very competitive in second place gave them control of the points table – Schumacher twelve points clear of his arch rival Hakkinen and Ferrari with over double the points haul of McLaren. From a depressingly familiar start in Melbourne the picture had changed dramatically. Ferrari had been reliable and canny, capitalized on the mechanical problems and mistakes of McLaren and won three of the four races. The car was obviously good, and Irvine had been able to reduce his deficit to Schumacher to just three-tenths of a second in qualifying, roughly half what it had traditionally been. The car was happy to hit the kerbs without becoming destabilized and the aerodynamics were the best they had been for years.

It was Michael's fourth win in Monaco and, more significantly, his sixteenth win for Ferrari, making him the most successful driver in the company's history. Although there was still no championship he had eclipsed Niki Lauda and Alberto Ascari, who were both double champions with the team.

Ferrari had also been enjoying that little bit of luck which comes your way when it really is your year. Now they just needed stability and progress. For sure there would be races where McLaren would be too strong for them, like the next event at Barcelona, but after that they were on the three tracks which had always looked after them – Montreal, Magny Cours and Silverstone – and on which they had a real chance of consolidating their position. By then the championship would be half finished. There was a long way to go, but more than a few people within the team allowed themselves to believe that this might just be the year.

SEVENTEEN SIDELINED

Despite the euphoria of Monaco, by late May it was clear that the Ferrari management were evaluating other drivers and Irvine other teams, although both sides would not admit it publicly. Irvine did not enjoy the same level of support as before from Jean Todt, but he did have one important ally: Gianni Agnelli. The old man, whose pronouncements are often seen as forerunners to official announcements, gave Irvine a vote of confidence when he said, 'It would be a shame if he left Ferrari. He's good and he's in the right position. They tell me that he's very popular with the ladies and that he doesn't hold himself back, but that's another quality and another reason to stay in Italy. I like him and I want him to stay.'

Irvine's response was straightforward. 'He's right because I too want to stay at Ferrari. About ten days ago I spelled this desire out to the management. Ferrari is the best team in Formula 1 and the car keeps getting better.'

For his part, Schumacher kept to the line that he and Eddie were a winning team and why should Ferrari want to change that? 'Eddie is the quickest team-mate I ever had,' he said on more than one occasion. 'Any talk of problems between us is rubbish.'

But Todt was not prepared to move on the pivotal issue of Irvine being allowed to race against Schumacher and chase victories. Irvine could stay on the same terms or he could leave and find himself a better deal elsewhere. The future for Ferrari lay with Schumacher, not with what Irvine might achieve for the team. With little room for manoeuvre Irvine found himself forced to look elsewhere and to face up to a life beyond Maranello. His Ferrari career was in its final stretch, but before it ended he would highlight the unfairness of his situation.

Whatever was being said publicly, the relationship was increasingly strained and the week before the Canadian Grand Prix it reached breaking point when an interview with Irvine appeared in the Italian weekly magazine *Autosprint*. It was not Irvine's dismissive words about the abilities of Hakkinen and Coulthard which upset Ferrari, although they served to get Ron Dennis into a lather as a result of which he came out with some damning assessments of Irvine's character and abilities. What really upset Ferrari was Irvine's openness in the interview about Ferrari's system of team orders and what he was obliged to do to help Schumacher. Having confirmed that he was contractually obliged to move over for Schumacher, he went further. 'If he is two places behind and I'm leading I have to slow down and try to let him get closer to the guy who's running second, which could cost me first and second place.'

The interview read as a tirade from a disaffected man. Possibly Eddie was feeling put out as a result of learning that Ferrari were in serious discussions with Rubens Barrichello. It made a lot of sense; FIAT was keen to have a Brazilian in the team to help with its important South American markets and Barrichello, still only twenty-seven despite having seven years' F1 experience, was a good prospect as a points-scoring partner to Schumacher.

However, in their two seasons together as team-mates at Jordan, Irvine had gradually edged Barrichello into the shade, frequently out-qualifying and out-racing the highly rated Brazilian. Nevertheless, Todt believed that Barrichello's dip in form had been due to the pressures on him as Brazil's leading driver following the death of his close friend Ayrton Senna in 1994. Rubens had pulled himself together in the past two seasons and his form had improved significantly during his time with Jackie Stewart's team. Todt also saw in the Brazilian a more consistent qualifier than Irvine. With increasing emphasis being placed on the start in Formula 1, Rubens might offer the team more tactical possibilities in the opening stages of a race.

But there was even more to it than that. Barrichello was negotiating to replace Irvine, but he was not being offered the same deal. What he would end up with was an agreement that whoever was fastest would be number one and the other would agree to work for the team. Cynics would say it amounted to the same thing but, to use Irvine's example, if the other driver were to qualify alongside Schumacher and beat him into the first corner, then according to Ferrari's explanation of the deal they were brokering with Barrichello, the team would not intervene and switch the order around. It may sound like smoke and mirrors but, on the face of it, it came to represent a shift in the team's policy. And Irvine would not be the one to benefit.

Ironically Irvine had managed to out-qualify Schumacher at the Spanish Grand Prix but then inadvertently blocked his team-mate at the start, allowing Villeneuve to slip through. Schumacher was unable to pass his old rival until the pit stops and the McLarens drove away to their first one-two of the season, while Schumacher and Irvine rolled in third and fourth. Although the performance of the Ferrari at this traditionally McLaren track gave grounds for optimism, Schumacher was less than happy about the way the weekend had gone. It had been one of the rare occasions when he had gone down a blind alley in practice, finding himself forced to switch to Irvine's tyre choice and settings at the last minute before qualifying and not making the most of the car. Irvine had qualified second behind Hakkinen, with Schumacher fourth behind Coulthard. For once there seemed to be no good reason for this, other than Irvine having simply outperformed Schumacher.

Irvine's poor start relegated him to fifth behind his team-mate, but there is no doubt that had they got away normally he would have been forced to employ team tactics and let

Schumacher ahead of him – something which he felt truly bad about doing now.

In Montreal Irvine again got the upper hand, thanks to a superb drive through to third place from dead last, following a collision with Coulthard early on. His charging drive through the field, reminiscent of the best of Nigel Mansell, had everyone on the edges of their seats. Even better for Irvine was that Schumacher made a dreadful mistake and crashed while leading the race, just as Hakkinen had done in Imola. For once there was no question of dodging the blame.

'It was all my fault,' said Michael. 'I knew that place was dusty and that makes me even more to blame. I must apologize to the team. Once a year I make a mistake and let's hope that was it.'

It was a cruel end to what had otherwise been a perfect weekend for Michael. He felt he had a clear advantage in the car and in qualifying needed just one lap to secure pole position. At the time his lap was 0.7 seconds faster than Hakkinen's best. While Michael sat in his car for the rest of the session watching the monitors, the Finn improved steadily, ending up a mere 0.02 seconds slower. It was a classic example of the way Schumacher is able to get on to the pace immediately, while his rivals need more runs to find their optimum speed.

In a mirror reversal of Imola, Hakkinen capitalized on Schumacher's error in the race, scoring ten points and taking the lead of the drivers' championship for the first time in the season. Schumacher now stood four points behind. Perhaps more ominously for Ferrari, Hakkinen said after the race that the McLaren had now conquered its reliability problems. 'Now we can finally start to develop this car in terms of finding more speed; something which so far this year we have been unable to do.'

It was Ron Dennis who had said after the double retirements in Australia that he would rather make a fast car reliable than a reliable car fast. Yet it had taken McLaren almost three months to get on top of their complex new car and it had involved biting the bullet and incorporating a few reliable elements from the 1998 car in place of the troublesome new parts. Meanwhile, Ferrari had taken its reliable car and not only closed the performance gap, but seized a clear advantage. In Canada the Ferrari was around three-tenths of a second faster than the McLaren, perhaps more, considering that Irvine's fastest race lap was half a second faster than Hakkinen's. But now McLaren was ready to turn the screw, to find more in every area of the car, more grip from its suspension, more power from its Mercedes engine.

Meanwhile, although most newspapers took Michael's *mea culpa* at face value, some of the Italian press drew a line connecting Michael's 'gross errors' over the past four seasons: the crash while leading in Monaco in 1996, the collision with Villeneuve at Jerez in 1997 and in 1998 the slam into the back of Coulthard at Spa and the stall on the line at Suzuka. *La Gazzetta dello Sport* described him as a 'Jekyll and Hyde' character, capable of 'acts of genius' as well as 'incredible errors'. One Ferrari team member observed wearily, 'For the Italian press the line between being a hero and being a wanker is very narrow.'

In the closing stages of the French Grand Prix, Irvine stared into the spray from his team-mate's car and thought hard about his situation. He had lost thirty-five seconds in a pit stop when the Ferrari mechanics had mistakenly put a set of dry tyres on his car, realized their mistake and replaced them with a set of wets. He had also lost time due to a spin. But having passed dozens of cars in the slippery conditions he had caught up to the back of Schumacher in fifth place and, although he was much faster than his team-mate, he knew that the rules at Ferrari meant he was barred from passing him. Ralf Schumacher was just ahead of his brother in fourth place and Irvine knew that he was there for the taking, but as Michael was struggling with a gearbox problem and a mismatched set of tyres, Irvine watched the two extra points he might be able to make drift away.

He had made a decision, he later told his friends. From now

on he was only going to play the team game when he was expressly ordered to by the management. In other words he would drive his race and make them tell him to back off. He wasn't going to play Michael's little games any more. From now on it was a case of no call on the radio, no pull-over.

On the grid at Silverstone Schumacher confided that the start would be everything. Lining up in second place, behind Hakkinen but with a car which was clearly as fast as the McLaren, Michael knew that the British Grand Prix was a vital opportunity to close down the eight-point gap in the championship between himself and Hakkinen, provided he got the start right. If Hakkinen were to get away and control the race, he might well drop to twelve points behind the Finn with tracks like Hockenheim and Austria coming up which favoured the McLaren. He needed a good result at Silverstone and it would be decided in the start.

Like so many other times when the pressure has been on him, he made a poor start, losing ground to Coulthard and to Irvine. Fourth into the first corner having taken longer to get up to speed, he immediately began to look for a way past his team-mate. But back on the grid the cars of Zanardi and Villeneuve were stuck in a dangerous place. The marshals would be unable to move them in the ninety seconds before the leaders came around. In the race control tower the order was given for the race to be stopped.

Out on the circuit Schumacher was finding Irvine difficult to pass. Instead of letting Michael through, he was making him work for it, blocking him while all the time Hakkinen could be seen drawing away. Schumacher tried a move into Becketts corner, but Irvine countered and down the long straight they weaved at each other, Irvine illustrating the theory he had out-lined earlier in the season about getting ahead of Schumi at the start and how strong an adversary he would prove to be if he were allowed to race the German. He would get the call, he knew that, but he was determined to make Schumacher and his allies in the management work for this one.

As the cars hammered down the straight, the engines at

their 18,000 rpm maximum, the team tried in vain to tell its drivers by radio that the race had been red-flagged. Forty seconds had elapsed since the start of the race and for nearly half of that time the team had called its drivers to back off and cruise around to the grid for a restart. Oblivious to all this and to the promise Irvine had made to himself, Schumacher made a dive for the inside into Stowe corner. He came from a long way back, went very deep onto the brakes and went shooting past Irvine's car on a trajectory which took him straight off the track. The car hurtled across the sand trap and struck the tyre barrier hard, breaking Schumacher's right leg in two places. He tried to climb out, adrenalin masking the pain, but he realized that his leg was broken and slumped back down to await help.

Ferrari later explained that a bleed nipple had come loose on the rear brakes, meaning that at the critical moment when Michael applied the brakes all the pressure would have gone from the rear brakes, allowing only the front brakes to slow the car down. Looking at the TV pictures, experienced people thought Schumacher had 'grabbed' a brake, in other words, been too sharp on the brake pedal and locked the wheels up, whilst others thought he had suffered a stuck throttle, driving the rear wheels on while the fronts were locked. But when the car was returned to the Ferrari garage and the rear wheels taken away for the tyres to be stripped, some observers noted that there was no trace of any brake fluid on the rear wheel rims. If the bleed nipple had failed or been insufficiently tightened, there would surely have been quite a cascade of fluid over the inside part of the rim. Ferrari maintained its line, but voices in the paddock over the coming weeks speculated that Schumacher had made a mistake which had cost him yet another world title. To this day Schumacher and the Ferrari management insist that the brakes caused the accident and that any other theory is 'bullshit', so we have to take them at their word.

But as the first time that Schumacher had hurt himself in a racing car and as the moment which lost yet another world title for Schumacher and Ferrari, the incident will remain one of the defining moments of the Schumacher story, like Adelaide 1994, Jerez 1997 and Spa 1998.

While Michael lay in Northampton General Hospital preparing for surgery to fit a metal plate and screws into his leg, which would speed up the healing process on his tibia and fibula, Eddie Irvine was holding forth in the press conference, oblivious to the extent of his team-mate's injuries. He talked of Michael's accident, about him being back at the next race and about the number one/number two roles in the quest for the title. Apparently no-one from Ferrari had managed to get a message through to him that Michael's leg was broken in two places and that it would be at least eight weeks before he could drive again. Irvine had finished second in the race having thrown away the win by misjudging his entry to the pit-stop area. Mika Hakkinen's race had ended when one of his rear wheels came loose, and David Coulthard had kept his head to collect the win. Ralf Schumacher, who was informed by his Williams team before the restart of the race of the precise nature of his brother's condition, was appalled to hear Irvine talk so blithely in the press conference. Irvine later apologized, saying that he did not know Michael's situation, but it did not stop Ralf from unleashing a vitriolic attack on the Irishman. 'Irvine should learn to keep quiet or to think before he speaks. In the last few weeks he's done nothing but moan about Michael's privileged status as if he didn't have the chance to show what he's worth. Michael has always been the faster of the two. I would like to say to Mr Irvine that he should stop complaining and show that he is faster.'

In hospital the day after his operation, Schumacher was low. He knew that the accident had put paid to his chances of winning the world title and he knew that this had been his best chance of doing it since joining Ferrari. His next opportunity would be in 2000, a full five years since he last won the title. This is a staggering figure, considering the extent of his superiority as a driver during that period. It might be a glorious pursuit, but it was seriously in danger of becoming a failure.

The shock of hurting himself for the first time in his career inevitably made him consider retiring from the sport. It was an unusual experience for a man who spends little time indulging in negative thoughts. Here he was, having done so much work over the past three months to build a realistic championship challenge and now that was gone with only a long and painful fight back from injury in prospect. Schumacher claimed that he was 'being positive, not depressed' about his situation and that he was 'focused on getting back into a Ferrari and racing before the end of the season'. Beside him in his room were thirty-five red roses from Luca di Montezemolo, one for each of Michael's Grand Prix wins.

Outside the hospital the talk was all of Irvine's new-found role as Ferrari number one. Thanks to his strong start to the season, his consistent podium finishes and Hakkinen's misfortunes, Eddie was now just eight points behind the McLaren driver. He had not visited his team-mate in hospital, although he spoke to him on the telephone, joking about the time he had broken his leg as a child by falling off his skateboard. Irvine's sister Sonia visited Michael, but Eddie claimed that it would be sheer hypocrisy for him to do so; after all, they both knew that Michael's misfortune had been Eddie's big break. He was sitting in the best Ferrari either of them had ever driven, with the full support of the Ferrari team behind him. What he didn't have any more was the working relationship with a team-mate who knows how to pull the team forwards and how to get the most from the car. As events were to transpire, this would prove his biggest problem.

Schumacher left hospital in Northampton on Tuesday morning at 8.30 a.m. and followed a complicated decoy pattern to escape the massive media hordes and meet up with his private jet. The amount of interest his accident had generated was staggering, with major news organizations from around the world camped out at the hospital, desperate for any new crumb of information on the patient's condition. Jean Todt had stayed with him more or less since the accident, missing the end of the race and delivering a harsh verdict on Irvine's pit-stop error, which he said lost him the race. 'How would he know,' said Irvine. 'He wasn't even there.'

Although Ferrari has always denied it, there were clear signs in the aftermath of the Silverstone accident that Todt, and possibly Schumacher too, felt that Irvine's obstructive driving, although not the cause of the accident, had been a contributory factor. The body language between the manager and his driver deteriorated, the sniping between the two increased, often with the press rushing from one to another. Todt had been losing patience with the Irishman's increasingly immodest outbursts in the press, with the ongoing saga of negotiations for the following year and Irvine's mantra of being the unfairly treated number two. When asked why he had not intervened on the opening lap battle and told Irvine to get out of the way, Todt pointed out that there were no team orders on the opening lap of a race.

Now both found themselves in a situation rich with irony. Irvine was on his way out of Ferrari. He had a lucrative offer to lead the new Jaguar team, which was to be created from Ford's purchase of the Stewart team. Todt meanwhile was forced to back a driver he was about to replace for the following year and who, if he won the title, would be taking the number one away with him. Irvine had met with Todt and di Montezemolo shortly after the race at Silverstone and they had told him that they would not be renewing his contract for 2000. Ferrari and Barrichello were close to an agreement and yet now the understudy who had complained about not being allowed to win found himself leading the team he had criticized, with a very real chance of winning the world title for which Schumacher had been striving for three and a half years. Irvine was out of Ferrari for the following year, but in terms of the rest of 1999 he was in a win-win situation. If he won the title he'd be a hero, would put Schumacher and Todt to shame and add a few million to his earning power. If he could take the title battle down to the last race, even if he lost, he would have achieved, on a fraction of the salary and little of the support, precisely what Schumacher had achieved for Ferrari in the 1997 and 1998 seasons!

'He's left me a great weight of expectation,' said Irvine, arriving for a test in Monza and parking his Fiat hire car in Schumacher's space. 'Now I will find out what it means to have that much pressure on me. I have always driven for Michael as the contract says. Now everything has changed. I will drive for myself, for Ferrari's world title, for my world title.'

Irvine won the next race in Austria and a week later he won again in Hockenheim, on Mercedes's home soil. Both victories owed everything to McLaren mistakes, but both required Irvine and Ferrari to make the most of the opportunities offered to them. In Austria, Hakkinen and Coulthard, with no clear team orders from McLaren, collided on the opening lap, sending Hakkinen to the back of the field. He mounted a spirited fightback, but could only manage third place. Ross Brawn, now fully at the disposal of Irvine for race strategy, kept his driver out on a light fuel load long enough to make an advantage over Coulthard, and Ferrari won the race in the pit stops. Coulthard was demoralized by his mistake in hitting Hakkinen, just as he was about to conclude a new contract with McLaren, and he was so tense that he was unable to challenge the Ferrari. Irvine was now just two points behind in the championship.

In Germany, seven days later, he took an eight-point lead after Hakkinen crashed out of the race with a mysterious rear tyre failure, which the team denied was caused by running low tyre pressures. But the same thing had happened to Coulthard the day before and the conclusion was that McLaren had been looking for a performance advantage and had tripped over themselves. Irvine's new team-mate, Mika Salo, played the loyal number two, moving over for the Ferrari number one, as Irvine had done many times before for Schumacher. Ferrari scored a glorious one-two and Irvine was so moved by Salo's gesture that he gave him his winner's trophy, a magnificent sporting gesture to round out a magnificent day.

Schumacher watched the events of these seven days unfold with mixed emotions and put on a brave face when talking about his feelings. 'Irvine did a good job,' he said after Austria, 'He didn't make any mistakes, especially at the end when Coulthard was pressuring him.'

But Todt was less enthusiastic. 'Irvine is paid to win,' he said brusquely. 'He did his duty, but he should also have won in England. Ever since he has had a more driveable car Eddie has demonstrated that he can do great things. He's in the running for the title, but to win it he'll have to win more.' For once, Todt did not go up on the podium himself, preferring to send Brawn, the architect of the success, to collect the trophy for the winning team. This, he claimed was all pre-arranged and had nothing to do with his relationship with Irvine.

If Todt was managing to hide his enthusiasm at Irvine's success, di Montezemolo was not about to miss an opportunity to show how great Ferrari was. 'This is a Ferrari team which never gives up,' gushed its president. 'Last week I got together all five hundred employees to tell them that they had to keep believing and they did. We are not Schumacher-dependent; despite losing our number-one driver we are able to put Irvine in a position to win.'

Before the German Grand Prix, Schumacher made the first of a series of errors of judgement in his new role as observer from the sidelines, which made him appear uncharitable and ungracious. In a live link-up around the Hockenheim track on race day he wished Heinz-Harald Frentzen well and said that Ferrari would struggle to win the race. Irvine was able to capitalize on this and claim that Michael clearly had a lot less faith in Ferrari than he did. In reality Irvine's future was already sealed. He was on his way to Jaguar for a salary in the region of £6 million per year, and with his sporting and financial future settled he could focus on enjoying the challenge of the championship.

Hakkinen had now scored just four points in the last three races, all of which he had been in a position to win. In the same period Irvine had scored twenty-four. By recent standards it was generally a low-scoring year. Traditionally two drivers score most of the victories and amass large points tallies. By the same stage in 1998, Hakkinen had sixty-six points to Schumacher's fifty-eight. This time around Irvine had fifty-two and Hakkinen forty-four, a mere twelve more than Schumacher. With six races to go and sixty points available, Schumacher reasoned that he might still be able to win this title after all. Four days after the German Grand Prix he was examined to see whether he might test at Fiorano over the weekend before the Hungarian Grand Prix. It was just twenty-five days since the accident.

At the Hospital de la Tour in Geneva, Professor Gerard Saillant told Schumacher that it was too soon to think about returning to the cockpit. However, a decision was taken to speed up the healing process by removing two screws from his leg and refixing the metal plate, the target now being for him to be ready to race at the Italian Grand Prix in Monza in two races' time.

'It's frustrating', said Schumacher, 'to see someone else driving my car. I've never been away from the cockpit for so long in my career. I started training about two weeks after Silverstone and things were going well for while. But then I had to take a step back, even though I really wanted to drive in Hungary. But it could have been worse. Having broken only my leg is nothing really.'

Di Montezemolo went on national radio in Italy to spell out Ferrari's position. 'I have told Michael I would like to have him back for Monza on 12 September and it seems to me that things are moving towards that happening. His role when he returns? It is already clear. At that point he will no longer have the possibility of winning the World Championship. We are very happy that Irvine now has a good chance of winning it. In any case what really matters with all due respect to Schumacher and Irvine is the victory of Ferrari. The drivers must follow orders and Schumacher has agreed to do this. I hope to have him back as soon as possible because his help is invaluable. Let's not forget with all due respect to Irvine that in fifty-four races they did together Michael outqualified Eddie fifty-one times.'

Meanwhile Schumacher worked hard on physiotherapy. The test at Monza would be in early September, just eight weeks after the accident; the doctors had predicted twelve to sixteen weeks for normal recovery. They had removed the two screws from his leg because they feared that there was a good chance of them coming loose under the extreme cornering forces of a Formula 1 car. Everything was focused on his return. He would return as soon as possible.

EIGHTEEN EXTREME TOLERANCES

Famiglia Cristiana is Italy's largest-selling family magazine, one which reaches the furthest corners of Italian life. Irvine sat down with their correspondent Pino Pagnatta during a test at Fiorano shortly before the Hungarian Grand Prix. Irvine's Italian, though improving rapidly, was still faltering; Pignatta's English little better. There was plenty of room for trouble and trouble is what resulted.

The magazine hit the news stands on the Wednesday as the teams arrived in the paddock at Budapest. It didn't take long before everyone knew about 'that' interview.

'At Ferrari I enjoy the work but I don't have many friends; with Todt I have a purely professional relationship, it lacks any feeling. He worships Schumacher. Todt is visibly happier if Schumacher wins, you can see it in his face. That's okay, all I care about is the points. But the chances for Ferrari are much higher now, after Michael's incident than before it.'

He was asked whether he planned to stay at Ferrari.

'Depends. If Schumi comes back as number one, I'm off.'

To Stewart-Ford?

'There's an offer, but nothing is decided. Let's wait and see whether Michael is still faster after his incident . . .'

So why did he throw away two world titles?

'Speed isn't enough. You need to avoid mistakes and he makes a lot of mistakes. Too many.'

The Italian press was not impressed by Irvine's outburst.

Corriere della Sera suggested that Schumi was entitled to think, 'Okay, well I won't make the mistake of helping you then.'

Irvine denied everything. He denied that relations with the team were frosty, he denied saying that he'd leave if Schumacher came back as number one, and he denied saying that Schumacher had thrown away two titles,

'I said three months ago that he makes mistakes; we all make mistakes. But Ferrari would not have been able to play for those titles at the last race if Michael weren't a great driver and now it would not be such a strong car if Michael hadn't worked so hard to develop it.' He said that he had not spoken to Michael for quite a while. 'I've been on my boat,' he smiled.

Hungary was a bad weekend for Ferrari. Irvine qualified well, just two-tenths behind Hakkinen for second place, but in the race he and the team were outclassed. McLaren strolled in for another one-two with Irvine twenty seconds adrift in third place. The team blamed a faulty sensor on the differential, but Irvine had been running second on the road fifteen laps before the end, until he caved in under pressure from Coulthard, lost control of the car and gave away second place and the extra two points that would have given him.

It was the start of Ferrari's decline. Neither Irvine nor Salo was able to get the most out of the car in Budapest, nor at Spa two weeks later nor at Monza for the Italian Grand Prix. At the European Grand Prix at the Nürburgring freak weather conditions intervened and Ferrari had another chaotic pit-stop mistake which left the Irishman with only three wheels on his car. These four races were to prove decisive in the final tally, as Irvine scored a mere eight points to Hakkinen's eighteen, from a possible maximum of forty. They also created the impression that neither driver wanted to win this world title, as both sides gave away points and chances and both Frentzen and Coulthard drew close to them in the table.

This period illustrated perhaps that Irvine was not a natural team leader, not a man who could pull the team along behind him like Schumacher. But it also illustrated how important it is to have two good drivers working together to get the most out of a car. As Ferrari technical director Ross Brawn explains, 'All credit to Eddie, he picked up the baton after Michael's accident and ran with it, but after a few races it began to dry up a little bit because we didn't have Michael there. Eddie is a good driver, gives good input, but with Michael there we are so much stronger. It would be the same the other way around; if Eddie wasn't there Michael wouldn't be as strong. Michael appreciates the input of another driver. He's never been arrogant or complacent enough not to pay close attention to what the other driver is doing.'

Schumacher, having dispelled thoughts of retirement, became increasingly desperate to return to the cockpit. He went for a test at Mugello in late August, which went well. Michael lapped faster than Irvine had done during the test and this gave him the confidence to test at Monza the following week. Di Montezemolo was desperate for him to try to make it for Ferrari's home race. Sadly after just one lap, he knew that it would be impossible, the shocks from hitting the kerbs, as you have to at Monza to be fast, proving too painful on his still damaged leg. Regretfully he ruled himself out of the Italian and European Grands Prix. Many people suggested that his decision was based more on not wanting to help Irvine become Ferrari's first champion for twenty years. But behind the scenes there was a dilemma. Ferrari knew that Irvine would not be with them in 2000 and they wanted to ensure that the development of the car would move forwards during the closing stages of the 1999 season and that they could test new parts, which they would not want Irvine to know about as he was leaving the team. Consequently they badly needed Schumacher to work on the car, to evaluate the direction which the development was taking.

Montezemolo reaffirmed that Schumacher would return as soon as he was fit and spelled out what the team orders would be. 'The lead driver is Eddie and Schumacher will come back to help him because Ferrari wants to win both World Championships.'

Throughout this time, Schumacher kept his thoughts to

himself, speaking regularly on the telephone with Todt, Brawn and di Montezemolo, while his thoughts on Ferrari, Irvine and the championship filtered out from the sidelines. When Schumacher's manager Willi Weber made some dismissive comments about Irvine in the German press, the Ferrari press office took the unprecedented step of issuing a statement distancing itself from his comments and saying that a 'business manager' is not competent to discuss the performances of drivers. It was the first time that a wedge had been driven between the two sides.

This was compounded following an interview Schumacher gave to the German media on the eve of the Nürburgring race where he said, 'Ferrari has done a lot of work in recent tests and I think that at Nürburgring they will be stronger. But in any case I do not believe that they will be strong enough to be able to beat McLaren. For Ferrari it will be really hard. For this reason, if everything is normal, McLaren will win. It is not going to be Eddie's year. Only bad luck can stop Mika [Hakkinen] from beating him and the only way Ferrari will finish with a championship is if McLaren give it to them.'

It was a cruel swipe, both at Irvine and the Ferrari team, coming as it did before a stern test on Mercedes's home circuit. It seemed strange that Ferrari's best-paid employee should chose publicly to denigrate the team that paid him so much. That he might be frustrated with Irvine's situation and by the heavy weather he had made of his opportunity was understandable, but surely it would have been far better to keep his feelings to himself. It was a mean and quite unnecessary swipe which quite rightly bounced back in his face. Irvine capitalized by saying, 'What Michael says is not important. Anyway it shows that he has less faith in the Ferrari team than I have.'

Shortly after the Nürburgring race, after the intense post-mortem at Ferrari into why Irvine had been given only three wheels at his pit stop and after a solemn promise from Montezemolo that such a mistake would never happen again, Schumacher went for his planned check-up with the doctors in Paris. This would establish whether he was fit enough to compete in the final two races of the season at Malaysia and Japan. Ferrari were now eight points adrift in the constructors' table and Irvine two points behind in the drivers'. The team was seriously at risk of ending the season with nothing. They knew that developments they had made on the car before the Nürburgring were a huge improvement, although the weather conditions and the pit-stop fiasco had disguised that. Getting Schumacher back for the final rounds was their only hope of salvaging something from the season. But a strange thing happened. News filtered out in Germany that Schumacher would not race again, then, after Schumacher's examination by Professor Saillant, Ferrari's press office issued the following, very pointed statement.

'This afternoon Michael Schumacher underwent a medical examination in Paris. This showed that the bones have healed sufficiently for him to resume normal activities. Tomorrow Schumacher will drive an F399 at the Mugello circuit for a series of shakedowns. Michael Schumacher has informed Ferrari of his decision not to take part in the remaining two Grands Prix of the season as he feels he is not sufficiently fit to cope with the demands of the race.'

Schumacher was unhappy that this press release created a 'false impression'. As he explained it, 'It's not true that I am okay. I'm not okay. The doctors said I was alright to do normal things in the sense of what a normal man would do, like make a sandwich or go to the office, but not like a man who has to drive a Formula 1 car for three hundred kilometres. My physical condition would not allow that. '

He was caught in the horns of a dilemma. If by coming back he were to help Irvine to the drivers' title, he would have undone all that he had been striving for since deciding to join Ferrari in 1995. He would have had a major part to play in the return of glory to Ferrari, but he would not be the one to claim it. In that sense his entire Ferrari experience would have been rendered pointless. But if he were to stand back, claiming that he was not fit enough to last a full Grand Prix weekend and

Ferrari were to slog on as they had for the past four races, not getting the most out of the car, they would almost certainly lose both championships and he would have indirectly caused it by doing nothing to help.

Worse still there were accusations that Ferrari were deliberately not helping Irvine to win, heightened by the pit-stop fiasco at the Nürburgring. The people on the inside might know that this was not the case, but the outward projection was of a team in disarray, with no fresh ideas and no clear desire to assist their number-two driver become champion. Schumacher's return would wipe away all such talk. It would be a sign of Ferrari's commitment. Schumacher was clearly fit enough to test and set competitive times, so why not race? Losing both championships would be a disaster for Jean Todt, the manager closest to him, and would be a severe embarrassment for Luca di Montezemolo, after all that he had said about how Schumacher had made Ferrari great again. It would look very bad.

Ferrari were clearly disappointed with their driver's decision. They could not and would not force him to drive, that decision could only come from the driver, but the wording of Ferrari's statement left little to the imagination; the all-clear from the doctors, then the fact he would test the following day, then the decision not to come and help the team out of the mire. There was also deep dissatisfaction at Ferrari with the way information about their driver's condition and his thoughts on it seemed to be driven from Germany and not centralized by Ferrari. Schumacher had not played straight with the press department about his condition or his plans since the accident and there was a great deal of confusion in the media at large about what was going on.

The test at Mugello intensified the problem. Schumacher was fast straight away and in the two days covered a total of 350 km, more than a Grand Prix distance, but in short bursts of a few laps at a time. At the end of the second day, the answer was still no. 'I'm the only one who can evaluate my condition,' he said angrily when asked how he could claim not to be ready. 'I'm not happy about the decision, but believe me it was inevitable.' He said his next test would probably be in December.

In Germany the press was split by Schumacher's decision: *Bild* sided with the driver, but *Die Welt* called him an 'ego maniac who shows full commitment only when his own interests are being served'. And *Frankfurt Rundschau* said, 'He doesn't want to play Irvine's water carrier even if officially he says the opposite.'

The Italian press was horrified by the way Schumacher had chosen to ignore the challenge (*la sfida*), and abandon Ferrari in its time of need, an act as close to treason as it is possible to find in Italy. Writing in *La Gazzetta dello Sport*, Pino Allievi concluded, 'It is difficult to discuss the dignity of a man who says no to a challenge, claiming he is not ready. But there are ways and ways. And Schumacher, once again, has chosen the wrong one.'

But then things changed. After an audience with the Pope in Rome, together with fellow drivers Jean Alesi and Giancarlo Fisichella, Schumacher went up to Fiorano, where he set the fastest time of the year for the F399 and announced that he had changed his mind. He would drive in Malaysia and Japan to help Ferrari in the fight for both championships.

What brought about the sudden change of heart? How much pressure was brought to bear on him from Luca di Montezemolo, who was more aware than anyone at Ferrari about the bad impression that his driver had created in the previous week? Without him there was no chance of winning either title and another barren season would make things difficult for the top management. Also there is evidence that di Montezemolo grew tired of his driver not playing straight with them. At a debrief session shortly after the season ended, di Montezemolo revealed that at one stage during the critical period when Michael was still refusing to drive, he had called Schumacher's house and the phone was answered by daughter Gina-Maria, who told the president that Michael was busy, putting on his football boots! If he could play football, he could help Ferrari.

On arrival in Malaysia, Ferrari vigorously denied that the president had put any pressure on him. Schumacher himself admitted that di Montezemolo had called him every day, but maintained that what made him change his mind was seeing how good the car was and realizing after three days' intensive testing that his fitness was not as bad as he thought. For sure, Ferrari put him in a situation where he could not refuse them. After two days at Mugello and then another test at Fiorano, how could he possibly deny them any more?

When he arrived at the new Sepang circuit, near Kuala Lumpur, Michael put on a brave show of being pleased to be back. He said all the right things in the press conferences, but clearly the time away from the treadmill had given him pause for reflection on all that comes with being Grand Prix racing's benchmark driver. The media hassle quickly got to him, the repetition of stupid petty questions. But he clearly enjoyed driving the car and soon established himself as the fastest man on this new track. Freed from the intense pressure which had accompanied him at every race since 1993, he was able to express himself fully in the car, while the championship contenders showed how much tension can affect lap times. While McLaren struggled to find the right set up on the Saturday, Ferrari snatched the front row, with Schumacher on pole by almost a second. If he could do this with one leg, what might he achieve with two? And the ten-million-dollar question was, would he let Irvine pass him in the race?

'My main priority is to win the race and help the team win the constructors' championship,' he said that evening. 'But we all know that if I am in a certain position relative to Eddie then I will help him.'

The race was a masterpiece of team driving. Schumacher dictated the pace from the start, allowed Irvine to pass him for the lead twice and completely destroyed Mika Hakkinen's morale by holding him up for lap after lap. He delivered the perfect result, with Irvine winning, himself second and Hakkinen third. The team was now ideally placed to clinch the constructors' title and Irvine would take a four-point lead into the final race at Suzuka. Most people had refused to believe that he would pull over to let Irvine past. Indeed many felt that it was to avoid having to do this that he had stayed away. By doing all the hard work and then selflessly moving over, he managed to project the image of a team player, a man capable of humility and self-sacrifice. It was a gesture of supreme commitment to Ferrari, a selflessness which seemed at odds with everything he had appeared to stand for throughout his turbulent career. Was it the moment when he found redemption for Jerez? Possibly, but being Schumacher he did it not once, but twice, as if relishing the opportunity to confound people's perceptions of him. Malaysia was payback time for all that Ferrari and Irvine had done for him, but it was also a moment when he came to terms with himself. He was the moral victor, but Ferrari and Irvine were the actual victors.

But there was trouble brewing. Throughout the weekend there had been dark rumours that Ferrari was up to its old tricks again, running something very close to traction control. Photographers out on the tracks swore blind they had heard the system on the car in the slower corners. On top of that McLaren had spotted a possible problem with the turning vanes on the side of the car. Ferrari had been covering them up, because their new design was a big gain for them. Unfortunately, they had made a very basic error in the manufacture and fitting of them and when the FIA technical man, on a tip-off from McLaren, checked the vanes, he found that they were 10 mm outside the correct measurement. The stewards of the meeting called Ferrari's technical director Ross Brawn, who admitted that the vanes did not comply and the stewards had no alternative but to disqualify both cars. Ferrari appealed, but it was hard to see how they could win. After all, Brawn had not only admitted the mistake but given a press conference about it, showing the vane and illustrating the problem with it.

A week later in a Paris appeal court, Ferrari's lawyers successfully argued that the measurement had been taken incorrectly and that in conjunction with a rule saying there is a 5 mm tolerance allowable on such measurements, the Ferraris were after all legal. It was all very neat and tidy and extremely clever, but it stank to high heaven. Predictably the reaction from McLaren was strong. 'It seems to be the perception that Ferrari winning the World Championship is better than McLaren,' said Ron Dennis. 'Everyone wants to have an exciting race at Suzuka, but I believe the price we have paid for that is too high.'

So Ferrari was back in it. Malaysia had been a great triumph for Michael. Whatever the reasons for him making the comeback, out on the track he had shown just how far ahead of his rivals he was. But in the way he conducted himself that weekend he had also shown a sporting side to his character and a humility which many people thought did not exist. As he accepted the congratulations of his team and of well-wishers after the race, he was honest in his feelings about what he had done. 'I admit it is a difficult role to play, but I'm not fighting for the championship myself and so in a sense it's easier to drive without the need to win at all costs. Ferrari has given me a lot in the last few years and I couldn't possibly hold back now that I am well again. I'm sure that Ferrari will do the same for me in future.'

Ross Brawn summed up the way Ferrari felt about Schumacher's comeback. 'I think that the commitment he made to the team in Malaysia showed his true nature. Unfortunately he is often misunderstood and there are a lot of sceptics who said, "Oh he won't do anything for them, he'll do his own thing." They don't understand the guy. He was a true team player and he did what was asked of him by the team. No, he did more than was asked of him by the team. Michael is a great guy and everyone in the team loves him. It's the same with Benetton. You ask anyone who was there with him what he's like and no-one has a bad word to say about him because they know the real Michael Schumacher. Unfortunately, he has a different persona to the outside world sometimes.'

The McLaren team did not feel that Schumacher's performance had been particularly sporting; here he was, by his own admission not a contender for the championship, deliberately interfering, holding up one of the genuine contenders to benefit his own team-mate. It had been a tough lesson for everyone, but the rules of Formula 1 do not forbid tactical driving like that and Ferrari had ruthlessly exploited the absence of such rules.

The evening before the final Grand Prix at Suzuka, Schumacher was relaxed about what lay ahead in the race. He had qualified on pole position again, but this time Irvine was down in fifth on the grid. Hakkinen was second fastest, which meant once again that the start could well decide the championship. Irvine needed Schumacher to win the race. Before the start, Michael spoke honestly about his feelings on Irvine becoming champion. 'I would prefer it to be me who was champion, but on the other side I would like to think that if Eddie wins it will be because of all the work I have put in over the past four years, so I will claim a little slice of it for myself.'

Not for the first time when it really mattered Schumacher messed up the start, allowing Hakkinen to take a lead he would never lose. With a heavy fuel load, the plan had been for Schumacher to contain the field and allow Irvine to make up places, then to beat Hakkinen to the victory. But the Finn was too sharp at the start and McLaren were too clever tactically. Ferrari finished second and third, which clinched the constructors' championship, but Irvine missed out by two points. Cynics said afterwards that Schumacher did not try particularly hard to win the race, but Irvine defended his team-mate's performance. 'He did better than anyone else could have done. I could never have given him the support he gave me. In the end the Ferrari wasn't quick enough.'

But David Coulthard let slip that before the race Schumacher had privately told two of the senior figures at McLaren-Mercedes, one of whom is believed to be Norbert Haug, that he would not mind if Hakkinen became champion. Coulthard accused Schumacher of throwing up 'a giant smoke-screen to deflect the outcome of the race'.

Coulthard was responding to a vicious attack on him by Schumacher after the race. The Scot had fallen a lap behind and briefly held Schumacher up while he was chasing Hakkinen. In an astonishing tirade after the race, Schumacher claimed he lost ten seconds, when in fact it was more like two and a half. 'McLaren should wonder why they ask a driver to do things like this,' he raged. 'It was a different thing in Malaysia, when I was racing for position. You can play tactics but when you've been lapped you should make way. Judging from the way he behaved today, I'm not sure I should believe that Spa last year was really done on purpose.'

Coulthard took the criticism badly, particularly the reference to Spa, which he thought had been sorted out at the time. 'Michael thinks he operates on a higher plane,' he said, 'but he should watch what he says. I have never tried to endanger another driver on the track and if he doesn't apologize for what he said I shall sue for slander.'

Coulthard had a point. He had hardly obstructed the Ferrari, in fact it was only for two corners that Schumacher found it difficult to pass. The McLaren did back him up into the tight hairpin, so much so that Rubens Barrichello closed up and almost passed Schumacher, but with the season over and the constructors' title won, was it really necessary for Schumacher to make such an attack? It is unlikely that Michael did it to detract attention from his own performance; after all, most drivers in his position would have done the same thing and driven for the team title, rather than the drivers' title for a team-mate. The attack was not born in the heat of the moment either because Schumacher was still going on about it an hour later in interviews. It undid much of the good he had done himself and his image in Malaysia.

Worse was to come, as barely a week after the Japanese Grand Prix Irvine's true feelings came to light with the serialization of his book in the *News of the World*. Over three extraordinary pages he confirmed many of the things which he had denied during the season. He claimed that Schumacher cost him the title, that Ferrari gave its priority to Michael even though it was Irvine who had the chance of winning. Instead of helping him win it, they were more concerned with Schumacher's comeback tests and put too much energy into those at his expense. He also confirmed that his blocking of Schumacher on the opening lap at Silverstone was deliberate.

And so after four seasons with Ferrari, Michael Schumacher was still no closer to the World Championship which would give his time there the legitimacy he craved. There were upsides: he had won more races for Ferrari than anyone in history, and many of them were classics which had cemented his image as the outstanding driver of his generation and increased his already considerable appeal. Although his three-month absence showed that interest in Formula 1 around the world did not depend on him, it also showed how sorely the Formula 1 circus missed him and his fighting spirit. And in his dramatic and highly controversial comeback, he had helped Ferrari to win its first constructors' championship since the death of its founder Enzo Ferrari in 1988.

But the jury was still out on his character. The Jerez incident was gone but not forgotten, and there had been many other controversial moments since then which he had not handled well. Though he had come close several times to finding redemption for Jerez, he had also shown himself capable of ignoring all the lessons of that controversial episode. But whatever the judgement on his character, there is no doubt about where he stands as a racing driver.

We should leave the final analysis to the man who has observed Michael Schumacher most closely as a driver over the past four years: Eddie Irvine.

'To beat Michael in equal equipment isn't possible. To do it in a better car is possible. And that's what Hakkinen's done, what Damon Hill has done and what Jacques Villeneuve's done.

'Michael's the best by a mile. People still don't realize how good he is.'

INDEX

rules, 131–2, 172
Ryan, Davey, 173

safety, 154, 157–8
Saillant, Professor Gerard, 263, 269
Salo, Mika, 142, 164, 261, 266
San Marino, *see* Imola
São Paulo: (1995), 63, 119; (1998), 107, 108, 126, 134, 169; (1999), 244, 248
Sauber, 142, 198, 204, 211
Scarperia, 67
Schmidt, Michael, 72, 88–9
Schrempp, Jurgen, 199
Schumacher, Corinna, *wife*, 17, 39, 48, 56, 102, 104, 243
Schumacher, Gina-Maria, *daughter*, 17, 56, 79, 93, 102, 104, 244, 271
Schumacher, Michael: accident, 256–60, 263, 264, 269; Adelaide (1994), 19, 21, 29, 44, 54–5, 61, 63, 76, 163, 258; (1995), 90; appearance, 76–8; arrogance, 38–9, 81, 86, 95, 101, 160, 162, 166; Austria (1998), 110, 168, 173–80, 238; background, 91, 96–8, 101, 193; Barcelona (1994), 116, 119; (1998), 135; beatable, 82; Benetton, 12, 14, 23, 28, 61, 64, 86, 112–13, 116, 131–2, 171, 198; *Bild*, 199, 201, 224; and Brawn; 111; Budapest (1998), 118, 167–86, 195; Buenos Aires (1998), 107–25, 126, 164, 198, 201, 210, 211; bullfight, 44; car mechanic, 96, 193; cats, 102; character, 75–6, 84–106, 120–5, 196, 220; community service, 72; concentration, 28; consistency, 163, 183; contempt for rivals, 81–2, 94, 164; contract, 106, 187, 202, 238, 247; and Coulthard, 90, 154, 203–13, 255, 267; crowds, 105, 106; 'devil in him', 154; driving style, 14, 49–50, 111, 113, 115–17, 154; earnings, 17, 38, 54, 59, 81, 87, 96, 104, 106, 155, 187; 'fall from grace', 42, 68; fans, 78, 97, 203, 217; fatherhood, 17, 39, 48, 56, 79, 93, 103; fear, 76; and Ferrari, 15, 32, 38, 64, 91, 99, 117, 165, 171, 183, 193, 196, 244–7, 268, 277; FIA hearing (1997), 53, 74, 80; FIAT spokesman, 99; film, 145–7; Fiorano villa, 188–9; first world title (1994), 114; fitness, 29, 76–7, 111, 121–2, 189; football, 90, 102, 271; Formula 1 début

(1991), 85, 93, 97, 198; Formula 3, 97, 161, 198; and Frentzen, 154, 157–8, 160–2, 164–5, 210; fuel, 64, 119; generosity, 88, 95; 'gets away with it', 156; go-karts, 60, 81, 96–7, 111, 124–5, 162, 164–5, 193; Grand Prix Drivers' Association, 75, 154, 157, 211; and Hakkinen, 154, 203, 213, 235; and Hill, 13, 14–15, 18, 62, 78, 86, 89–90, 101, 154, 157, 158–9, 256; Hockenheim (1994), 63; (1998), 167–8, 175, 213; humour, 88–9, 90; hypocrisy, 154; and illegal devices, 23–4, 61, 86, 172–3, 177–80; immaturity, 87; Imola (1998), 135; (1999), 247–9; improvisation, 115; intelligence, 28, 87; and Irvine, 237–50, 251–64, 265–77; isolation, 39; Italian lessons, 103; jealousy of, 154, 155, 173; Jerez (1997), 11, 21–30, 31–40, 41–52, 72–3, 76, 79–80, 82, 101, 127, 156, 158–9, 162–3, 216, 228, 246, 255, 258, 273, 277; Jerez press conferences (1997), 17–19, 35, 40, 234; Jordan, 93–4, 198; McLaren-Mercedes offer, 188, 198, 199–202; Magny Cours (1998), 116, 161, 167, 168–70; (1999), 255–6; Maranello press conference (1997), 54, 56; Marlboro spokesman, 96; 'maximize everything', 112, 166; Melbourne (1994), 218; (1998), 213; mentally driven, 87; Mercedes, 198–203, 208; merchandising, 38, 187; 'miraculous starts', 24, 61–2, 115–16; Monte Carlo (1996), 66, 255; (1997), 110; (1998), 101, 138, 139–53, 156, 224; (1999), 7, 250; and Montezemolo, 33–5, 44–7, 54, 65, 84; Montreal (1998), 154–65; (1999), 254–5; Monza (1996), 34, 45, 79; Monza (1998), 203, 213–17, 220; motorcycle, 99; *Newsweek*, 19–20, 66; nickname, 60, 62, 63–4; Norway home, 56, 68, 105, 122, 240; Nürburgring (1995), 91; (1997), 12, 89–90; (1998), 103, 218–20, 220, 248; 'on a pedestal', 114; 'on the limit', 113, 123; parents, 96, 97, 104, 211; 'Pele of Formula 1', 109; penalties and suspensions, 16, 62, 63–4, 72, 119, 155, 158, 163, 169–71; plane, 103, 259; press relations, 100, 197; private life, 85,

THRUST
By Richard Noble

'One of the great stories of sporting triumph over adversity ever told' *Motoring News*

They said it couldn't be done. Sceptics warned that as a car approached 750 m.p.h., the shock waves generated when it hit the sound barrier would either force it off the ground like an aeroplane or tear it apart.

Richard Noble, the modern embodiment of the swashbuckling British speed-seeker of yesteryear, was used to that kind of blinkered thinking. He had held the title of the Fastest Man on Earth since 1983, when his *Thrust2* car set a new world land-speed record at 633 m.p.h. Critics had argued that he would fail then, too. Noble likes nothing better than a fight and in the late 1990s, as a gripping Anglo-American race began to create the world's first supersonic car, he was determined to risk everything to achieve this world first for Britain.

On 15 October 1997 Noble's *ThrustSSC*, driven by ice-cool RAF Squadron Leader Andy Green, smashed through the sound barrier to create the first supersonic land-speed record at 763 m.p.h. The *ThrustSSC* team had beaten the Americans, thumbed its nose at the sceptics, and realized what seemed like an impossible dream. It was a triumph for British engineering, technology and derring-do.

This is not a tale of unbroken success, but a story of disappointment and struggle, and of the entangled emotions behind one of the greatest engineering achievements of the twentieth century.

'Compelling and a fitting eulogy to one of Britain's last great motoring heroes' *Mirror*

A Bantam Paperback

0 553 81208 4